# NEW LATIN GRAMMAR

## by
## CHARLES E. BENNETT

Bolchazy-Carducci Publishers, Inc.

Cover illustration:

A Roman schoolgirl with a stylus and wax tablet
from a Pompeiian mural ca. A.D. 70
(Museo Nationale, Naples)


Printed in the United States of America
## 2004
by United Graphics


# Bolchazy-Carducci Publishers, Inc.
1000 Brown Street
Wauconda, Illinois 60084
http://www.bolchazy.com


ISBN 0-86516-261-1


Reprint of the 1908 Allyn and Bacon edition

# PREFACE.

THE present work is a revision of that published in 1908. No radical alterations have been introduced, although a number of minor changes will be noted. I have added an Introduction on the origin and development of the Latin language, which it is hoped will prove interesting and instructive to the more ambitious pupil. At the end of the book will be found an Index to the Sources of the Illustrative Examples cited in the Syntax.

C. E. B.

ITHACA, NEW YORK,
May 4, 1918. _____

## PREFACE TO THE SECOND EDITION.

THE present book is a revision of my *Latin Grammar* originally published in 1895. Wherever greater accuracy or precision of statement seemed possible, I have endeavored to secure this. The rules for syllable division have been changed and made to conform to the prevailing practice of the Romans themselves. In the Perfect Subjunctive Active, the endings *-īs*, *-īmus*, *-ītis* are now marked long. The theory of vowel length before the suffixes **-gnus**, **-gna**, **-gnum**, and also before **j**, has been discarded. In the Syntax I have recognized a special category of Ablative of Association, and have abandoned the original doctrine as to the force of tenses in the Prohibitive.

Apart from the foregoing, only minor and unessential modifications have been introduced. In its main lines the work remains unchanged.

ITHACA, NEW YORK,
October 16, 1907.

# FROM THE PREFACE TO THE FIRST EDITION.

THE object of this book is to present *the essential facts* of Latin grammar in a direct and simple manner, and within the smallest compass consistent with scholarly standards. While intended primarily for the secondary school, it has not neglected the needs of the college student, and aims to furnish such grammatical information as is ordinarily required in undergraduate courses.

The experience of foreign educators in recent years has tended to restrict the size of school-grammars of Latin, and has demanded an incorporation of the main principles of the language in compact manuals of 250 pages. Within the past decade, several grammars of this scope have appeared abroad which have amply met the most exacting demands.

The publication in this country of a grammar of similar plan and scope seems fully justified at the present time, as all recent editions of classic texts summarize in introductions the special idioms of grammar and style peculiar to individual authors. This makes it feasible to dispense with the enumeration of many *minutiae* of usage which would otherwise demand consideration in a student's grammar.

In the chapter on Prosody, I have designedly omitted all special treatment of the lyric metres of Horace and Catullus, as well as of the measures of the comic poets. Our standard editions of these authors all give such thorough consideration to versification that repetition in a separate place seems superfluous.

ITHACA, NEW YORK,
December 15, 1894.

# TABLE OF CONTENTS.

———•◦•———

## PART I.

### SOUNDS, ACCENT, QUANTITY, ETC.

## PART II.

### INFLECTIONS.

# PART III.

## PARTICLES.

# PART IV.

## WORD FORMATION.

### I. DERIVATIVES.

# PART V.

## SYNTAX.

# Part VI.

## PROSODY.

## SUPPLEMENTS TO THE GRAMMAR.

# INTRODUCTION.

## THE LATIN LANGUAGE.

1. **The Indo-European Family of Languages**. — Latin belongs to one group of a large family of languages, known as *Indo-European*.[1] This Indo-European family of languages embraces the following groups :

### ASIATIC MEMBERS OF THE INDO-EUROPEAN FAMILY.

*a. The Sanskrit*, spoken in ancient India. Of this there were several stages, the oldest of which is the Vedic, or language of the Vedic Hymns. These Hymns are the oldest literary productions known to us among all the branches of the Indo-European family. A conservative estimate places them as far back as 1500 B.C. Some scholars have even set them more than a thousand years earlier than this, *i.e.* anterior to 2500 B.C. The Sanskrit, in modified form, has always continued to be spoken in India, and is represented to-day by a large number of dialects descended from the ancient Sanskrit, and spoken by millions of people.

*b. The Iranian*, spoken in ancient Persia, and closely related to the Sanskrit. There were two main branches of the Iranian group, *viz.* the Old Persian and the Avestan. The Old Persian was the official language of the court, and appears in a number of so-called cuneiform [2] inscriptions, the earliest of which date from the time of Darius I (sixth century B.C.). The other branch of the Iranian, the Avestan,[3] is the language of the Avesta or sacred books of the Parsees, the followers of Zoro-

---

[1] Sometimes also called *Aryan* or *Indo-Germanic*.

[2] Cuneiform means "wedge-shaped." The name applies to the form of the strokes of which the characters consist.

[3] The name Zend is often given to this.

aster, founder of the religion of the fire-worshippers.  Portions of these sacred books may have been composed as early as 1000 B.C.

Modern Persian is a living representative of the old Iranian speech.  It has naturally been much modified by time, particularly through the introduction of many words from the Arabic.

*c. The Armenian*, spoken in Armenia, the district near the Black Sea and Caucasus Mountains.  This is closely related to the Iranian, and was formerly classified under that group.  It is now recognized as entitled to independent rank.  The earliest literary productions of the Armenian language date from the fourth and fifth centuries of the Christian era.  To this period belong the translation of the Scriptures and the old Armenian Chronicle.  The Armenian is still a living language, though spoken in widely separated districts, owing to the scattered locations in which the Armenians are found to-day.

*d. The Tokharian.*  This language, only recently discovered and identified as Indo-European, was spoken in the districts east of the Caspian Sea (modern Turkestan).  While in some respects closely related to the three Asiatic branches of the Indo-European family already considered, in others it shows close relationship to the European members of the family.  The literature of the Tokharian, so far as it has been brought to light, consists mainly of translations from the Sanskrit sacred writings, and dates from the seventh century of our era.

### EUROPEAN MEMBERS OF THE INDO-EUROPEAN FAMILY.

*e. The Greek.*  The Greeks had apparently long been settled in Greece and Asia Minor as far back as 1500 B.C.  Probably they arrived in these districts much earlier.  The earliest literary productions are the Iliad and the Odyssey of Homer, which very likely go back to the ninth century B.C.  From the sixth century B.C. on, Greek literature is continuous.  Modern Greek, when we consider its distance in time from antiquity, is remarkably similar to the classical Greek of the fourth and fifth centuries B.C.

*f. The Italic Group.* The Italic Group embraces the
Umbrian, spoken in the northern part of the Italian peninsula
(in ancient Umbria); the Latin, spoken in the central part (in
Latium); the Oscan, spoken in the southern part (in Samnium,
Campania, Lucania, etc.). Besides these, there were a number
of minor dialects, such as the Marsian, Volscian, etc. Of all
these (barring the Latin), there are no remains except a few
scanty inscriptions. Latin literature begins shortly after
250 B.C. in the works of Livius Andronicus, Naevius, and Plautus, although a few brief inscriptions are found belonging to a
much earlier period.

*g. The Celtic.* In the earliest historical times of which we
have any record, the Celts occupied extensive portions of northern Italy, as well as certain areas in central Europe; but after
the second century B.C., they are found only in Gaul and the
British Isles. Among the chief languages belonging to the
Celtic group are the Gallic, spoken in ancient Gaul; the Breton,
still spoken in the modern French province of Brittany; the
Irish, which is still extensively spoken in Ireland among the
common people; the Welsh; and the Gaelic of the Scotch
Highlanders.

*h. The Teutonic.* The Teutonic group is very extensive. Its
earliest representative is the Gothic, preserved for us in the
translation of the scriptures by the Gothic Bishop Ulfilas (about
375 A.D.). Other languages belonging to this group are the Old
Norse, once spoken in Scandinavia, and from which are descended the modern Icelandic, Norwegian, Swedish, Danish;
German; Dutch; Anglo-Saxon, from which is descended the
modern English.

*i. The Balto-Slavic.* The languages of this group belong to
eastern Europe. The Baltic division of the group embraces the
Lithuanian and Lettic, spoken to-day by the people living on
the eastern shores of the Baltic Sea. The earliest literary productions of these languages date from the sixteenth century.
The Slavic division comprises a large number of languages, the
most important of which are the Russian, the Bulgarian, the

Serbian, the Bohemian, the Polish. All of these were late in developing a literature, the earliest to do so being the Old Bulgarian, in which we find a translation of the Bible dating from the ninth century.

*j. The Albanian*, spoken in Albania and parts of Greece, Italy, and Sicily. This is most nearly related to the Balto-Slavic group, and is characterized by the very large proportion of words borrowed from Latin, Turkish, Greek, and Slavic. Its literature does not begin till the seventeenth century.

2. **Home of the Indo-European Family.** — Despite the many outward differences of the various languages of the foregoing groups, a careful examination of their structure and vocabulary demonstrates their intimate relationship and proves overwhelmingly their descent from a common parent. We must believe, therefore, that at one time there existed a homogeneous clan or tribe of people speaking a language from which all the above enumerated languages are descended. The precise location of the home of this ancient tribe cannot be determined. For a long time it was assumed that it was in central Asia north of the Himalaya Mountains, but this view has long been rejected as untenable. It arose from the exaggerated importance attached for a long while to Sanskrit. The great antiquity of the earliest literary remains of the Sanskrit (the Vedic Hymns) suggested that the inhabitants of India were geographically close to the original seat of the Indo-European Family. Hence the home was sought in the elevated plateau to the north. To-day it is thought that central or southeastern Europe is much more likely to have been the cradle of the Indo-European parent-speech, though anything like a logical demonstration of so difficult a problem can hardly be expected.

As to the size and extent of the original tribe whence the Indo-European languages have sprung, we can only speculate. It probably was not large, and very likely formed a compact racial and linguistic unit for centuries, possibly for thousands of years.

The time at which Indo-European unity ceased and the various individual languages began their separate existence, is likewise shrouded in obscurity. When we consider that the separate existence of the Sanskrit may antedate 2500 B.C., it may well be believed that people speaking the Indo-European parent-speech belonged to a period as far back as 5000 B.C., or possibly earlier.

3. **Stages in the Development of the Latin Language.** — The earliest remains of the Latin language are found in certain very archaic inscriptions. The oldest of these belong to the sixth and seventh centuries B.C. Roman literature does not begin till several centuries later, *viz.* shortly after the middle of the third century B.C. We may recognize the following clearly marked periods of the language and literature:

*a. The Preliterary Period*, from the earliest times down to 240 B.C., when Livius Andronicus brought out his first play. For this period our knowledge of Latin depends almost exclusively upon the scanty inscriptions that have survived from this remote time. Few of these are of any length.

*b. The Archaic Period*, from Livius Andronicus (240 B.C.) to Cicero (81 B.C.). Even in this age the language had already become highly developed as a medium of expression. In the hands of certain gifted writers it had even become a vehicle of power and beauty. In its simplicity, however, it naturally marks a contrast with the more finished diction of later days. To this period belong:

> Livius Andronicus, about 275–204 B.C. (Translation of Homer's Odyssey; Tragedies).
> Plautus, about 250–184 B.C. (Comedies).
> Naevius, about 270–199 B.C. (" Punic War "; Comedies).
> Ennius, 239–169 B.C. (" Annals "; Tragedies).
> Terence, about 190–159 B.C. (Comedies).
> Lucilius, 180–103 B.C. (Satires).
> Pacuvius, 220–about 130 B.C. (Tragedies).
> Accius, 170–about 85 B.C. (Tragedies).

*c. The Golden Age*, from Cicero (81 B.C.) to the death of Augustus (14 A.D.). In this period the language, especially in the hands of Cicero, reaches a high degree of stylistic perfection. Its vocabulary, however, has not yet attained its greatest fullness and range. Traces of the diction of the Archaic Period are often noticed, especially in the poets, who naturally sought their effects by reverting to the speech of olden times. Literature reached its culmination in this epoch, especially in the great poets of the Augustan Age. The following writers belong here :

> Lucretius, about 95–55 B.C. (Poem on Epicurean Philosophy).
>
> Catullus, 87–about 54 B.C. (Poet).
>
> Cicero, 106–43 B.C. (Orations; Rhetorical Works; Philosophical Works; Letters).
>
> Caesar, 102–44 B.C. (Commentaries on Gallic and Civil Wars).
>
> Sallust, 86–36 B.C. (Historian).
>
> Nepos, about 100–about 30 B.C. (Historian).
>
> Virgil, 70–19 B.C. (" Aeneid "; " Georgics "; " Bucolics ").
>
> Horace, 65–8 B.C. (Odes; Satires; Epistles).
>
> Tibullus, about 54–19 B.C. (Poet).
>
> Propertius, about 50–about 15 B.C. (Poet).
>
> Ovid, 43 B.C.–17 A.D. (" Metamorphoses " and other poems).
>
> Livy, 59 B.C.–17 A.D. (Historian).

*d. The Silver Latinity*, from the death of Augustus (14 A.D.) to the death of Marcus Aurelius (180 A.D.). This period is marked by a certain reaction against the excessive precision of the previous age. It had become the practice to pay too much attention to standardized forms of expression, and to leave too little play to the individual writer. In the healthy reaction against this formalism, greater freedom of expression now manifests itself. We note also the introduction of idioms from the colloquial language, along with many poetical words and usages. The following authors deserve mention:

> Phaedrus, flourished about 40 A.D. (Fables in Verse)
> Velleius Paterculus, flourished about 30 A.D. (Historian).
> Lucan, 39–65 A.D. (Poem on the Civil War).
> Seneca, about 1–65 A.D. (Tragedies; Philosophical Works).
> Pliny the Elder, 23–79 A.D. ("Natural History").
> Pliny the Younger, 62–about 115 A.D. ("Letters").
> Martial, about 45–about 104 A.D. (Epigrams).
> Quintilian, about 35–about 100 A.D. (Treatise on Oratory and Education).
> Tacitus, about 55–about 118 A.D. (Historian).
> Juvenal, about 55–about 135 A.D. (Satirist).
> Suetonius, about 75–about 150 A.D. ("Lives of the Twelve Caesars").
> Minucius Felix, flourished about 160 A.D. (First Christian Apologist).
> Apuleius, 125–about 200 A.D. ("Metamorphoses," or "Golden Ass").

*e. The Archaizing Period.* This period is characterized by a conscious imitation of the Archaic Period of the second and first centuries B.C.; it overlaps the preceding period, and is of importance from a linguistic rather than from a literary point of view. Of writers who manifest the archaizing tendency most conspicuously may be mentioned Fronto, from whose hand we have a collection of letters addressed to the Emperors Antoninus Pius and Marcus Aurelius; also Aulus Gellius, author of the "Attic Nights." Both of these writers flourished in the second half of the second century A.D.

*f. The Period of the Decline*, from 180 to the close of literary activity in the sixth century A.D. This period is characterized by rapid and radical alterations in the language. The features of the conversational idiom of the lower strata of society invade the literature, while in the remote provinces, such as **Gaul**, Spain, Africa, the language suffers from the incorporation of local peculiarities. Representative writers of this period are :

Tertullian, about 160–about 240 A.D. (Christian Writer).

Cyprian, about 200–258 A.D. (Christian Writer).

Lactantius, flourished about 300 A.D. (Defense of Christianity).

Ausonius, about 310–about 395 A.D. (Poet).

Jerome, 340–420 A.D. (Translator of the Scriptures).

Ambrose, about 340–397 (Christian Father).

Augustine, 354–430 (Christian Father — "City of God").

Prudentius, flourished 400 A.D. (Christian Poet).

Claudian, flourished 400 A.D. (Poet).

Boëthius, about 480–524 A.D. ("Consolation of Philosophy").

4. **Subsequent History of the Latin Language.** — After the sixth century A.D. Latin divides into two entirely different streams. One of these is the literary language maintained in courts, in the Church, and among scholars. This was no longer the language of people in general, and as time went on, became more and more artificial. The other stream is the colloquial idiom of the common people, which developed ultimately in the provinces into the modern so-called Romance idioms. These are the Italian, Spanish, Portuguese, French, Provençal (spoken in Provence, *i.e.* southeastern France), the Rhaeto-Romance (spoken in the Canton of the Grisons in Switzerland), and the Roumanian, spoken in modern Roumania and adjacent districts. All these Romance languages bear the same relation to the Latin as the different groups of the Indo-European family of languages bear to the parent speech.

# Part I.

---•---

## SOUNDS, ACCENT, QUANTITY.

---•---

### THE ALPHABET.

**1.** The Latin Alphabet is the same as the English, except that the Latin has no **w**.

1. **K** occurs only in *Kalendae* and a few other words; **y** and **z** were introduced from the Greek about 50 B.C., and occur only in foreign words — chiefly Greek.

2. With the Romans, who regularly employed only capitals, **I** served both as vowel and consonant; so also **V**. For us, however, it is more convenient to distinguish the vowel and consonant sounds, and to write **i** and **u** for the former, **j** and **v** for the latter. Yet some scholars prefer to employ **i** and **u** in the function of consonants as well as vowels.

### CLASSIFICATION OF SOUNDS.

**2.** 1. The Vowels are **a, e, i, o, u, y**. The other letters are Consonants. The Diphthongs are **ae, oe, ei, au, eu, ui**.

2. Consonants are further subdivided into Mutes, Liquids, Nasals, and Spirants.

3. The Mutes are **p, t, c, k, q; b, d, g; ph, th, ch**. Of these, —

   *a)* **p, t, c, k, q** are voiceless,[1] *i.e.* sounded *without* voice or vibration of the vocal cords.
   *b)* **b, d, g** are voiced,[2] *i.e.* sounded *with* vibration of the vocal cords.

---

[1] For 'voiceless,' 'surd,' 'hard,' or 'tenuis' are sometimes used.
[2] For 'voiced,' 'sonant,' 'soft,' or 'media' are sometimes used.

*c*) **ph, th, ch** are aspirates. These are confined almost exclusively to words derived from the Greek, and were equivalent to **p + h, t + h, c + h,** *i.e.* to the corresponding voiceless mutes with a following breath, as in Eng. *loop-hole, hot-house, block-house.*

4. The Mutes admit of classification also as

| | |
|---|---|
| Labials, | **p, b, ph.** |
| Dentals (or Linguals), | **t, d, th.** |
| Gutturals (or Palatals), | **c, k, q, g, ch.** |

5. The Liquids are **l, r.** These sounds were voiced.

6. The Nasals are **m, n.** These were voiced. Besides its ordinary sound, **n**, when followed by a guttural mute also had another sound, — that of **ng** in *sing*, — the so-called **n** *adulterīnum;* as, —

    **anceps,** *double,* pronounced **angceps.**

7. The Spirants (sometimes called Fricatives) are **f, s, h.** These were voiceless.

8. The Semivowels are **j** and **v.** These were voiced.

9. Double Consonants are **x** and **z.** Of these, **x** was equivalent to **cs,** while the equivalence of **z** is uncertain. See § 3. 3.

10. The following table will indicate the relations of the consonant sounds: —

| | VOICELESS. | VOICED. | ASPIRATES. | |
|---|---|---|---|---|
| | **p,** | **b,** | **ph,** | (Labials). |
| Mutes, | **t,** | **d,** | **th,** | (Dentals). |
| | **c, k, q,** | **g,** | **ch,** | (Gutturals). |
| Liquids, | | **l, r,** | | |
| Nasals, | | **m, n,** | | |
| | **f,** | | | (Labial). |
| Spirants, | **s,** | | | (Dental). |
| | **h,** | | | (Guttural). |
| Semivowels, | | **j, v.** | | |

*a.* The Double Consonants, **x** and **z,** being compound sounds do not admit of classification in the above table.

## SOUNDS OF THE LETTERS.

**3.** The following pronunciation (often called Roman) is substantially that employed by the Romans at the height of their civilization; *i.e.* roughly, from 50 B.C. to 50 A.D.

### 1. Vowels.

ā as in *father* ;                ă as in the first syllable of *ahá* ;
ē as in *they* ;                  ĕ as in *met* ;
ī as in *machine* ;               ĭ as in *pin* ;
ō as in *note* ;                  ŏ as in *obey, melody* ;
ū as in *rude* ;                  ŭ as in *put* ;
y like French *u*, German *ü*.

### 2. Diphthongs.

ae like *ai* in *aisle* ;         eu with its two elements, ĕ and ŭ,
oe like *oi* in *oil* ;              pronounced in rapid succession ;
ei as in *rein* ;                 ui occurs almost exclusively in *cui*
au like *ow* in *how* ;              and *huic*. These words may be
                                     pronounced as though written
                                     *kwee* and *wheek*.

### 3. Consonants.

**b, d, f, h, k, l, m, n, p, qu** are pronounced as in English, except that **bs, bt** are pronounced *ps, pt*.

**c** is always pronounced as *k*.

**t** is always a plain *t*, never with the sound of *sh* as in Eng. *oration*.

**g** always as in *get* ; when **ngu** precedes a vowel, **gu** has the sound of *gw*, as in **anguis, languidus**.

**j** has the sound of *y* as in *yet*.

**r** was probably slightly trilled with the tip of the tongue

**s** always voiceless as in *sin* ; in **suādeō, suāvis, suēscō,** and in compounds and derivatives of these words, **su** has the sound of *sw*.

**v** like *w*.

**x** always like *ks* ; never like Eng. *gz* or *z*.

**z** uncertain in sound; possibly like Eng. *zd*, possibly like *z*. The latter sound is recommended.

The aspirates **ph, ch, th** were pronounced very nearly like our stressed Eng. *p, c, t* — so nearly so, that, for practical purposes, the latter sounds suffice.

Doubled letters, like **ll, mm, tt,** *etc.*, should be so pronounced that both members of the combination are distinctly articulated.

## SYLLABLES.

**4.** There are as many syllables in a Latin word as there are separate vowels and diphthongs.

In the division of words into syllables, —

1. A single consonant is joined to the following vowel; as, **vo-lat, ge-rit, pe-rit, a-dest.**

2. Doubled consonants, like **tt, ss,** *etc.*, are always separated; as, **vit-ta, mis-sus.**

3. Other combinations of two or more consonants are regularly separated, and the first consonant of the combination is joined with the preceding vowel; as, **ma-gis-trī, dig-nus, mōn-strum, sis-te-re.**

4. An exception to Rule 3 occurs when the two consonants consist of a mute followed by l or r (**pl, cl, tl; pr, cr, tr,** *etc.*). In such cases both consonants are regularly joined to the following vowel; as, **a-grī, vo-lu-cris, pa-tris, mā-tris.** Yet if the l or r introduces the second part of a compound, the two consonants are separated; as, **ab-rumpō, ad-lātus.**

5. The double consonant **x** is joined to the preceding vowel; as, **ax-is, tēx-ī.**

## QUANTITY.

**5. A. Quantity of Vowels.**

A vowel is *long* or *short* according to the length of time required for its pronunciation No absolute rule can be given for determining the quantity of Latin vowels. This knowledge must be gained, in large measure, by experience; but the following principles are of aid: —

1. **A vowel is long,**[1] —

   *a)* before **nf** or **ns**; as, **īnfāns, īnferior, cōnsūmō, cēnseō, īnsum.**

   *b)* when the result of contraction; as, **nīlum** for **nihilum.**

2. **A vowel is short,** —

   *a)* before **nt, nd**; as, **amant, amandus.** A few exceptions occur in compounds whose first member has a long vowel; as, **nōn-dum (nōn dum).**

   *b)* before another vowel, or **h**; as, **meus, trahō.** Some exceptions occur, chiefly in proper names derived from the Greek; as, **Aenēās.**

---

[1] In this book, long vowels are indicated by a horizontal line above them; as, **ā, ī, ō,** *etc.* Vowels not thus marked are short. Occasionally a curve is set above short vowels; as, **ĕ, ŭ.**

## B. Quantity of Syllables.

Syllables are distinguished as *long* or *short* according to the length of time required for their pronunciation.

1. **A syllable is long,** [1] —

   *a*) if it contains a long vowel; as, **māter, rēgnum, dīus.**

   *b*) if it contains a diphthong; as, **causae, foedus.**

   *c*) if it contains a short vowel followed by **x, z,** or any two con-sonants (except a mute with l or r); as, **axis, gaza, restō.**

2. **A syllable is short,** if it contains a short vowel followed by a vowel or by a single consonant; as, **mea, amat.**

3. Sometimes a syllable varies in quantity, *viz.* when its vowel is short and is followed by a mute with l or r, *i.e.* by pl, cl, tl; pr, cr, tr, *etc.*; as, **ăgrī, volŭcris.**[2] Such syllables are called *common.* In prose they were regularly short, but in verse they might be treated as long at the option of the poet.

NOTE. — These distinctions of *long* and *short* are not arbitrary and artificial, but are purely natural. Thus, a syllable containing a short vowel followed by two consonants, as **ng,** is long, because such a syllable requires *more time* for its pronunciation; while a syllable containing a short vowel followed by one consonant is short, because it takes *less time* to pronounce it. In case of the common syllables, the mute and the liquid blend so easily as to produce a combination which takes no more time than a single consonant. Yet by separating the two elements (as **ag-rī**) the poets were able to use such syllables as long.

## ACCENT.

**6.** 1. Words of two syllables are accented upon the first; as, **tégit mórem.**

2. Words of more than two syllables are accented upon the penul (next to the last) if that is a long syllable, otherwise upon the antepenult (second from the last); as, **amávī, amántis, míserum.**

3. When the enclitics -**que, -ne, -ve, -ce, -met, -dum** are appended to words, if the syllable preceding the enclitic is long (either originally or as a result of adding the enclitic) it is accented; as, **miserōque, hominísque.** But if the syllable still remains short after the enclitic has been added, it is not accented unless the word originally took the accent on the antepenult. Thus, **pórtaque**; but **míseráque.**

---

[1] To avoid confusion, the quantity of *syllables* is not indicated by any sign.

[2] But if the l or r introduces the second part of a compound, the preceding syllable is always long; as, **abrumpō.**

4. Sometimes the final -e of -ne and -ce disappears, but without affecting the accent; as, **tantŏn, istĭc, illŭc.**

5. In **utrắque,** *each,* and **plērắque,** *most,* -que is not properly an enclitic; yet these words accent the penult, owing to the influence of their other cases, — **utérque, utrúmque, plērúmque.**

## VOWEL CHANGES.[1]

**7.** 1. **In Compounds,** —

*a*) ĕ before a single consonant becomes ĭ; as, —
**colligō** for **con-legō.**

*b*) ă before a single consonant becomes ĭ; as, —
**adigō** for **ad-agō.**

*c*) ă before two consonants becomes ĕ; as, —
**expers** for **ex-pars.**

*d*) ae becomes ī; as, —
**conquīrō** for **con-quaerō.**

*e*) au becomes ū, sometimes ō; as, —
**conclūdō** for **con-claudō**;<br>**explōdō** for **ex-plaudō.**

2. **Contraction.** Concurrent vowels were frequently contracted into one long vowel. The first of the two vowels regularly prevailed; as, —

| | | | |
|---|---|---|---|
| **trēs** | for **tre-es**; | **cōpia** | for **co-opia** |
| **mālō** | for **ma(v)elō**; | **cōgō** | for **co-agō**; |
| **amāstī** | for **amā(v)istī**; | **cōmō** | for **co-emō**; |
| **dēbeō** | for **dē(h)abeō**; | **jūnior** | for **ju(v)enior.** |
| **nīl** | for **nihil**; | | |

3. **Parasitic Vowels.** In the environment of liquids and nasals a parasitic vowel sometimes develops; as, —

**vinculum** for earlier **vinclum.**

So **perīculum, saeculum.**

4. **Syncope.** Sometimes a vowel drops out by syncope; as, —

**ārdor** for **āridor** (compare *āridus*);<br>**valdē** for **validē** (compare *validus*).

---

[1] Only the simplest and most obvious of these are here treated.

## CONSONANT CHANGES.[1]

**8.** 1. **Rhotacism.** An original **s** between vowels became **r**; as, —

arbōs, Gen. arboris (for arbosis);
genus, Gen. generis (for genesis);
dirimō (for dis-emō).

2. **dt, tt, ts** each give **s** or **ss**; as, —

pēnsum  for pend-tum;
versum  for vert-tum;
mīles   for mīlet-s;
sessus   for sedtus;
passus   for pattus.

3. Final consonants were often omitted; as, —

cor  for cord;
lac  for lact.

4. **Assimilation of Consonants.** Consonants are often assimilated to a following sound. Thus: **accurrō** (adc-); **aggerō** (adg-); **asserō** (ads-); **allātus** (adl-); **apportō** (adp-); **attulī** (adt-); **arrīdeō** (adr-); **afferō** (adf-); **occurrō** (obc-); **suppōnō** (subp-); **offerō** (obf-); **corruō** (comr-); **collātus** (coml-); *etc.*

5. **Partial Assimilation.** Sometimes the assimilation is only partial. Thus: —

*a*) **b** before **s** or **t** becomes **p**; as, —
scrīpsī (scrīb-sī),      scrīptum (scrīb-tum).

*b*) **g** before **s** or **t** becomes **c**; as, —
āctus (āg-tus).

*c*) **m** before a dental or guttural becomes **n**; as, —
eundem (eum-dem);   prīnceps (prīm-ceps).

## PECULIARITIES OF ORTHOGRAPHY.

**9.** Many words have variable orthography.

1. Sometimes the different forms belong to different periods of the language. Thus, **quom, voltus, volnus, volt,** *etc.*, were the prevail-

---

[1] Only the simplest and most obvious of these are here treated.

ing forms almost down to the Augustan age; after that, **cum, vultus, vulnus, vult,** *etc.* So **optumus, maxumus, lubet, lubīdō,** *etc.,* down to about the same era; later, **optimus, maximus, libet, libīdō,** *etc.*

2. In some words the orthography varies at one and the same period of the language. Examples are **exspectō, expectō; exsistō, existō; epistula, epistola; adulēscēns, adolēscēns; paulus, paullus; cottīdiē, cotīdiē**; and, particularly, prepositional compounds, which often made a concession to the etymology in the spelling, as, —

| | | | |
|---|---|---|---|
| ad-gerō | or aggerō; | ad-serō | or asserō; |
| ad-liciō | or alliciō; | in-lātus | or illātus; |
| ad-rogāns | or arrogāns; | sub-moveō | or summoveō; |

and many others.

3. Compounds of **jaciō** were usually written **ēiciō, dēiciō, adiciō, obiciō,** *etc.,* but were probably pronounced as though written **adjiciō, objiciō,** *etc.*

4. Adjectives and nouns in **-quus, -quum; -vus, -vum; -uus, -uum** preserved the earlier forms in **-quos, -quom; -vos, -vom; -uos, -uom,** down through the Ciceronian age; as, **antīquos, antīquom; saevos; perpetuos; equos; servos.** Similarly verbs in the 3d plural present indicative exhibit the terminations **-quont, -quontur; -vont, -vontur; -uont, -uontur,** for the same period; as, **relinquont, loquontur; vīvont, metuont.**

The older spelling, while generally followed in editions of Plautus and Terence, has not yet been adopted in our prose texts.

# PART II.

———◆———

## INFLECTIONS.

———◆———

**10**. The Parts of Speech in Latin are the same as in English, *viz.* Nouns, Adjectives, Pronouns, Verbs, Adverbs, Prepositions, Conjunctions, and Interjections; but the Latin has no article.

**11**. Of these eight parts of speech the first four are capable of **Inflection**, *i.e.* of undergoing change of form to express modifications of meaning. In case of Nouns, Adjectives, and Pronouns, this process is called **Declension**; in case of verbs, **Conjugation**.

———◆———

## Chapter I. — *Declension.*

### A. NOUNS.

**12**. A Noun is the name of a *person, place, thing,* or *quality;* as, **Caesar,** *Caesar;* **Rōma,** *Rome;* **penna,** *feather;* **virtūs,** *courage.*

1. Nouns are either Proper or Common. Proper nouns are permanent names of persons or places; as, **Caesar, Rōma.** Other nouns are Common; as, **penna, virtūs.**

2. Nouns are also distinguished as Concrete or Abstract.

    *a*) Concrete nouns are those which designate individual objects; as, **mōns,** *mountain;* **pēs,** *foot;* **diēs,** *day;* **mēns,** *mind.*

Under concrete nouns are included, also, collective nouns; as, **legiō,** *legion* ; **comitātus,** *retinue.*

*b*) Abstract nouns designate qualities ; as, **cōnstantia,** *steadfastness;* **paupertās,** *poverty.*

## GENDER OF NOUNS.

**13.** There are three Genders, — Masculine, Feminine, and Neuter. Gender in Latin is either natural or grammatical.

### Natural Gender.

**14.** The gender of nouns is natural when it is based upon sex. Natural gender is confined entirely to names of persons ; and these are —

1. Masculine, if they denote males ; as, —
   **nauta,** *sailor* ; **agricola,** *farmer.*
2. Feminine, if they denote females ; as, —
   **māter,** *mother* ; **rēgīna,** *queen.*

### Grammatical Gender.

**15.** Grammatical gender is determined not by sex, but by the general signification of the word, or the ending of its Nominative Singular. By grammatical gender, nouns denoting things or qualities are often Masculine or Feminine, simply by virtue of their signification or the ending of the Nominative Singular. The following are the general principles for determining grammatical gender : —

*A. Gender determined by Signification.*

1. Names of *Rivers,* *Winds,* and *Months* are Masculine ; as, —

   **Sēquana,** *Seine;* **Eurus,** *east wind;* **Aprīlis,** *April.*

2. Names of *Trees,* and such names of *Towns* and *Islands* as end in -**us,** are Feminine ; as, —

   **quercus,** *oak;* **Corinthus,** *Corinth;* **Rhodus,** *Rhodes.*

Other names of towns and islands follow the gender of their endings (see *B*, below) ; as, —

    **Delphī,** m. ; **Leuctra,** n. ; **Tībur,** n. ; **Carthāgō,** f.

3. Indeclinable nouns, also infinitives and phrases, are Neuter; as, —

    **nihil,** *nothing;* **nefās,** *wrong;* **amāre,** *to love.*

Note. — Exceptions to the above principles sometimes occur; as, **Allia (the** river), f.

    *B.*   *Gender determined by Ending of Nominative Singular.*

The gender of other nouns is determined by the ending of the Nominative Singular.[1]

Note 1. — *Common Gender.* Certain nouns are sometimes Masculine, sometimes Feminine. Thus, **sacerdōs** may mean either *priest* or *priestess,* and is Masculine or Feminine accordingly. So also **cīvis,** *citizen* ; **parēns,** *parent;* etc. The gender of such nouns is said to be *common.*

Note 2. — Names of animals usually have grammatical gender, according to the ending of the Nominative Singular, but the one form may designate either the male or female; as, **ānser,** m., *goose* or *gander.* So **vulpēs,** f., *fox;* **aquila,** f., *eagle.*

### NUMBER.

16. The Latin has two Numbers, — the Singular and Plural. The Singular denotes one object; the Plural, more than one.

### CASES.

17. There are six Cases in Latin : —

        **Nominative,** Case of Subject ;
        **Genitive,**   Objective with *of,* or Possessive ;
        **Dative,**     Objective with *to* or *for ;*
        **Accusative,** Case of Direct Object ;
        **Vocative,**   Case of Address ;
        **Ablative,**   Objective with *by, from, in, with.*

---

[1] The great majority of all Latin nouns come under this category. The principles for determining their gender are given under the separate declensions.

1. LOCATIVE. Vestiges of another case, the **Locative** (denoting place where), occur in names of towns and in a few other words.

2. OBLIQUE CASES. The Genitive, Dative, Accusative, and Ablative are called **Oblique Cases.**

3. STEM AND CASE-ENDINGS. The different cases are formed by appending certain **case-endings** to a fundamental part called the **Stem.**[1] Thus, **portam** (Accusative Singular) is formed by adding the case-ending -m to the stem **porta-**. But in most cases the final vowel of the stem has coalesced so closely with the actual case-ending that the latter has become more or less obscured. The *apparent case-ending* thus resulting is called a **termination.**

## THE FIVE DECLENSIONS.

**18.** There are five Declensions in Latin, distinguished from each other by the final letter of the Stem, and also by the Termination of the Genitive Singular, as follows : —

| DECLENSION. | FINAL LETTER OF STEM. | GEN. TERMINATION. |
| --- | --- | --- |
| **First** | ā | -ae |
| **Second** | ŏ | -ī |
| **Third** | ĭ / Some consonant | -ĭs |
| **Fourth** | ŭ | -ūs |
| **Fifth** | ē | -ĕī |

### Cases alike in Form.

**19.** 1. The Vocative is regularly like the Nominative, except in the singular of nouns in -us of the Second Declension.

2. The Dative and Ablative Plural are always alike.

3. In Neuters the Accusative and Nominative are always alike, and in the Plural end in -ă.

4. In the Third, Fourth, and Fifth Declensions, the Accusative Plural is regularly like the Nominative.

---

[1] The Stem is often derived from a more primitive form called the **Root.** Thus, the stem **porta-** goes back to the root per-, por-. Roots are usually monosyllabic. The addition made to a root to form a stem is called a **Suffix.** Thus in **porta-** the suffix is -ta.

## FIRST DECLENSION.

### ā-Stems.

**20.** Pure Latin nouns of the First Declension regularly end, in the Nominative Singular, in -ă, weakened from -ā, and are of the Feminine Gender. They are declined as follows: —

**Porta,** *gate;* stem, **portā-.**

#### SINGULAR.

| CASES. | | MEANINGS. | TERMINATIONS. |
|---|---|---|---|
| *Nom.* | porta | *a gate* (as subject) | -ă |
| *Gen.* | portae | *of a gate* | -ae |
| *Dat.* | portae | *to* or *for a gate* | -ae |
| *Acc.* | port**am** | *a gate* (as object) | -am |
| *Voc.* | porta | *O gate!* | ·ă |
| *Abl.* | portā | *with, by, from, in a gate* | -ā |

#### PLURAL.

| | | | |
|---|---|---|---|
| *Nom.* | portae | *gates* (as subject) | -ae |
| *Gen.* | portā**rum** | *of gates* | -ārum |
| *Dat.* | portīs | *to* or *for gates* | -īs |
| *Acc.* | portā**s** | *gates* (as object) | -ās |
| *Voc.* | portae | *O gates!* | -ae |
| *Abl.* | portīs | *with, by, from, in gates* | -īs |

1. The Latin has no article, and **porta** may mean either *a gate* or *the gate;* and in the Plural, *gates* or *the gates.*

### Peculiarities of Nouns of the First Declension.

**21.** 1. EXCEPTIONS IN GENDER. Nouns denoting males are Masculine; as, **nauta,** *sailor;* **agricola,** *farmer;* also, **Hadria,** *Adriatic Sea.*

2. Rare Case-Endings, —

*a*) An old form of the Genitive Singular in -**ās** is preserved in the combination **pater familiās,** *father of a family;* also in **māter familiās, fīlius familiās, fīlia familiās.** But the regular form of the Genitive in -ae is also admissible in these expressions; as, **pater familiae.**

*b*) In poetry a Genitive in -**āī** also occurs; as, **aulāī.**

*c*) The Locative Singular ends in -ae; as, **Rōmae**, *at Rome*.

*d*) A Genitive Plural in **-um** instead of **-ārum** sometimes occurs; as, **Dardanidum** instead of **Dardanidārum**. This termination **-um** is not a contraction of **-ārum**, but represents an entirely different case-ending.

*e*) Instead of the regular ending **-īs**, we usually find **-ābus** in the Dative and Ablative Plural of **dea**, *goddess*, and **fīlia**, *daughter*, especially when it is important to distinguish these nouns from the corresponding forms of **deus**, *god*, and **fīlius**, *son*. A few other words sometimes have the same peculiarity; as, **lībertābus** (from **līberta**, *freedwoman*), **equābus** (*mares*), to avoid confusion wiih **lībertīs** (from **lībertus**, *freedman*) and **equīs** (from **equus**, *horse*).

### Greek Nouns.

**22.** These end in **-ē** (Feminine); **-ās** and **-ēs** (Masculine). In the Plural they are declined like regular Latin nouns of the First Declension. In the Singular they are declined as follows:—

| **Archiās,** *Archias.* | **Epitomē,** *epitome.* | **Comētēs,** *comet.* |
|---|---|---|
| *Nom.* Archiās | epitomē | comētēs |
| *Gen.* Archiae | epitomēs | comētae |
| *Dat.* Archiae | epitomae | comētae |
| *Acc.* Archiam (or -ān) | epitomēn | comētēn |
| *Voc.* Archiā | epitomē | comētē (or -ă) |
| *Abl.* Archiā | epitomē | comētē (or -ā) |

1. But most Greek nouns in **-ē** become regular Latin nouns in **-a**, and are declined like **porta**; as, **grammatica**, *grammar*; **mūsica**, *music*; **rhētorica**, *rhetoric*.

2. Some other peculiarities occur, especially in poetry.

### SECOND DECLENSION.

#### ŏ-Stems.

**23.** Pure Latin nouns of the Second Declension end in **-us, -er, -ir**, Masculine; **-um**, Neuter. Originally **-us** in the Nominative of the Masculine was **-os**; and **-um** of the Neuters **-om**. So also in the Accusative.

Nouns in -**us** and -**um** are declined as follows: —

Hortus, *garden*;
stem, hortŏ-.

Bellum, *war*;
stem, bellŏ-.

SINGULAR.

|       |         | TERMINATION. |        | TERMINATION. |
|-------|---------|--------------|--------|--------------|
| *Nom.* | hortus  | -us          | bellum | -um          |
| *Gen.* | hortī   | -ī           | bellī  | -ī           |
| *Dat.* | hortō   | -ō           | bellō  | -ō           |
| *Acc.* | hortum  | -um          | bellum | -um          |
| *Voc.* | horte   | -e           | bellum | -um          |
| *Abl.* | hortō   | -ō           | bellō  | -ō           |

PLURAL.

|       |          |         |          |        |
|-------|----------|---------|----------|--------|
| *Nom.* | hortī    | -ī      | bella    | -a     |
| *Gen.* | hortōrum | -ōrum   | bellōrum | -ōrum  |
| *Dat.* | hortīs   | -īs     | bellīs   | -īs    |
| *Acc.* | hortōs   | -ōs     | bella    | -a     |
| *Voc.* | hortī    | -ī      | bella    | -a     |
| *Abl.* | hortīs   | -īs     | bellīs   | -īs    |

Nouns in -**er** and -**ir** are declined as follows: —

Puer, *boy*;
stem, puerŏ-.

Ager, *field*;
stem, agrŏ-.

Vir, *man*;
stem, virŏ-

SINGULAR.

|       |         |         |        | TERMINATION. |
|-------|---------|---------|--------|--------------|
| *Nom.* | puer    | ager    | vir    | Wanting      |
| *Gen.* | puerī   | agrī    | virī   | -ī           |
| *Dat.* | puerō   | agrō    | virō   | -ō           |
| *Acc.* | puerum  | agrum   | virum  | -um          |
| *Voc.* | puer    | ager    | vir    | Wanting      |
| *Abl.* | puerō   | agrō    | virō   | -ō           |

PLURAL.

|       |          |         |         |        |
|-------|----------|---------|---------|--------|
| *Nom.* | puerī    | agrī    | virī    | -ī     |
| *Gen.* | puerōrum | agrōrum | virōrum | -ōrum  |
| *Dat.* | puerīs   | agrīs   | virīs   | -īs    |
| *Acc.* | puerōs   | agrōs   | virōs   | -ōs    |
| *Voc.* | puerī    | agrī    | virī    | -ī     |
| *Abl.* | puerīs   | agrīs   | virīs   | -īs    |

1. Note that in words of the type of **puer** and **vir** the final vowel of the stem has disappeared in the Nominative and Vocative Singular.

In the Nominative and Vocative Singular of **ager**, the stem is further modified by the development of **e** before **r**

2. The following nouns in **-er** are declined like **puer** : **adulter**, *adulterer* ; **gener**, *son-in-law* ; **Līber**, *Bacchus* ; **socer**, *father-in-law* ; **vesper**, *evening* ; and compounds in **-fer** and **-ger**, as **signifer**, **armiger**.

### Nouns in *-vus*, *-vum*, *-quus*.

**24.** Nouns ending in the Nominative Singular in **-vus**, **-vum**, **-quus**, exhibited two types of inflection in the classical Latin, — an earlier and a later, — as follows : —

### *Earlier Inflection* (*including Caesar and Cicero*).

**Servos**, m., *slave.*      **Aevom**, n., *age.*      **Equos**, m., *horse.*

SINGULAR.

|       |        |        |        |
|-------|--------|--------|--------|
| *Nom.* | servos | aevom  | equos  |
| *Gen.* | servī  | aevī   | equī   |
| *Dat.* | servō  | aevō   | equō   |
| *Acc.* | servom | aevom  | equom  |
| *Voc.* | serve  | aevom  | eque   |
| *Abl.* | servō  | aevō   | equō   |

### *Later Inflection* (*after Cicero*).

SINGULAR.

|       |        |        |        |
|-------|--------|--------|--------|
| *Nom.* | servus | aevum  | equus  |
| *Gen.* | servī  | aevī   | equī   |
| *Dat.* | servō  | aevō   | equō   |
| *Acc.* | servum | aevum  | equum  |
| *Voc.* | serve  | aevum  | eque   |
| *Abl.* | servō  | aevō   | equō   |

1. The Plural of these nouns is regular, and always uniform.

### Peculiarities of Inflection in the Second Declension.

**25.** 1. Proper names in **-ius** regularly form the Genitive Singular in **-ī** (instead of **-iī**), and the Vocative Singular in **-ī** (for **-ie**) ; as, **Vergilī**, *of Virgil*, or *O Virgil* (instead of **Vergiliī**, **Vergilie**). In such words the accent stands upon the penult, even though that be short. Nouns in **-aius**, **-ejus** form the Gen. in **-aī**, **-eī**, as **Pompejus**, **Pompeī**.

2. Nouns in **-ius** and **-ium**, until after the beginning of the reign of Augustus (31 B.C.), regularly formed the Genitive Singular in **-ī** (instead of **-iī**) ; as, —

| | | |
|---|---|---|
| *Nom.* | ingenium | fīlius |
| *Gen.* | ingénī | fīlī |

These Genitives accent the penult, even when it is short.

3. **Fīlius** forms the Vocative Singular in -ī (for -ie); *viz.* **fīlī,** *O son!*

4. **Deus,** *god,* lacks the Vocative Singular. The Plural is inflected as follows: —

| | | |
|---|---|---|
| *Nom.* | dī | (deī) |
| *Gen.* | deōrum | (deum) |
| *Dat.* | dīs | (deīs) |
| *Acc.* | deōs | |
| *Voc.* | dī | (deī) |
| *Abl.* | dīs | (deīs) |

5. The Locative Singular ends in -ī; as, **Corinthī,** *at Corinth.*

6. The Genitive Plural has **-um,** instead of **-ōrum,** —

   *a)* in words denoting money and measure; as, **talentum,** *of talents;* **modium,** *of pecks;* **sēstertium,** *of sesterces.*

   *b)* in **duumvir, triumvir, decemvir;** as, **duumvirum.**

   *c)* sometimes in other words; as, **līberum,** *of the children;* **socium,** *of the allies.*

**Exceptions to Gender in the Second Declension.**

**26.** 1. The following nouns in **-us** are Feminine by exception: —

   *a)* Names of **towns, islands, trees** — according to the general rule laid down in § 15. 2; also some names of countries; as **Aegyptus,** *Egypt.*

   *b)* Five special words, —

         **alvus,** *belly;*
         **carbasus,** *flax;*
         **colus,** *distaff;*
         **humus,** *ground;*
         **vannus,** *winnowing-fan.*

   *c)* A few Greek Feminines; as, —

         **atomus,** *atom;*
         **diphthongus,** *diphthong.*

2. The following nouns in **-us** are Neuter: —

         **pelagus,** *sea;*
         **vīrus,** *poison;*
         **vulgus,** *crowd.*

### Greek Nouns of the Second Declension.

**27.** These end in -os, -ōs, Masculine or Feminine; and
-on, Neuter.   They are mainly proper names, and are declined as follows : —

| Barbitos, m. and f., *lyre.* | Androgeōs, m., *Androgeos.* | Īlion, n., *Troy.* |
|---|---|---|
| *Nom.* barbitos | Androgeōs | Īlion |
| *Gen.* barbitī | Androgeō, -ī | Īliī |
| *Dat.* barbitō | Androgeō | Īliō |
| *Acc.* barbiton | Androgeō, -ōn | Īlion |
| *Voc.* barbite | Androgeōs | Īlion |
| *Abl.* barbitō | Androgeō | Īliō |

1. Nouns in -os sometimes form the Accusative Singular in -um,
instead of -on ; as, Dēlum, *Delos.*

2. The Plural of Greek nouns, when it occurs, is usually regular.

3. For other rare forms of Greek nouns the lexicon may be consulted.

### THIRD DECLENSION.

**28.** Nouns of the Third Declension end in -a, -e, -ī, -ō,
-y, -c, -l, -n, -r, -s, -t, -x.   The Third Declension includes
several distinct classes of Stems, —

I. Pure Consonant-Stems.

II. ĭ-Stems.

III. Consonant-Stems which have partially adapted
themselves to the inflection of ĭ-Stems.

IV. A very few stems ending in a long vowel or a
diphthong.

V. Irregular Nouns.

### I. Consonant-Stems.

**29.** 1. In these the stem appears in its unaltered form
in all the oblique cases, so that the actual case-endings
may be clearly recognized.

2. Consonant-Stems fall into several natural subdivisions, according as the stem ends in a **Mute, Liquid, Nasal,** or **Spirant.**

## *A. Mute-Stems.*

**30.** Mute-Stems may end, —

1. In a Labial (**p**) ; as, **prīncep -s.**
2. In a Guttural (**g** or **c**) ; as, **rēmex (rēmeg -s) ; dux (duc -s).**
3. In a Dental (**d** or **t**) ; as, **lapis (lapid -s) ; mīles (mīlet -s).**

### 1. STEMS IN A LABIAL MUTE (p).

**31. Prīnceps,** m., *chief.*

#### SINGULAR.

|       |            | TERMINATION. |
|-------|------------|--------------|
| *Nom.* | prīnceps   | -s           |
| *Gen.* | prīncipis  | -is          |
| *Dat.* | prīncipī   | -ī           |
| *Acc.* | prīncipem  | -em          |
| *Voc.* | prīnceps   | -s           |
| *Abl.* | prīncipe   | -e           |

#### PLURAL.

|       |              |        |
|-------|--------------|--------|
| *Nom.* | prīncipēs   | -ēs    |
| *Gen.* | prīncipum   | -um    |
| *Dat.* | prīncipibus | -ibus  |
| *Acc.* | prīncipēs   | -ēs    |
| *Voc.* | prīncipēs   | -ēs    |
| *Abl.* | prīncipibus | -ibus  |

### 2. STEMS IN A GUTTURAL MUTE (g, c).

**32.** In these the termination **-s** of the Nominative Singular unites with the guttural, thus producing **-x.**

**Rēmex,** m., *rower.*          **Dux,** c., *leader.*

| | SINGULAR. | PLURAL. | SINGULAR. | PLURAL. |
|-------|-----------|-----------|-----------|-----------|
| *Nom.* | rēmex    | rēmigēs   | dux       | ducēs     |
| *Gen.* | rēmigis  | rēmigum   | ducis     | ducum     |
| *Dat.* | rēmigī   | rēmigibus | ducī      | ducibus   |
| *Acc.* | rēmigem  | rēmigēs   | ducem     | ducēs     |
| *Voc.* | rēmex    | rēmigēs   | dux       | ducēs     |
| *Abl.* | rēmige   | rēmigibus | duce      | ducibus   |

### 3. Stems in a Dental Mute (d, t).

**33**. In these the final **d** or **t** of the stem disappears in the Nomina‑ tive Singular before the ending **-s**.

| | **Lapis**, m., *stone.* | | **Mīles**, m., *soldier.* | |
|---|---|---|---|---|
| | SINGULAR. | PLURAL. | SINGULAR. | PLURAL. |
| *Nom.* | lapis | lapidēs | mīles | mīlitēs |
| *Gen.* | lapidis | lapidum | mīlitis | mīlitum |
| *Dat.* | lapidī | lapidibus | mīlitī | mīlitibus |
| *Acc.* | lapidem | lapidēs | mīlitem | mīlitēs |
| *Voc.* | lapis | lapidēs | mīles | mīlitēs |
| *Abl.* | lapide | lapidibus | mīlite | mīlitibus |

### B. Liquid Stems.

**34**. These end in **-l** or **-r**.

| | **Vigil**, m., *watchman.* | **Victor**, m., *conqueror.* | **Aequor**, n., *sea.* |
|---|---|---|---|
| | | SINGULAR. | |
| *Nom.* | vigil | victor | aequor |
| *Gen.* | vigilis | victōris | aequoris |
| *Dat.* | vigilī | victōrī | aequorī |
| *Acc.* | vigilem | victōrem | aequor |
| *Voc.* | vigil | victor | aequor |
| *Abl.* | vigile | victōre | aequore |
| | | PLURAL. | |
| *Nom.* | vigilēs | victōrēs | aequora |
| *Gen.* | vigilum | victōrum | aequorum |
| *Dat.* | vigilibus | victōribus | aequoribus |
| *Acc.* | vigilēs | victōrēs | aequora |
| *Voc.* | vigilēs | victōrēs | aequora |
| *Abl.* | vigilibus | victōribus | aequoribus |

1. Masculine and Feminine stems ending in a liquid form the Nomi‑ native and Vocative Singular without termination.

2. The termination is also lacking in the Nominative, Accusative and Vocative Singular of **all neuters** of the Third Declension.

## C. *Nasal Stems.*

**35.** These end in -n,[1] which often disappears in the Nom. Sing.

**Leō**, m., *lion.*  **Nōmen**, n., *name*

| SINGULAR. | PLURAL. | SINGULAR. | PLURAL. |
|---|---|---|---|
| *Nom.* leō | leōnēs | nōmen | nōmina |
| *Gen.* leōnis | leōnum | nōminis | nōminum |
| *Dat.* leōnī | leōnibus | nōminī | nōminibus |
| *Acc.* leōnem | leōnēs | nōmen | nōmina |
| *Voc.* leō | leōnēs | nomen | nōmina |
| *Abl.* leōne | leōnibus | nōmine | nōminibus |

### D. s-*Stems.*

**36. Mōs**, m., *custom.*  **Genus**, n., *race.*  **Honor**, m., *honor.*

SINGULAR.

| | | | |
|---|---|---|---|
| *Nom.* | mōs | genus | honor |
| *Gen.* | mōris | generis | honōris |
| *Dat.* | mōrī | generī | honōrī |
| *Acc.* | mōrem | genus | honōrem |
| *Voc.* | mōs | genus | honor |
| *Abl.* | mōre | genere | honōre |

PLURAL.

| | | | |
|---|---|---|---|
| *Nom.* | mōrēs | genera | honōrēs |
| *Gen.* | mōrum | generum | honōrum |
| *Dat.* | mōribus | generibus | honōribus |
| *Acc.* | mōrēs | genera | honōrēs |
| *Voc.* | mōrēs | genera | honōrēs |
| *Abl.* | mōribus | generibus | honōribus |

1. Note that the final **s** of the stem becomes **r** (between vowels) in the oblique cases. In many words (**honor, color,** and the like) the **r** of the oblique cases has, by analogy, crept into the Nominative, displacing the earlier **s**, though the forms **honōs, colōs,** *etc.,* also occur, particularly in early Latin and in poetry.

[1] There is only one stem ending in -**m**.—**hiems** hiemis. *winter*

## II. Ĭ-Stems.

### A. *Masculine and Feminine* Ĭ-*Stems.*

**37.** These regularly end in -**is** in the Nominative Singular, and always have -**ium** in the Genitive Plural. Originally the Accusative Singular ended in -**im**, the Ablative Singular in -**ī**, and the Accusative Plural in -**īs**; but these endings have been largely displaced by **-em, -e,** and **-ēs,** the endings of Consonant-Stems.

**38.** **Tussis,** f., *cough*; **Īgnis,** m., *fire*; **Hostis,** c., *enemy*;
stem, **tussi-.**          stem, **īgni-.**          stem, **hosti-.**

**SINGULAR.**

|       |              |              |                 | TERMINATION. |
|-------|--------------|--------------|-----------------|--------------|
| *Nom.* | tussis       | īgnis        | hostis          | -is          |
| *Gen.* | tussis       | īgnis        | hostis          | -is          |
| *Dat.* | tussī        | īgnī         | hostī           | -ī           |
| *Acc.* | tussim       | īgnem        | hostem          | -im, -em     |
| *Voc.* | tussis       | īgnis        | hostis          | -is          |
| *Abl.* | tussī        | īgnī or e    | hoste           | -ī, -e       |

**PLURAL.**

|       |              |              |                 |              |
|-------|--------------|--------------|-----------------|--------------|
| *Nom.* | tussēs       | īgnēs        | hostēs          | -ēs          |
| *Gen.* | tussium      | īgnium       | hostium         | -ium         |
| *Dat.* | tussibus     | īgnibus      | hostibus        | -ibus        |
| *Acc.* | tussīs or -ēs | īgnīs or -ēs | hostīs or -ēs   | -īs, -ēs     |
| *Voc.* | tussēs       | īgnēs        | hostēs          | -ēs          |
| *Abl.* | tussibus     | īgnibus      | hostibus        | -ibus        |

1. To the same class belong —

| | | |
|---|---|---|
| apis, *bee.* | crātis, *hurdle.* | † *secūris, *axe.* |
| auris, *ear.* | *febris, *fever.* | sēmentis, *sowing.* |
| avis, *bird.* | orbis, *circle.* | † *sitis, *thirst.* |
| axis, *axle.* | ovis, *sheep.* | torris, *brand.* |
| *būris, *plough-beam.* | pelvis, *basin.* | † *turris, *tower.* |
| clāvis, *key.* | puppis, *stern.* | trudis, *pole.* |
| collis, *hill.* | restis, *rope.* | vectis, *lever.* |
| | and many others. | |

Words marked with a star regularly have Acc. -**im**; those marked with a † regularly have Abl. -**ī**. Of the others, many at times show -**im** and -**ī**. Town and river names in -**is** regularly have -**im**, -**ī**.

2. Not all nouns in -is are Ĭ-Stems. Some are genuine consonant-stems, and have the regular consonant terminations throughout, notably, **canis**, *dog*; **juvenis**, *youth*.[1]

3. Some genuine Ĭ-Stems have become disguised in the Nominative Singular; as, **pars**, *part*, for par(ti)s; **anas**, *duck*, for ana(ti)s; so also **mors**, *death*; **dōs**, *dowry*; **nox**, *night*; **sors**, *lot*; **mēns**, *mind*; **ars**, *art*; **gēns**, *tribe*; and some others.

### B. Neuter Ĭ-Stems.

**39.** These end in the Nominative Singular in -e, -al, and -ar. They always have -ī in the Ablative Singular, -ia in the Nominative, Accusative, and Vocative Plural, and -ium in the Genitive Plural, thus holding more steadfastly to the i-character than do Masculine and Feminine Ĭ-Stems.

| | **Sedīle**, *seat*;<br>stem, **sedīli-**. | **Animal**, *animal*;<br>stem, **animāli-**. | **Calcar**, *spur*;<br>stem, **calcāri-** |
| --- | --- | --- | --- |

#### SINGULAR.

| | | | | TERMINATION. |
| --- | --- | --- | --- | --- |
| *Nom.* | sedīle | animal | calcar | -e or wanting |
| *Gen.* | sedīlis | animālis | calcāris | -is |
| *Dat.* | sedīlī | animālī | calcārī | -ī |
| *Acc.* | sedīle | animal | calcar | -e or wanting |
| *Voc.* | sedīle | animal | calcar | -e or wanting |
| *Abl.* | sedīlī | animālī | calcārī | -ī |

#### PLURAL.

| | | | | |
| --- | --- | --- | --- | --- |
| *Nom.* | sedīlia | animālia | calcāria | -ia |
| *Gen.* | sedīlium | animālium | calcārium | -ium |
| *Dat.* | sedīlibus | animālibus | calcāribus | -ibus |
| *Acc.* | sedīlia | animālia | calcāria | -ia |
| *Voc.* | sedīlia | animālia | calcāria | -ia |
| *Abl.* | sedīlibus | animālibus | calcāribus | -ibus |

1. In most words of this class the final -i of the stem is lost in the Nominative Singular; in others it appears as -e.

2. Proper names in -e form the Ablative Singular in -e; as, **Sōracte**, *Mt. Soracte*; so also sometimes **mare**, *sea*.

---

[1] **Mēnsis**, *month*, originally a consonant stem (**mēns-**), has in the Genitive Plural both **mēnsium** and **mēnsum**. The Accusative Plural is **mēnsēs**.

### III. Consonant-Stems that have partially adapted themselves to the Inflection of Ĭ-Stems.

**40.** Many Consonant-Stems have so far adapted them-selves to the inflection of ĭ-stems as to take -ium in the Genitive Plural, and -īs in the Accusative Plural. Their true character as Consonant-Stems, however, is shown by the fact that they never take -im in the Accusative Singu-lar, or -ī in the Ablative Singular. The following words are examples of this class: —

|  | **Caedēs**, f., *slaughter*; stem, **caed-**. | **Arx**, f., *citadel*; stem, **arc-**. | **Linter**, f., *skiff*; stem, **lintr-**. |
|---|---|---|---|
| | | **SINGULAR.** | |
| *Nom.* | caedēs | arx | linter |
| *Gen.* | caedis | arcis | lintris |
| *Dat.* | caedī | arcī | lintrī |
| *Acc.* | caedem | arcem | lintrem |
| *Voc.* | caedēs | arx | linter |
| *Abl.* | caede | arce | lintre |
| | | **PLURAL.** | |
| *Nom.* | caedēs | arcēs | lintrēs |
| *Gen.* | caedium | arcium | lintrium |
| *Dat.* | caedibus | arcibus | lintribus |
| *Acc.* | caedēs, -īs | arcēs, -īs | lintrēs, -īs |
| *Voc.* | caedēs | arcēs | lintrēs |
| *Abl.* | caedibus | arcibus | lintribus |

1. The following classes of nouns belong here : —

   *a)* Nouns in -ēs, with Genitive in -is ; as, **nūbēs, aedēs, clādēs,** *etc.*

   *b)* Many monosyllables in -s or -x preceded by one or more consonants ; as, **urbs, mōns, stirps, lanx.**

   *c)* Most nouns in -ns and -rs ; as, **cliēns, cohors.**

   *d)* **Ūter, venter ; fūr, līs, mās, mūs, nix ;** and the Plurals **faucēs, penātēs, Optimātēs, Samnītēs, Quirītēs.**

   *e)* Sometimes nouns in -tās with Genitive -tātis ; as, **cīvitās, aetās. Cīvitās** *usually* has **cīvitātium.**

### IV. Stems in -ī, -ū, and Diphthongs.

**41.**  Vīs, f., Sūs, c., Bōs, c., Juppiter, m.,
*force ;* *swine ;* *ox, cow ;* *Jupiter ;*
stem, vī-. stem, sū-. stem, bou-. stem, Jou-.

SINGULAR.

| | | | |
|---|---|---|---|
| *Nom.* | vīs | sūs | bōs | Juppiter |
| *Gen.* | — | suis | bovis | Jovis |
| *Dat.* | — | suī | bovī | Jovī |
| *Acc.* | vim | suem | bovem | Jovem |
| *Voc.* | vīs | sūs | bōs | Juppiter |
| *Abl.* | vī | sue | bove | Jove |

PLURAL.

| | | | |
|---|---|---|---|
| *Nom.* | vīrēs | suēs | bovēs |
| *Gen.* | vīrium | suum | { bovum / boum |
| *Dat.* | vīribus | { suibus / subus | { bōbus / būbus |
| *Acc.* | vīrēs | suēs | bovēs |
| *Voc.* | vīrēs | suēs | bovēs |
| *Abl.* | vīribus | { suibus / subus | { bōbus / būbus |

1. Notice that the oblique cases of **sūs** have ŭ in the root syllable.

2. **Grūs** is declined like **sūs**, except that the Dative and Ablative Plural are always **gruibus**.

3. **Juppiter** is for **Jou-pater**, and therefore contains the same stem as in **Jov-is, Jov-ī,** *etc.*

**Nāvis** was originally a diphthong stem ending in **au-**, but it has passed over to the ĭ-stems (§ 37). Its ablative often ends in -ĭ.

### V. Irregular Nouns.

**42.**  Senex, m., *old man.*  Carō, f., *flesh.*  Os, n., *bone.*

SINGULAR.

| | | | |
|---|---|---|---|
| *Nom.* | senex | carō | os |
| *Gen.* | senis | carnis | ossis |
| *Dat.* | senī | carnī | ossī |
| *Acc.* | senem | carnem | os |
| *Voc.* | senex | carō | os |
| *Abl.* | sene | carne | osse |

PLURAL.

| *Nom.* | senēs | carnēs | ossa |
|---|---|---|---|
| *Gen.* | senum | carnium | ossium |
| *Dat.* | senibus | carnibus | ossibus |
| *Acc.* | senēs | carnēs | ossa |
| *Voc.* | senēs | carnēs | ossa |
| *Abl.* | senibus | carnibus | ossibus |

1. **Iter, itineris,** n., *way,* is inflected regularly throughout from the stem **itiner-.**

2. **Supellex, supellectilis,** f., *furniture,* is confined to the Singular. The oblique cases are formed from the stem **supellectil-.** The ablative has both -ī and -e.

3. **Jecur,** n., *liver,* forms its oblique cases from two stems, — **jecor-** and **jecinor-.** Thus, Gen. **jecoris** or **jecinoris.**

4. **Femur,** n., *thigh,* usually forms its oblique cases from the stem **femor-,** but sometimes from the stem **femin-.** Thus, Gen. **femoris** or **feminis.**

### General Principles of Gender in the Third Declension.

**43.** 1. Nouns in **-ō, -or, -ōs, -er, -ĕs** are Masculine.

2. Nouns in **-ās, -ēs, -is, -ys, -x, -s** (preceded by a consonant); **-dō, -gō** (Genitive **-inis**); **-iō** (abstract and collective), **-ūs** (Genitive **-ūtis** or **-ūdis**) are Feminine.

3. Nouns ending in **-a, -e, -i, -y, -c, -l, -n, -t, -ar, -ur, -ŭs** are Neuter.

### Chief Exceptions to Gender in the Third Declension.

**44.** **Exceptions to the Rule for Masculines.**

1. Nouns in **-ō.**

    *a.* Feminine: **carō,** *flesh.*

2. Nouns in **-or.**

    *a.* Feminine: **arbor,** *tree.*

    *b.* Neuter: **aequor,** *sea;* **cor,** *heart;* **marmor,** *marble.*

3. Nouns in **-ōs.**

    *a.* Feminine: **dōs,** *dowry.*

    *b.* Neuter: **ōs** (**ōris**), *mouth.*

4. Nouns in **-er.**

    *a.* Feminine: **linter,** *skiff.*

*h.* Neuter: **cadāver**, *corpse*; **iter**, *way*; **tūber**, *tumor*; **ūber**, *udder*. Also botanical names in -er; as, **acer**, *maple*.

5. Nouns in -ĕs.
   *a.* Feminine: **seges**, *crop*.

## 45. Exceptions to the Rule for Feminines.

1. Nouns in -ās.
   *a.* Masculine: **vās**, *bondsman.*
   *b.* Neuter: **vās**, *vessel.*

2. Nouns in -ēs.
   *a.* Masculine: **ariēs**, *ram*; **pariēs**, *wall*; **pēs**, *foot.*

3. Nouns in -is.
   *a.* Masculine: all nouns in -nis and -guis; as, **amnis**, *river*; **īgnis**, *fire*; **pānis**, *bread*; **sanguis**, *blood*; **unguis**, *nail.* Also—

     **axis**, *axle.*        **piscis**, *fish.*
     **collis**, *hill.*        **postis**, *post.*
     **fascis**, *bundle.*     **pulvis**, *dust.*
     **lapis**, *stone.*       **orbis**, *circle.*
     **mēnsis**, *month.*     **sentis**, *brier.*

4. Nouns in -x.
   *a.* Masculine: **apex**, *peak*; **cōdex**, *tree-trunk*; **grex**, *flock*; **imbrex**, *tile*; **pollex**, *thumb*; **vertex**, *summit*; **calix**, *cup.*

5. Nouns in -s preceded by a consonant.
   *a.* Masculine: **dēns**, *tooth*; **fōns**, *fountain*; **mōns**, *mountain*; **pōns**, *bridge.*

6. Nouns in -dō.
   *a.* Masculine: **cardō**, *hinge*; **ōrdō**, *order.*

## 46. Exceptions to the Rule for Neuters.

1. Nouns in -l.
   *a.* Masculine: **sōl**, *sun*; **sāl**, *salt.*

2. Nouns in -n.
   *a.* Masculine: **pecten**, *comb.*

3. Nouns in -ur.
   *a.* Masculine: **vultur**, *vulture.*

4. Nouns in -ŭs.
   *a.* Masculine: **lepus**, *hare.*

### Greek Nouns of the Third Declension.

**47.** The following are the chief peculiarities of these : —

1. The ending -ă in the Accusative Singular; as, **aetheră,** *aether* ; **Salamīnă,** *Salamis.*

2. The ending -**ĕs** in the Nominative Plural; as, **Phrygĕs,** *Phrygians.*

3. The ending -**ăs** in the Accusative Plural ; as, **Phrygăs,** *Phrygians.*

4. Proper names in -**ās** (Genitive -antis) have -**ā** in the Vocative Singular; as, **Atlās (Atlantis),** Vocative **Atlā,** *Atlas.*

5. Neuters in -**ma** (Genitive -**matis**) have -**īs** instead of -**ibus** in the Dative and Ablative Plural; as, **poēmatīs,** *poems.*

6. **Orpheus,** and other proper names ending in -**eus,** form the Vocative Singular in -**eu** (**Orpheu,** *etc.*). But in prose the other cases usually follow the second declension; as, **Orpheī, Orpheō,** *etc.*

7. Proper names in -**ēs,** like **Periclēs,** form the Genitive Singular sometimes in -**is,** sometimes in -**ī,** as, **Periclis** or **Periclī.**

8. Feminine proper names in -**ō** have -**ūs** in the Genitive, but -**ō** in the other oblique cases ; as, —

| | | | |
|---|---|---|---|
| *Nom.* | Dīdō | *Acc.* | Dīdō |
| *Gen.* | Dīdūs | *Voc.* | Dīdō |
| *Dat.* | Dīdō | *Abl.* | Dīdō |

9. The regular Latin endings often occur in Greek nouns.

### FOURTH DECLENSION.

#### ŭ-Stems.

**48.** Nouns of the Fourth Declension end in -**us** Mascu line, and -**ū** Neuter. They are declined as follows : —

| | **Frūctus,** m., *fruit.* | | **Cornū,** n., *horn.* | |
|---|---|---|---|---|
| | SINGULAR. | PLURAL. | SINGULAR. | PLURAL. |
| *Nom.* | frūctus | frūctūs | cornū | cornua |
| *Gen.* | frūctūs | frūctuum | cornūs | cornuum |
| *Dat.* | frūctuī | frūctibus | cornū | cornibus |
| *Acc.* | frūctum | frūctūs | cornū | cornua |
| *Voc.* | frūctus | frūctūs | cornū | cornua |
| *Abl.* | frūctū | frūctibus | cornū | cornibus |

### Peculiarities of Nouns of the Fourth Declension.

**49.** 1. Nouns in -us, particularly in early Latin, often form the Genitive Singular in -ī, following the analogy of nouns in -us of the Second Declension; as, senātī, ōrnātī. This is usually the case in Plautus and Terence.

2. Nouns in -us sometimes have -ū in the Dative Singular, instead of -uī; as, frūctū (for frūctuī).

3. The ending -ubus, instead of -ibus, occurs in the Dative and Ablative Plural of artūs (Plural), *limbs*; tribus, *tribe*; and in dissyllables in -cus; as, artubus, tribubus, arcubus, lacubus. But with the exception of tribus, all these words admit the forms in -ibus as well as those in -ubus.

4. Domus, *house*, is declined according to the Fourth Declension, but has also the following forms of the Second: —

domī (locative), *at home*;    domum, *homewards, to one's home*;
domō, *from home*;             domōs, *homewards, to their (etc.) homes*

5. The only Neuters of this declension in common use are: cornū, *horn*; genū, *knee*; and verū, *spit*.

### Exceptions to Gender in the Fourth Declension.

**50.** The following nouns in -us are Feminine: acus, *needle*; domus, *house*; manus, *hand*; porticus, *colonnade*; tribus, *tribe*; Īdūs (Plural), *Ides*; also names of trees (§ 15. 2).

## FIFTH DECLENSION.

### ē-Stems.

**51.** Nouns of the Fifth Declension end in -ēs, and are declined as follows : —

|  | Diēs, m., *day.* | | Rēs, f., *thing.* | |
|---|---|---|---|---|
|  | SINGULAR. | PLURAL. | SINGULAR. | PLURAL. |
| *Nom.* | diēs | diēs | rēs | rēs |
| *Gen.* | diēī | diērum | rĕī | rērum |
| *Dat.* | diēī | diēbus | rĕī | rēbus |
| *Acc.* | diem | diēs | rem | rēs |
| *Voc.* | diēs | diēs | rēs | rēs |
| *Abl.* | diē | diēbus | rē | rēbus |

30 INFLECTIONS.

### Peculiarities of Nouns of the Fifth Declension.

**52.** 1. The ending of the Genitive and Dative Singular is -ĕī, instead of -ēī, when a consonant precedes; as, spĕī, rĕī, fidĕī.

2. A Genitive ending -ī (for -ĕī) is found in plēbī (from plēbēs = plēbs) in the expressions tribūnus plēbī, *tribune of the people*, and plēbī scītum, *decree of the people*; sometimes also in other words.

3. A Genitive and Dative form in -ē sometimes occurs; as, aciē.

4. With the exception of diēs and rēs, most nouns of the Fifth Declension are not declined in the Plural. But aciēs, seriēs, speciēs, spēs, and a few others are used in the Nominative and Accusative Plural.

### Gender in the Fifth Declension.

**53.** Nouns of the Fifth Declension are regularly Feminine, except diēs, *day*, and merīdiēs, *mid-day*. But diēs is sometimes Feminine in the Singular, particularly when it means an *appointed day*.

### DEFECTIVE NOUNS.

**54.** Here belong —

1. Nouns used in the Singular only.
2. Nouns used in the Plural only.
3. Nouns used only in certain cases.
4. Indeclinable Nouns.

### Nouns used in the Singular only.

**55.** Many nouns, from the nature of their signification, are regularly used in the Singular only. Thus: —

1. **Proper names**; as, Cicerō, *Cicero*; Italia, *Italy*.
2. **Nouns denoting material**; as, aes, *copper*; lac, *milk*.
3. **Abstract nouns**; as, ignōrantia, *ignorance*; bonitās, *goodness*.
4. But the above classes of words are sometimes used in the Plural. Thus: —

> a) Proper names, — to denote different members of a family, or specimens of a type; as, Cicerōnēs, *the Ciceros*; Catōnēs, *men like Cato*.

*b*) Names of materials, — to denote objects made of the material, or different kinds of the substance; as, **aera**, *bronzes* (*i.e.* bronze figures); **ligna**, *woods*.

*c*) Abstract nouns, — to denote instances of the quality; as, **ignōrantiae**, *cases of ignorance*.

#### Nouns used in the Plural only.

**56.** Here belong —

1. Many geographical names; as, **Thēbae**, *Thebes*; **Leuctra**, *Leuctra*; **Pompejī**, *Pompeii*.

2. Many names of festivals; as, **Megalēsia**, *the Megalesian festival*.

3. Many special words, of which the following are the most important: —

| | |
|---|---|
| **angustiae**, *narrow pass.* | **mānēs**, *spirits of the dead.* |
| **arma**, *weapons.* | **moenia**, *city walls.* |
| **dēliciae**, *delight.* | **minae**, *threats.* |
| **dīvitiae**, *riches.* | **nūptiae**, *marriage.* |
| **Īdūs**, *Ides.* | **posterī**, *descendants.* |
| **indūtiae**, *truce.* | **reliquiae**, *remainder.* |
| **īnsidiae**, *ambush.* | **tenebrae**, *darkness.* |
| **majōrēs**, *ancestors.* | **verbera**, *blows.* |

Also in classical prose regularly —

| | |
|---|---|
| **cervīcēs**, *neck.* | **nārēs**, *nose.* |
| **fidēs**, *lyre.* | **vīscerā**, *viscera.* |

#### Nouns used only in Certain Cases.

**57.** 1. **Used in only One Case.** Many nouns of the Fourth Declension are found only in the Ablative Singular; as, **jussū**, *by the order*; **injussū**, *without the order*; **nātū**, *by birth*.

2. **Used in Two Cases.**

*a.* **Fors** (*chance*), Nom. Sing.; **forte**, Abl. Sing.

*b.* **Spontis** (*free-will*), Gen. Sing.; **sponte**, Abl. Sing.

3. **Used in Three Cases.** **Nēmō**, *no one* (Nom.), has also the Dat. **nēminī** and the Acc. **nēminem**. The Gen. and Abl. are supplied by the corresponding cases of **nūllus**; *viz.* **nūllīus** and **nūllō**.

4. **Impetus** has the Nom., Acc., and Abl. Sing., and the Nom and Acc. Plu.; *viz.* **impetus, impetum, impetū, impetūs**.

5. *a.* **Precī, precem, prece**, lacks the Nom. and Gen. Sing.

*b.* **Vicis, vicem, vice**, lacks the Nom. and Dat. Sing.

6. **Opis, dapis**, and **frūgis**, — all lack the Nom. Sing.

7. Many monosyllables of the Third Declension lack the Gen. Plu.; as, **cor, lūx, sōl, aes, ōs (ōris), rūs, sāl, tūs**.

### Indeclinable Nouns.

**58.** Here belong —

| | |
|---|---|
| **fās**, n., *right.* | **nefās**, n., *impiety.* |
| **īnstar**, n., *likeness.* | **nihil**, n., *nothing.* |
| **māne**, n., *morning.* | **secus**, n., *sex.* |

1. With the exception of **māne** (which may serve also as Ablative, *in the morning*), the nouns in this list are simply Neuters confined in use to the Nominative and Accusative Singular.

### Heteroclites.

**59.** These are nouns whose forms are partly of one declension, and partly of another. Thus: —

1. Several nouns have the entire Singular of one declension, while the Plural is of another; as, —

**vās, vāsis** (*vessel*);    Plu., **vāsa, vāsōrum, vāsīs,** *etc.*

**jūgerum, jūgerī** (*acre*);    Plu., **jūgera, jūgerum, jūgeribus,** *etc.*

2. Several nouns, while belonging in the main to one declension, have certain special forms belonging to another. Thus: —

*a)* Many nouns of the First Declension ending in **-ia** take also a Nom. and Acc. of the Fifth; as, **māteriēs, māteriem,** *material,* as well as **māteria, māteriam**.

*b)* **Famēs**, *hunger,* regularly of the Third Declension, has the Abl. **famē** of the Fifth.

*c)* **Requiēs, requiētis**, *rest,* regularly of the Third Declension, takes an Acc. of the Fifth, **requiem**, in addition to **requiētem**.

*d)* Besides **plēbs, plēbis,** *common people,* of the Third Declension, we find **plēbēs, plēbēī** (also **plēbī**, see § 52. 2), of the Fifth.

## Heterogeneous Nouns.

**60.** Heterogeneous nouns vary in Gender. Thus: —

1. Several nouns of the Second Declension have two forms, — one Masc. in -us, and one Neuter in -um; as, **clipeus, clipeum,** *shield;* **carrus, carrum,** *cart.*

2. Other nouns have one gender in the Singular, another in the Plural; as, —

| SINGULAR. | PLURAL. |
|---|---|
| **balneum,** n., *bath;* | **balneae,** f., *bath-house.* |
| **epulum,** n., *feast;* | **epulae,** f., *feast.* |
| **frēnum,** n., *bridle;* | **frēnī,** m. (rarely **frēna,** n.), *bridle.* |
| **jocus,** m., *jest;* | **joca,** n. (also **jocī,** m.), *jests.* |
| **locus,** m., *place;* | **loca,** n., *places;* **locī,** m., *passages* or *topics in an author.* |
| **rāstrum,** n., *rake;* | **rāstrī,** m.; **rāstra,** n., *rakes.* |

*a.* Heterogeneous nouns may at the same time be heteroclites, as in case of the first two examples above.

### Plurals with Change of Meaning.

**61.** The following nouns have one meaning in the Singular, and another in the Plural: —

| SINGULAR. | PLURAL. |
|---|---|
| **aedēs,** *temple;* | **aedēs,** *house.* |
| **auxilium,** *help;* | **auxilia,** *auxiliary troops.* |
| **carcer,** *prison;* | **carcerēs,** *stalls for racing-chariot;* |
| **castrum,** *fort;* | **castra,** *camp.* |
| **cōpia,** *abundance;* | **cōpiae,** *troops, resources.* |
| **fīnis,** *end;* | **fīnēs,** *borders, territory.* |
| **fortūna,** *fortune;* | **fortūnae,** *possessions, wealth.* |
| **grātia,** *favor, gratitude;* | **grātiae,** *thanks.* |
| **impedīmentum,** *hindrance;* | **impedīmenta,** *baggage.* |
| **littera,** *letter* (of the alphabet); | **litterae,** *epistle; literature* |
| **mōs,** *habit, custom;* | **mōrēs,** *character.* |
| **opera,** *help, service;* | **operae,** *laborers.* |
| **(ops) opis,** *help;* | **opēs,** *resources.* |
| **pars,** *part;* | **partēs,** *party; rôle.* |
| **sāl,** *salt;* | **sălēs,** *wit.* |

## *B.* ADJECTIVES.

**62.** Adjectives denote *quality*. They are declined like nouns, and fall into two classes, —

   1. Adjectives of the First and Second Declensions.
   2. Adjectives of the Third Declension.

### ADJECTIVES OF THE FIRST AND SECOND DECLENSIONS.

**63.** In these the Masculine is declined like **hortus, puer,** or **ager,** the Feminine like **porta,** and the Neuter like **bellum.** Thus, Masculine like **hortus** : —

**Bonus,** *good.*

SINGULAR.

| | MASCULINE. | FEMININE | NEUTER. |
|---|---|---|---|
| *Nom.* | bonus | bona | bonum |
| *Gen.* | bonī | bonae | bonī |
| *Dat.* | bonō | bonae | bonō |
| *Acc.* | bonum | bonam | bonum |
| *Voc.* | bone | bona | bonum |
| *Abl.* | bonō | bonā | bonō |

PLURAL.

| | | | |
|---|---|---|---|
| *Nom.* | bonī | bonae | bona |
| *Gen.* | bonōrum | bonārum | bonōrum |
| *Dat.* | bonīs | bonīs | bonīs |
| *Acc.* | bonōs | bonās | bona |
| *Voc.* | bonī | bonae | bona |
| *Abl.* | bonīs | bonīs | bonīs |

   1. The Gen. Sing. Masc. and Neut. of Adjectives in -ius ends in -iī (not in -ī as in case of Nouns; see § 25. 1 ; 2). So also the Voc. Sing. of such Adjectives ends in -ie, not in ī. Thus **eximius** forms Gen. **eximiī**; Voc. **eximie.**

   2. Distributives (see § 78. 1. *c*) regularly form the Gen. Plu. Masc. and Neut. in **-um** instead of **-ōrum** (compare § 25. 6); as, **dēnum, centēnum**; but always **singulōrum.**

**64.** Masculine like **puer** : —

### Tener, *tender.*

#### SINGULAR.

|  | MASCULINE. | FEMININE. | NEUTER. |
|---|---|---|---|
| *Nom.* | tener | teneɪa | tenerum |
| *Gen.* | tenerī | tenerae | tenerī |
| *Dat.* | tenerō | tenerae | tenerō |
| *Acc.* | tenerum | teneram | tenerum |
| *Voc.* | tener | tenera | tenerum |
| *Abl.* | tenerō | tenerā | tenerō |

#### PLURAL.

|  | MASCULINE | FEMININE | NEUTER |
|---|---|---|---|
| *Nom.* | tenerī | tenerae | tenera |
| *Gen.* | tenerōrum | tenerārum | tenerōrum |
| *Dat.* | tenerīs | tenerīs | tenerīs |
| *Acc.* | tenerōs | tenerās | tenera |
| *Voc.* | tenerī | tenerae | tenera |
| *Abl.* | tenerīs | tenerīs | tenerīs |

**65.** Masculine like **ager** : —

### Sacer, *sacred.*

#### SINGULAR.

|  | MASCULINE. | FEMININE. | NEUTER. |
|---|---|---|---|
| *Nom.* | sacer | sacra | sacrum |
| *Gen.* | sacrī | sacrae | sacrī |
| *Dat.* | sacrō | sacrae | sacrō |
| *Acc.* | sacrum | sacram | sacrum |
| *Voc.* | sacer | sacra | sacrum |
| *Abl.* | sacrō | sacrā | sacrō |

#### PLURAL.

|  | MASCULINE | FEMININE | NEUTER |
|---|---|---|---|
| *Nom.* | sacrī | sacrae | sacra |
| *Gen.* | sacrōrum | sacrārum | sacrōrum |
| *Dat.* | sacrīs | sacrīs | sacrīs |
| *Acc.* | sacrōs | sacrās | sacra |
| *Voc.* | sacrī | sacrae | sacra |
| *Abl.* | sacrīs | sacrīs | sacrīs |

1. Most adjectives in -er are declined like **sacer.**  The following,
however, are declined like **tener** : **asper.** *rough;* **lacer,** *torn;* **līber,** *free;*

miser, *wretched*; prŏspẹr, *prosperous*; compounds in -fer and -ger; sometimes dexter, *right*.

2. Satur, *full*, is declined: satur, satura, saturum.

### Nine Irregular Adjectives.

**66.** Here belong —

| | |
|---|---|
| alius, *another*; | alter, *the other*; |
| ūllus, *any*; | nūllus, *none*; |
| uter, *which?* (of two); | neuter, *neither*; |
| sōlus, *alone*; | tōtus, *whole*; |

ūnus, *one, alone*.

They are declined as follows: —

#### SINGULAR.

| | Masculine. | Feminine. | Neuter. | Masculine. | Feminine. | Neuter. |
|---|---|---|---|---|---|---|
| *Nom.* | alius | alia | aliud | alter | altera | alterum |
| *Gen.* | alterĭus | alterĭus | alterĭus [1] | alterĭus | alterĭus | alterĭus |
| *Dat.* | aliī | aliī | aliī | alterī | alterī [2] | alterī |
| *Acc.* | alium | aliam | aliud | alterum | alteram | alterum |
| *Voc.* | —— | —— | —— | —— | —— | —— |
| *Abl.* | aliō | aliā | aliō | alterō | alterā | alterō |
| *Nom.* | uter | utra | utrum | tōtus | tōta | tōtum |
| *Gen.* | utrĭus | utrĭus | utrĭus | tōtĭus | tōtĭus | tōtĭus |
| *Dat.* | utrī | utrī | utrī | tōtī | tōtī | tōtī |
| *Acc.* | utrum | utram | utrum | tōtum | tōtam | tōtum |
| *Voc.* | —— | —— | —— | —— | —— | —— |
| *Abl.* | utrō | utrā | utrō | tōtō | tōtā | tōtō |

1. All these words lack the Vocative. The Plural is regular.
2. **Neuter** is declined like **uter**.

### ADJECTIVES OF THE THIRD DECLENSION.

**67.** These fall into three classes, —

1. Adjectives of three terminations in the Nominative Singular, — one for each gender.

2. Adjectives of two terminations.

3. Adjectives of one termination.

---

[1] This is practically always used instead of **alīus** in the Genitive.

[2] A Dative Singular Feminine **alterae** also occurs.

*a.* With the exception of Comparatives, and a few other words mentioned below in § 70. 1, all Adjectives of the Third Declension follow the inflection of Ĭ-stems; *i.e.* they have the Ablative Singular in -ī, the Genitive Plural in -ium, the Accusative Plural in īs (as well as -ēs) in the Masculine and Feminine, and the Nominative and Accusative Plural in -ia in Neuters.

### Adjectives of Three Terminations.

**68.**  These are declined as follows : —

Ācer, *sharp.*

SINGULAR.

|       | MASCULINE. | FEMININE. | NEUTER. |
|-------|-----------|-----------|---------|
| *Nom.* | ācer    | ācris    | ācre   |
| *Gen.* | ācris   | ācris    | ācris  |
| *Dat.* | ācrī    | ācrī     | ācrī   |
| *Acc.* | ācrem   | ācrem    | ācre   |
| *Voc.* | ācer    | ācris    | ācre   |
| *Abl.* | ācrī    | ācrī     | ācrī   |

PLURAL.

|       | MASCULINE. | FEMININE. | NEUTER. |
|-------|-----------|-----------|---------|
| *Nom.* | ācrēs      | ācrēs      | ācria  |
| *Gen.* | ācrium     | ācrium     | ācrium |
| *Dat.* | ācribus    | ācribus    | ācribus |
| *Acc.* | ācrēs, -īs | ācrēs, -īs | ācria  |
| *Voc.* | ācrēs      | ācrēs      | ācria  |
| *Abl.* | ācribus    | ācribus    | ācribus |

1.  Like **ācer** are declined **alacer,** *lively;* **campester,** *level;* **celeber,** *famous;* **equester,** *equestrian;* **palūster.** *marshy;* **pedester,** *pedestrian;* **puter,** *rotten;* **salūber,** *wholesome;* **silvester,** *woody;* **terrester,** *terrestrial;* **volucer,** *winged;* also names of months in -ber, as **September.**

2.  **Celer, celeris, celere,** *swift,* retains the e before r, but lacks the Genitive Plural.

3.  In the Nominative Singular of Adjectives of this class the Feminine form is sometimes used for the Masculine.  This is regularly true of **salūbris, silvestris,** and **terrestris.**  In case of the other words in the list, the use of the Feminine for the Masculine is confined chiefly to early and late Latin, and to poetry.

## Adjectives of Two Terminations.

**69.** These are declined as follows:—

Fortis, *strong.*                Fortior, *stronger.*

### SINGULAR.

| | M. AND F. | NEUT. | M. AND F. | NEUT. |
|---|---|---|---|---|
| *Nom.* | fortis | forte | fortior | fortius |
| *Gen.* | fortis | fortis | fortiōris | fortiōris |
| *Dat.* | fortī | fortī | fortiōrī | fortiōrī |
| *Acc.* | fortem | forte | fortiōrem | fortius |
| *Voc.* | fortis | forte | fortior | fortius |
| *Abl.* | fortī | fortī | fortiōre | fortiōre |

### PLURAL.

| | M. AND F. | NEUT. | M. AND F. | NEUT. |
|---|---|---|---|---|
| *Nom.* | fortēs | fortia | fortiōrēs | fortiōra |
| *Gen.* | fortium | fortium | fortiōrum | fortiōrum |
| *Dat.* | fortibus | fortibus | fortiōribus | fortiōribus |
| *Acc.* | fortēs, -īs | fortia | fortiōrēs, -īs | fortiōra |
| *Voc.* | fortēs | fortia | fortiōrēs | fortiōra |
| *Abl.* | fortibus | fortibus | fortiōribus | fortiōribus |

1. **Fortior** is the Comparative of **fortis**. All Comparatives are regularly declined in the same way. The Acc. Plu. in -īs is rare.

## Adjectives of One Termination.

**70.**     Fēlīx, *happy.*                Prūdēns, *prudent.*

### SINGULAR.

| | M. AND F. | NEUT. | M. AND F. | NEUT. |
|---|---|---|---|---|
| *Nom.* | fēlīx | fēlīx | prūdēns | prūdēns |
| *Gen.* | fēlīcis | fēlīcis | prūdentis | prūdentis |
| *Dat.* | fēlīcī | fēlīcī | prūdentī | prūdentī |
| *Acc.* | fēlīcem | fēlīx | prūdentem | prūdēns |
| *Voc.* | fēlīx | fēlīx | prūdēns | prūdēns |
| *Abl.* | fēlīcī | fēlīcī | prūdentī | prūdentī |

### PLURAL.

| | M. AND F. | NEUT. | M. AND F. | NEUT. |
|---|---|---|---|---|
| *Nom.* | fēlīcēs | fēlīcia | prūdentēs | prūdentia |
| *Gen.* | fēlīcium | fēlīcium | prūdentium | prūdentium |
| *Dat.* | fēlīcibus | fēlīcibus | prūdentibus | prūdentibus |
| *Acc.* | fēlīcēs, -īs | fēlīcia | prūdentēs, -īs | prūdentia |
| *Voc.* | fēlīcēs | fēlīcia | prūdentēs | prūdentia |
| *Abl.* | fēlīcibus | fēlīcibus | prūdentibus | prūdentibus |

| | **Vetus,** *old.* | | **Plūs,** *more·* | |
|---|---|---|---|---|
| | | SINGULAR. | | |
| | M. AND F. | NEUT. | M. AND F. | NEUT. |
| *Nom.* | vetus | vetus | —— | plūs |
| *Gen.* | veteris | veteris | —— | plūris |
| *Dat.* | veterī | veterī | —— | —— |
| *Acc.* | veterem | vetus | —— | plūs |
| *Voc.* | vetus | vetus | —— | —— |
| *Abl.* | vetere | vetere | —— | plūre |
| | | PLURAL. | | |
| *Nom.* | veterēs | vetera | plūrēs | plūra |
| *Gen.* | veterum | veterum | plūrium | plūrium |
| *Dat.* | veteribus | veteribus | plūribus | plūribus |
| *Acc.* | veterēs | vetera | plūrēs, -īs | plūra |
| *Voc.* | veterēs | vetera | —— | —— |
| *Abl.* | veteribus | veteribus | plūribus | plūribus |

1. It will be observed that **vetus** is declined as a pure Consonant-Stem; *i.e.* Ablative Singular in -e, Genitive Plural in -um, Nominative Plural Neuter in -a, and Accusative Plural Masculine and Feminine in -ēs only. In the same way are declined **compos,** *controlling;* **dīves,** *rich;* **particeps,** *sharing;* **pauper,** *poor;* **prīnceps,** *chief;* **sōspes,** *safe;* **superstes,** *surviving.* Yet **dīves** always has Neut. Plu. **dītia.**

2. **Inops,** *needy,* and **memor,** *mindful,* have Ablative Singular **inopī, memorī,** but Genitive Plural **inopum, memorum.**

3. Participles in -āns and -ēns follow the declension of ĭ-stems. But they do not have -ī in the Ablative, except when employed as adjectives; when used as participles or as substantives, they have -e; as,—

> **ā sapientī virō,** *by a wise man;* but
> **ā sapiente,** *bv a philosopher.*
> **Tarquiniō rēgnante,** *under the reign of Tarquin.*

4. **Plūs,** in the Singular, is always a noun.

5. In the Ablative Singular, adjectives, when used as substantives,—
   *a*) usually retain the adjective declension; as,—

> **aequālis,** *contemporary,* Abl. **aequālī.**
> **cōnsulāris,** *ex-consul,* Abl. **cōnsulārī.**

So names of Months; as, **Aprīlī,** *April;* **Decembrī,** *December.*

*b*) But adjectives used as proper names have -e in the Ablative Singular; as, **Celere,** *Celer;* **Juvenāle,** *Juvenal.*

*c*) Patrials in -**ās**, -**ātis** and -**īs**, -**ītis**, when designating places, regularly have -**ī**; as, **in Arpīnātī**, *on the estate at Arpinum*; yet -**e**, when used of persons; as, **ab Arpīnāte**, *by an Arpīnatian*.

6. A very few indeclinable adjectives occur, the chief of which are **frūgī**, *frugal*; **nēquam**, *worthless*.

7. In poetry, adjectives and participles in -**ns** sometimes form the Gen. Plu. in -**um** instead of -**ium**; as, **venientum**, *of those coming*.

## COMPARISON OF ADJECTIVES.

**71.** 1. There are three degrees of Comparison, — the Positive, the Comparative, and the Superlative.

2. The Comparative is regularly formed by adding -**ior** (Neut. -**ius**), and the Superlative by adding -**issimus** (-**a**, -**um**), to the Stem of the Positive deprived of its final vowel; as, —

| | | | |
|---|---|---|---|
| altus, *high*, | altior, *higher*, | altissimus, | { *highest,* *very high.* |
| fortis, *brave*, | fortior, | fortissimus. | |
| fēlīx, *fortunate*, | fēlīcior, | fēlīcissimus. | |

So also Participles, when used as Adjectives; as, —

| | | |
|---|---|---|
| doctus, *learned*, | doctior, | doctissimus. |
| egēns, *needy*, | egentior, | egentissimus. |

3. Adjectives in -**er** form the Superlative by appending -**rimus** to the Nominative of the Positive. The Comparative is regular. Thus: —

| | | |
|---|---|---|
| asper, *rough*, | asperior, | asperrimus. |
| pulcher, *beautiful*, | pulchrior, | pulcherrimus. |
| ācer, *sharp*, | ācrior, | ācerrimus. |
| celer, *swift*, | celerior, | celerrimus. |

*a.* Notice mātūrus, mātūrior, mātūrissimus or mātūrrimus.

4. Five Adjectives in -**ilis** form the Superlative by adding -**limus** to the Stem of the Positive deprived of its final vowel. The Comparative is regular. Thus: —

| | | |
|---|---|---|
| facilis, *easy*, | facilior, | facillimus. |
| difficilis, *difficult*, | difficilior, | difficillimus. |
| similis, *like*, | similior, | simillimus. |
| dissimilis, *unlike*, | dissimilior, | dissimillimus. |
| humilis, *low*, | humilior, | humillimus. |

5. Adjectives in **-dicus**, **-ficus**, and **-volus** form the Comparative and Superlative as though from forms in **-dīcēns**, **-fiǒēns**, **-volēns**. Thus: —

| | | |
|---|---|---|
| maledicus, *slanderous*, | maledīcentior, | maledīcentissimus. |
| magnificus, *magnificent*, | magnificentior, | magnificentissimus. |
| benevolus, *kindly*, | benevolentior, | benevolentissimus. |

    *a.* Positives in **-dīcēns** and **-volēns** occur in early Latin; as, **maledīcēns, benevolēns**.

6. **Dīves** has the Comparative **dīvitior** or **dītior**; Superlative **dīvitissimus** or **dītissimus**.

### Irregular Comparison.

**72.** Several Adjectives vary the Stem in Comparison; *viz.* —

| | | |
|---|---|---|
| bonus, *good*, | melior, | optimus. |
| malus, *bad*, | pejor, | pessimus. |
| parvus, *small*, | minor, | minimus. |
| magnus, *large*, | major, | maximus. |
| multus, *much*, | plūs, | plūrimus. |
| frūgī, *thrifty*, | frūgālior, | frūgālissimus. |
| nēquam, *worthless*, | nēquior, | nēquissimus. |

### Defective Comparison.

**73.** 1. Positive lacking entirely, —

| | | |
|---|---|---|
| (Cf. **prae**, *in front of.*) | prior, *former*, | prīmus, *first* |
| (Cf. **citrā**, *this side of.*) | citerior, *on this side*, | citimus, *near*. |
| (Cf. **ultrā**, *beyond.*) | ulterior, *farther*, | ultimus, *farthest*. |
| (Cf. **intrā**, *within.*)˙ | interior, *inner*, | intimus, *inmost*. |
| (Cf. **prope**, *near.*) | propior, *nearer*, | proximus, *nearest*. |
| (Cf. **dē**, *down.*) | dēterior, *inferior*, | dēterrimus, *worst*. |
| (Cf. archaic **potis**, *possible.*) | potior, *preferable*, | potissimus, *chiefest.* |

2. Positive occurring only in special cases, —

| | | | |
|---|---|---|---|
| posterō diē, annō, *etc.*, *the following day, etc.*, | posterior, *later*, | postrēmus, | *latest*, *last*. |
| posterī, *descendants*, | | postumus, | *late-born*, *posthumous* |
| exterī, *foreigners*, nātiōnēs exterae, *foreign nations*. | exterior, *outer*, | extrēmus, extimus, | *outermost*. |

| | | |
|---|---|---|
| īnferī, *gods of the lower world,* | | īnfimus, |
| Mare Īnferum, *Mediterranean Sea,* | } īnferior, *lower,* | { īmus, } *lowest.* |
| superī, *gods above,* | | suprēmus, *last.* |
| Mare Superum, *Adriatic Sea,* | } superior, *higher,* | { summus, *highest.* |

3. Comparative lacking.

| | | |
|---|---|---|
| vetus, *old,* | ——[1] | veterrimus. |
| fīdus, *faithful,* | —— | fīdissimus. |
| novus, *new,* | ——[2] | novissimus,[3] *last.* |
| sacer, *sacred,* | —— | sacerrimus. |
| falsus, *false,* | —— | falsissimus. |

Also in some other words less frequently used.

4. Superlative lacking.

| | | |
|---|---|---|
| alacer, *lively,* | alacrior, | —— |
| ingēns, *great,* | ingentior, | —— |
| salūtāris, *wholesome,* | salūtārior, | —— |
| juvenis, *young,* | jūnior, | ——[4] |
| senex, *old,* | senior. | ——[5] |

*a.* The Superlative is lacking also in many adjectives in -ālis, -īlis, -ĭlis, -bilis, and in a few others.

### Comparison by *Magis* and *Maximē.*

**74.** Many adjectives do not admit terminational comparison, but form the Comparative and Superlative degrees by prefixing **magis** (*more*) and **maximē** (*most*). Here belong —

1. Many adjectives ending in -ālis, -āris, -idus, -īlis, -icus, imus, īnus, -ōrus.

2. Adjectives in -us, preceded by a vowel; as, **idōneus**, *adapted;* **arduus**, *steep;* **necessārius**, *necessary.*

*a.* Adjectives in -quus, of course, do not come under this rule. The first u in such cases is not a vowel, but a consonant.

---

[1] Supplied by **vetustior**, from **vetustus.**
[2] Supplied by **recentior.**
[3] For *newest,* **recentissimus** is used.
[4] Supplied by **minimus nātū.**
[5] Supplied by **maximus nātū.**

### Adjectives not admitting Comparison.

**75**. Here belong —

1. Many adjectives, which, from the nature of their signification, do not admit of comparison; as, **hodiernus**, *of to-day*; **annuus**, *annual*; **mortālis**, *mortal*.

2. Some special words; as, **mīrus**, **gnārus**, **merus**; and a few others.

### FORMATION AND COMPARISON OF ADVERBS.

**76**. Adverbs are for the most part derived from adjectives, and depend upon them for their comparison.

1. Adverbs derived from adjectives of the First and Second Declensions form the Positive by changing -ī of the Genitive Singular to -ē; those derived from adjectives of the Third Declension, by changing -is of the Genitive Singular to -iter; as, —

| | |
|---|---|
| cārus, | cārē, *dearly*; |
| pulcher, | pulchrē, *beautifully*; |
| ācer, | ācriter, *fiercely*; |
| levis, | leviter, *lightly*. |

*a.* But Adjectives in -ns, and a few others, add -er (instead of -iter), to form the Adverb; as, —

| | |
|---|---|
| sapiēns, | sapienter, *wisely*; |
| sollers, | sollerter, *skillfully*. |

Note **audāx**, audācter, *boldly*.

2. The Comparative of all Adverbs regularly consists of the Accusative Singular Neuter of the Comparative of the Adjective; while the Superlative of the Adverb is formed by changing the -ī of the Genitive Singular of the Superlative of the Adjective to -ē. Thus —

| | | | |
|---|---|---|---|
| (cārus) | cārē, *dearly*, | cārius, | cārissimē. |
| (pulcher) | pulchrē, *beautifully*, | pulchrius, | pulcherrimē. |
| (ācer) | ācriter, *fiercely*, | ācrius, | ācerrimē. |
| (levis) | leviter, *lightly*, | levius, | levissimē. |
| (sapiēns) | sapienter, *wisely*, | sapientius, | sapientissimē. |
| (audāx) | audācter, *boldly*, | audācius, | audācissimē. |

### Adverbs Peculiar in Comparison and Formation.

**77.** 1.

| | | |
|---|---|---|
| benĕ, *well,* | melius, | optimē. |
| malĕ, *ill,* | pejus, | pessimē. |
| magnopere, *greatly,* | magis, | maximē. |
| multum, *much,* | plūs, | plūrimum. |
| nōn multum, \} *little,* parum, | minus, | minimē. |
| diū, *long,* | diūtius, | diūtissimē. |
| nēquiter, *worthlessly,* | nēquius, | nēquissimē. |
| saepe, *often,* | saepius, | saepissimē. |
| mātūrē, *betimes,* | mātūrius, | { mātūrrimē. mātūrissimē. |
| prope, *near,* | propius, | proximē. |
| nūper, *recently,* | —— | nūperrimē. |
| —— | potius, *rather,* | potissimum, *especially.* |
| —— | prius, { *previously, before,* } | prīmum, *first.* |
| secus, *otherwise,* | sētius, *less.* | |

2. A number of adjectives of the First and Second Declensions form an Adverb in -ō, instead of -ē; as, —

crēbrō, *frequently;*      falsō, *falsely;*
continuō, *immediately;*      subitō, *suddenly;*
                rārō, *rarely;* and a few others.

*a.* cito, *quickly,* has -ŏ.

3. A few adjectives employ the Accusative Singular Neuter as the Positive of the Adverb; as, —

multum, *much;*      paulum, *little;*      facile, *easily.*

4. A few adjectives of the First and Second Declensions form the Positive in -iter; as, —

fīrmus, fīrmiter, *firmly;*      hūmānus, hūmāniter, *humanly;*
largus, largiter, *copiously;*      alius, aliter, *otherwise.*

*a.* violentus has violenter.

5. Various other adverbial suffixes occur, the most important of which are -tus and -tim; as, antīquitus, *anciently;* paulātim, *gradually.*

## NUMERALS.

**78.** Numerals may be divided into —

I. Numeral Adjectives, comprising —

    *a. Cardinals;* as, **ūnus,** *one;* **duo,** *two; etc.*
    *b. Ordinals;* as, **prīmus,** *first;* **secundus,** *second; etc.*
    *c. Distributives;* as, **singulī,** *one by one;* **bīnī,** *two by two; etc.*

II. Numeral Adverbs; as, **semel,** *once;* **bis,** *twice; etc.*

**79.** TABLE OF NUMERAL ADJECTIVES AND ADVERBS.

| | CARDINALS. | ORDINALS. | DISTRIBUTIVES. | ADVERBS. |
|---|---|---|---|---|
| 1. | ūnus, ūna, ūnum | prīmus, *first* | singulī, *one by one* | semel, *once* |
| 2. | duo, duae, duo | secundus, *second* | bīnī, *two by two* | bis |
| 3. | trēs, tria | tertius, *third* | ternī (trīnī) | ter |
| 4. | quattuor | quārtus, *fourth* | quaternī | quater |
| 5. | quīnque | quīntus, *fifth* | quīnī | quīnquiēs |
| 6. | sex | sextus | sēnī | sexiēs |
| 7. | septem | septimus | septēnī | septiēs |
| 8. | octō | octāvus | octōnī | octiēs |
| 9. | novem | nōnus | novēnī | noviēs |
| 10. | decem | decimus | dēnī | deciēs |
| 11. | ūndecim | ūndecimus | ūndēnī | ūndeciēs |
| 12. | duodecim | duodecimus | duodēnī | duodeciēs |
| 13. | tredecim | tertius decimus | ternī dēnī | terdeciēs |
| 14. | quattuordecim | quārtus decimus | quaternī dēnī | quaterdeciēs |
| 15. | quīndecim | quīntus decimus | quīnī dēnī | quīnquiēs deciēs |
| 16. | sēdecim / sexdecim | sextus decimus | sēnī dēnī | sexiēs deciēs |
| 17. | septendecim | septimus decimus | septēnī dēnī | septiēs deciēs |
| 18. | duodēvīgintī | duodēvīcēsimus | duodēvīcēnī | octiēs deciēs |
| 19. | ūndēvīgintī | ūndēvīcēsimus | ūndēvīcēnī | noviēs deciēs |
| 20. | vīgintī | vīcēsimus | vīcēnī | vīciēs |
| 21. | vīgintī ūnus / ūnus et vīgintī | vīcēsimus prīmus / ūnus et vīcēsimus | vīcēnī singulī / singulī et vīcēnī | vīciēs semel |
| 22. | vīgintī duo / duo et vīgintī | vīcēsimus secundus / alter et vīcēsimus | vīcēnī bīnī / bīnī et vīcēnī | vīciēs bis |
| 30. | trīgintā | trīcēsimus | trīcēnī | trīciēs |
| 40. | quadrāgintā | quadrāgēsimus | quadrāgēnī | quadrāgiēs |
| 50. | quīnquāgintā | quīnquāgēsimus | quīnquāgēnī | quīnquāgiēs |
| 60. | sexāgintā | sexāgēsimus | sexāgēnī | sexāgiēs |
| 70. | septuāgintā | septuāgēsimus | septuāgēnī | septuāgiēs |
| 80. | octōgintā | octōgēsimus | octōgēnī | octōgiēs |
| 90. | nōnāgintā | nōnāgēsimus | nōnāgēnī | nōnāgiēs |
| 100. | centum | centēsimus | centēnī | centiēs |

| | CARDINALS. | ORDINALS. | DISTRIBUTIVES. | ADVERBS. |
|---|---|---|---|---|
| 101. | centum ūnus / centum et ūnus | centēsimus prīmus / centēsimus et prīmus | centēnī singulī / centēnī et singulī | } centiēs semel |
| 200. | ducentī, -ae, -a | ducentēsimus | ducēnī | ducentiēs |
| 300. | trecentī | trecentēsimus | trecēnī | trecentiēs |
| 400. | quadringentī | quadringentēsimus | quadringēnī | quadringentiēs |
| 500. | quīngentī | quīngentēsimus | quīngēnī | quīngentiēs |
| 600. | sescentī | sescentēsimus | sescēnī | sescentiēs |
| 700. | septingentī | septingentēsimus | septingēnī | septingentiēs |
| 800. | octingentī | octingentēsimus | octingēnī | octingentiēs |
| 900. | nōngentī | nōngentēsimus | nōngēnī | nōngentiēs |
| 1,000. | mille | millēsimus | singula mīlia | mīliēs |
| 2,000. | duo mīlia | bis millēsimus | bīna mīlia | bis mīliēs |
| 100,000. | centum mīlia | centiēs millēsimus | centēna mīlia | centiēs mīliēs |
| 1,000,000. | deciēs centēna mīlia | deciēs centiēs millē-simus | deciēs centēna mīlia | deciēs centiēs mīliēs |

NOTE. —-ēnsimus and -iēns are often written in the numerals instead of -ēsimus and -iēs.

### Declension of the Cardinals.

**80.** 1. The declension of **ūnus** has already been given under § 66.

2. **Duo** is declined as follows: —

| *Nom.* | duo | duae | duo |
|---|---|---|---|
| *Gen.* | duōrum | duārum | duōrum |
| *Dat.* | duōbus | duābus | duōbus |
| *Acc.* | duōs, duo | duās | duo |
| *Abl.* | duōbus | duābus | duōbus |

*a.* So **ambō**, *both*, except that its final o is long.

3. **Trēs** is declined, —

| *Nom.* | trēs | tria |
|---|---|---|
| *Gen.* | trium | trium |
| *Dat.* | tribus | tribus |
| *Acc.* | trēs (trīs) | tria |
| *Abl.* | tribus | tribus |

4. The hundreds (except **centum**) are declined like the Plural of **bonus**.

5. **Mīlle** is regularly an adjective in the Singular, and indeclinable. In the Plural it is a substantive (followed by the Genitive of the objects enumerated; § 201. 1), and is declined, —

| *Nom.* mīlia | *Acc.* mīlia |
|---|---|
| *Gen.* mīlium | *Voc.* mīlia |
| *Dat.* mīlibus | *Abl.* mīlibus |

Thus **mīlle hominēs**, *a thousand men*; but **duo mīlia hominum,** *two thousand men*, literally *two thousands of men*.

    *a.* Occasionally the Singular admits the Genitive construction; as, **mīlle hominum.**

  6. Other Cardinals are indeclinable. Ordinals and Distributives are declined like Adjectives of the First and Second Declensions.

### Peculiarities in the Use of Numerals.

**81.** 1. The compounds from 21 to 99 may be expressed either with the larger or the smaller numeral first. In the latter case, **et** is used Thus:—

    **trīgintā sex** or **sex et trīgintā**, *thirty-six.*

  2. The numerals under 90, ending in 8 and 9, are often expressed by subtraction; as,—

**duodēvīgintī**, *eighteen* (but also **octōdecim**);

**ūndēquadrāgintā**, *thirty-nine* (but also **trīgintā novem** or **novem et trīgintā**).

  3. Compounds over 100 regularly have the largest number first; the others follow without **et**; as,—

**centum vīgintī septem**, *one hundred and twenty-seven.*

**annō octingentēsimō octōgēsimō secundō**, *in the year 882.*

Yet **et** may be inserted where the smaller number is either a digit or one of the tens; as,—

    **centum et septem**, *one hundred and seven;*

    **centum et quadrāgintā**, *one hundred and forty.*

  4. The Distributives are used—

    *a*) To denote *so much each, so many apiece*; as,—

    **bīna talenta eīs dedit**, *he gave them two talents each.*

    *b*) When those nouns that are ordinarily Plural in form, but Singular in meaning, are employed in a Plural sense; as,—

    **bīnae litterae**, *two epistles.*

    But in such cases, **ūnī** (not **singulī**) is regularly employed for *one*, and **trīnī** (not **ternī**) for *three*; as,—

    **ūnae litterae**, *one epistle;* **trīnae litterae**, *three epistles.*

    *c*) In multiplication; as,—

    **bis bīna sunt quattuor**, *twice two are four.*

    *d*) Often in poetry, instead of the cardinals; as,—

    **bīna hastīlia**, *two spears.*

### C. **PRONOUNS.**

**82.** A Pronoun is a word that indicates something with out naming it.

**83.** There are the following classes of pronouns: —

| | |
|---|---|
| I. Personal. | V. Intensive. |
| II. Reflexive. | VI. Relative. |
| III. Possessive. | VII. Interrogative. |
| IV. Demonstrative. | VIII. Indefinite. |

### I. PERSONAL PRONOUNS.

**84.** These correspond to the English *I, you, he, she, it etc.*, and are declined as follows: —

| *First Person.* | *Second Person.* | *Third Person.* |
|---|---|---|

SINGULAR.

| | | | |
|---|---|---|---|
| *Nom.* | ego, *I* | tū, *thou* | is, *he ;* ea, *she ;* id. *it* |
| *Gen.* | meī | tuī | (For declension see § 87.) |
| *Dat.* | mihi¹ | tibi¹ | |
| *Acc.* | mē | tē | |
| *Voc.* | —— | tū | |
| *Abl.* | mē | tē | |

PLURAL.

| | | |
|---|---|---|
| *Nom.* | nōs, *we* | vōs, *you* |
| *Gen.* | { nostrum / nostrī | { vestrum / vestrī |
| *Dat.* | nōbīs | vōbīs |
| *Acc.* | nōs | vōs |
| *Voc.* | —— | vōs |
| *Abl.* | nōbīs | vōbīs |

1. A Dative Singular mī occurs in poetry.

2. Emphatic forms in -**met** are occasionally found; as, **egomet,** *I myself;* **tibimet,** *to you yourself;* tū has **tūte** and **tūtemet** (written also **tūtimet**).

---

¹ The final ī is sometimes long in poetry.

3. In early Latin, **mēd** and **tēd** occur as Accusative and Ablative forms.

## II. REFLEXIVE PRONOUNS.

**85.** These refer to the subject of the sentence or clause in which they stand; like *myself, yourself*, in '*I see myself*' *etc.* They are declined as follows : —

|      | First Person. | Second Person. | Third Person. |
|------|---------------|----------------|---------------|
|      | Supplied by oblique cases of **ego**. | Supplied by oblique cases of **tū**. | |
| *Gen.* | meī, *of myself* | tuī, *of thyself* | suī |
| *Dat.* | mihi, *to myself* | tibi, *to thyself* | sibi [1] |
| *Acc.* | mē, *myself* | tē, *thyself* | sē *or* sēsē |
| *Voc.* | —— | —— | —— |
| *Abl.* | mē, *with myself, etc.* | tē, *with thyself, etc.* | sē *or* sēsē |

1. The Reflexive of the Third Person serves for *all genders* and for *both numbers*. Thus **suī** may mean, *of himself, herself, itself*, or *of themselves*; and so with the other forms.

2. All of the Reflexive Pronouns have at times a *reciprocal* force; as, —

    **inter sē pugnant**, *they fight with each other.*

3. In early Latin, **sēd** occurs as Accusative and Ablative.

## III. POSSESSIVE PRONOUNS.

**86.** These are strictly adjectives of the First and Second Declensions, and are inflected as such. They are —

| First Person. | Second Person. |
|---------------|----------------|
| meus, -a, -um, *my*; | tuus, -a, -um, *thy*; |
| noster, nostra, nostrum, *our*; | vester, vestra, vestrum, *your*; |

*Third Person.*

    suus, -a, -um, *his, her, its, their.*

1. **Suus** is exclusively Reflexive; as, —

    **pater līberōs suōs amat**, *the father loves his children.*

Otherwise, *his, her, its* are regularly expressed by the Genitive Singular of **is**, *viz.* **ejus**; and *their* by the Genitive Plural, **eōrum, eārum.**

---

[1] The final i is sometimes long in poetry.

2. The Vocative Singular Masculine of **meus** is **mī**.

3. The enclitic -**pte** may be joined to the Ablative Singular of the Possessive Pronouns for the purpose of emphasis. This is particularly common in case of **suō, suā**; as, **suōpte, suāpte**.

## IV. DEMONSTRATIVE PRONOUNS.

**87.** These point out an object as **here** or **there**, or as previously mentioned. They are —

> **hīc**, *this* (where I am) ;
> **iste**, *that* (where you are) ;
> **ille**, *that* (something distinct from the speaker) ;
> **is**, *that* (weaker than **ille**) ;
> **īdem**, *the same.*

**Hīc, iste**, and **ille** are accordingly the Demonstratives of the First, Second, and Third Persons respectively.

### Hīc, *this.*

| | SINGULAR. | | | PLURAL. | | |
|---|---|---|---|---|---|---|
| | MASCULINE. | FEMININE. | NEUTER. | MASCULINE. | FEMININE. | NEUTER. |
| *Nom.* | hīc | haec | hōc | hī | hae | haec |
| *Gen.* | hūjus [1] | hūjus | hūjus | hōrum | hārum | hōrum |
| *Dat.* | huic | huic | huic | hīs | hīs | hīs |
| *Acc.* | hunc | hanc | hōc | hōs | hās | haec |
| *Abl.* | hōc | hāc | hōc | hīs | hīs | hīs |

### Iste, *that, that of yours.*

| | SINGULAR. | | | PLURAL. | | |
|---|---|---|---|---|---|---|
| | MASCULINE. | FEMININE. | NEUTER. | MASCULINE. | FEMININE. | NEUTER. |
| *Nom.* | iste | ista | istud [2] | istī | istae | ista [2] |
| *Gen.* | istīus | istīus | istīus | istōrum | istārum | istōrum |
| *Dat.* | istī | istī | istī | istīs | istīs | istīs |
| *Acc.* | istum | istam | istud | istōs | istās | ista [2] |
| *Abl.* | istō | istā | istō | istīs | istīs | istīs |

**Ille** (archaic **olle**), *that, that one, he,* is declined like **iste**.[3]

---

[1] Forms of **hīc** ending in -s sometimes append -**ce** for emphasis; as, **hūjusce**, *this . . . here ;* **hōsce, hīsce.** When -**ne** is added, -**c** and -**ce** become -**cī**; as **huncine, hōscine.**

[2] For **istud, istūc** sometimes occurs; for **ista, istaec.**

[3] For **illud, illūc** sometimes occurs.

**Is**, *he, this, that.*

|  | SINGULAR. | | | PLURAL. | | |
|---|---|---|---|---|---|---|
|  | MASCULINE. | FEMININE. | NEUTER. | MASCULINE. | FEMININE. | NEUTER. |
| *Nom.* | is | ea | id | eī, iī, (ī) | eae | ea |
| *Gen.* | ejus | ejus | ejus | eōrum | eārum | eōrum |
| *Dat.* | eī | eī | eī | eīs, iīs | eīs, iīs | eīs, iīs |
| *Acc.* | eum | eam | id | eōs | eās | ea |
| *Abl.* | eō | eā | eō | eīs, iīs | eīs, iīs | eīs, iīs |

**Īdem**, *the same.*

|  | SINGULAR. | | | PLURAL. | | |
|---|---|---|---|---|---|---|
|  | MASCULINE. | FEMININE. | NEUTER. | MASCULINE. | FEMININE. | NEUTER. |
| *Nom.* | īdem | eadem | idem | eīdem / iīdem | eaedem | eadem |
| *Gen.* | ejusdem | ejusdem | ejusdem | eōrundem | eārundem | eōrundem |
| *Dat.* | eīdem | eīdem | eīdem | ·eīsdem | eīsdem | eīsdem |
| *Acc.* | eundem | eandem | idem | eōsdem | eāsdem | eadem |
| *Abl.* | eōdem | eādem | eōdem | eīsdem | eīsdem | eīsdem |

The Nom. Plu. Masc. also has **idem**, and the Dat. Abl. Plu. **īsdem** or **iīsdem**.

## V. THE INTENSIVE PRONOUN.

**88**. The Intensive Pronoun in Latin is **ipse**. It corresponds to the English *myself, etc.,* in ' *I myself, he himself.*'

|  | SINGULAR. | | | PLURAL. | | |
|---|---|---|---|---|---|---|
|  | MASCULINE. | FEMININE. | NEUTER. | MASCULINE. | FEMININE. | NEUTER. |
| *Nom.* | ipse | ipsa | ipsum | ipsī | ipsae | ipsa |
| *Gen.* | ipsīus | ipsīus | ipsīus | ipsōrum | ipsārum | ipsōrum |
| *Dat.* | ipsī | ipsī | ipsī | ipsīs | ipsīs | ipsīs |
| *Acc.* | ipsum | ipsam | ipsum | ipsōs | ipsās | ipsa |
| *Abl.* | ipsō | ipsā | ipsō | ipsīs | ipsīs | ipsīs |

## VI. THE RELATIVE PRONOUN.

**89**. The Relative Pronoun is **quī**, who.  It is declined:—

|  | SINGULAR. | | | PLURAL. | | |
|---|---|---|---|---|---|---|
|  | MASCULINE. | FEMININE. | NEUTER. | MASCULINE. | FEMININE. | NEUTER. |
| *Nom.* | quī | quae | quod | quī | quae | quae |
| *Gen.* | cūjus | cūjus | cūjus | quōrum | quārum | quōrum |
| *Dat.* | cui | cui | cui | quibus [2] | quibus [2] | quibus [2] |
| *Acc.* | quem | quam | quod | quōs | quās | quae |
| *Abl.* | quō [1] | quā [1] | quō [1] | quibus [2] | quibus [2] | quibus [2] |

[1] An ablative **quī** occurs in **quīcum**, *with whom.*      [2] Sometimes **quīs**.

## VII. INTERROGATIVE PRONOUNS.

**90.** The Interrogative Pronouns are **quis**, *who?* (substantive) and **quī**, *what? what kind of?* (adjective).

1. **Quis**, *who?*

|  | SINGULAR. | | PLURAL. |
|---|---|---|---|
|  | MASC. AND FEM. | NEUTER. |  |
| *Nom.* | quis | quid | The rare Plural |
| *Gen.* | cūjus | cūjus | follows the de- |
| *Dat.* | cui | cui | clension of the |
| *Acc.* | quem | quid | Relative Pronoun. |
| *Abl.* | quō | quō |  |

2. **Quī**, *what? what kind of?* is declined precisely like the Relative Pronoun ; *viz.* **quī, quae, quod**, *etc.*

    *a.* An old Ablative **quī** occurs, in the sense of *how? why?*

    *b.* **Quī** is sometimes used for **quis** in Indirect Questions.

    *c.* **Quis**, when limiting words denoting persons, is sometimes an adjective. But in such cases **quis homō** = *what man?* whereas **quī homō** = *what sort of man?*

    *d.* **Quis** and **quī** may be strengthened by adding -nam. Thus:—
Substantive : **quisnam**, *who, pray?* **quidnam**, *what, pray?*
Adjective :   **quīnam, quaenam, quodnam,** *of what kind, pray?*

## VIII. INDEFINITE PRONOUNS.

**91.** These have the general force of *some one, any one.*

| SUBSTANTIVES. | | | ADJECTIVES. | | |
|---|---|---|---|---|---|
| M. AND F. | NEUT. | | MASC. | FEM. | NEUT. |
| quis, | quid, | { *any one, anything.* | quī, | quae, qua, | quod, *any.* |
| aliquis, | aliquid, | { *some one, something.* | aliquī, | aliqua, | aliquod, *any.* |
| quisquam, | quidquam, | { *any one, anything.* | quisquam, | | quidquam, { *any (rare)* |
| quispiam, | quidpiam, | { *any one, anything.* | quispiam, | quaepiam, | quodpiam, *any.* |
| quisque, | quidque, *each.* | | quisque, | quaeque, | quodque, *each.* |
| quīvīs, quaevīs, quīlibet, quaelibet, | quidvīs, quidlibet, | { *any one (anything) you wish.* | quīvīs, quīlibet, | quaevīs, quaelibet, | quodvīs, quodlibet, { *any you wish* |
| quīdam, quaedam, | quiddam, | { *a certain person, or thing.* | quīdam, quaedam, | | quoddam, { *a certain.* |

1. In the Indefinite Pronouns, only the pronominal part is declined. Thus: Genitive Singular alicūjus, cūjuslibet, *etc.*

2. Note that aliquī has aliqua in the Nominative Singular Femi‑nine, also in the Nominative and Accusative Plural Neuter. Quī has both qua and quae in these same cases.

3. Quīdam forms Accusative Singular quendam, quandam; Geni‑tive Plural quōrundam, quārundam; the m being assimilated to n before d.

4. Aliquis may be used adjectively, and (occasionally) aliquī sub‑stantively.

5. In combination with nē, sī, nisi, num, either quis or quī may stand as a Substantive. Thus: sī quis or sī quī.

6. Ecquis, *any one*, though strictly an Indefinite, generally has interrogative force. It has both substantive and adjective forms, — substantive, ecquis, ecquid; adjective, ecquī, ecquae and ecqua, ecquod.

7. Quisquam is not used in the Plural.

8. There are two Indefinite Relatives, — quīcumque and quisquis, *whoever*. Quīcumque declines only the first part; quisquis declines both but has only quisquis, quidquid, quōquō, in common use.

## PRONOMINAL ADJECTIVES.

**92** The following adjectives, also, frequently have pro nominal force : —

1. alius, *another*;            alter, *the other;*
   uter, *which of two?* (interr.); neuter, *neither;*
      *whichever of two* (rel.) ;
   ūnus, *one;*            nūllus, *no one* (in oblique cases).

2. The compounds, —
   uterque, utraque, utrumque, *each of two;*
   utercumque, utracumque, utrumcumque, *whoever of two;*
   uterlibet, utralibet, utrumlibet, *either one you please;*
   utervīs, utravīs, utrumvīs, *either one you please;*
   alteruter, alterutra, alterutrum, *the one or the other.*

In these, uter alone is declined. The rest of the word remains unchanged, except in case of alteruter, which may decline both parts; as, —

*Nom.* alteruter      altera utra      alterum utrum
*Gen.* alterius utrīus, *etc.*

## Chapter II. — *Conjugation.*

**93.** A Verb is a word which asserts something; as, **est,** *he is;* **amat,** *he loves.* The Inflection of Verbs is called Conjugation.

**94.** Verbs have Voice, Mood, Tense, Number, and Person : —

    1. Two Voices, — Active and Passive.
    2. Three Moods, — Indicative, Subjunctive, Imperative.
    3. Six Tenses, —

|  |  |
|---|---|
| Present, | Perfect, |
| Imperfect, | Pluperfect, |
| Future, | Future Perfect. |

But the Subjunctive lacks the Future and Future Perfect; while the Imperative employs only the Present and Future.

    4. Two Numbers, — Singular and Plural.
    5. Three Persons, — First, Second, and Third.

**95.** These make up the so-called *Finite Verb.* Besides this, we have the following Noun and Adjective Forms:—

    1. Noun Forms, — Infinitive, Gerund, and Supine.
    2. Adjective Forms, — Participles (including the Gerundive).

**96.** The Personal Endings of the Verb are, —

|  | ACTIVE. | PASSIVE. |
|---|---|---|
| *Sing.* 1. | -ō; -m; -ī (Perf. Ind.); | -r. |
| 2. | -s; -stī (Perf. Ind.); -tō or wanting (Impv.); | -ris, -re; -re, -tor (Impv.). |
| 3. | -t; -tō (Impv.); | -tur; -tor (Impv.). |
| *Plu.* 1. | -mus; | -mur. |
| 2. | -tis; -stis (Perf. Ind.); -te, -tōte (Impv.); | -minī. |
| 3. | -nt; -ērunt (Perf. Ind.); -ntō (Impv.); | -ntur; -ntor (Impv.). |

### VERB STEMS.

**97.** Conjugation consists in appending certain endings to the Stem. We distinguish three different stems in a fully inflected verb, —

I.  **Present Stem,** from which are formed —
    1. Present, Imperfect, and Future Indicative, ⎫
    2. Present and Imperfect Subjunctive,    ⎬ Active and Passive.
    3. The Imperative,                ⎭ sive.
    4. The Present Infinitive,
    5. The Present Active Participle, the Gerund, and Gerundive.

II.  **Perfect Stem,** from which are formed —
    1. Perfect, Pluperfect, and Future Perfect Indicative, ⎫
    2. Perfect and Pluperfect Subjunctive,        ⎬ Active.
    3. Perfect Infinitive,                   ⎭

III.  **Participial Stem,** from which are formed —
    1. Perfect Participle,                   ⎫
    2. Perfect, Pluperfect, and Future Perfect Indicative, ⎬ Passive.
    3. Perfect and Pluperfect Subjunctive,        ⎭
    4. Perfect Infinitive,

Apparently from the same stem, though really of different origin, are the Supine, the Future Active Participle, the Future Infinitive Active and Passive.

## THE FOUR CONJUGATIONS.

**98.** There are in Latin four regular Conjugations, distinguished from each other by the vowel of the termination of the Present Infinitive Active, as follows : —

| CONJUGATION. | INFINITIVE TERMINATION. | DISTINGUISHING VOWEL. |
|:---:|:---:|:---:|
| I. | -āre | ā |
| II. | -ēre | ē |
| III. | -ĕre | ĕ |
| IV. | -īre | ī |

**99.** PRINCIPAL PARTS.   The Present Indicative, Present Infinitive, Perfect Indicative, and the Perfect Participle [1] constitute the **Principal Parts** of a Latin verb, — so called because they contain the different stems, from which the full conjugation of the verb may be derived.

---

[1] Where the Perfect Participle is not in use, the Future Active Participle, if it occurs, is given as one of the Principal Parts.

## CONJUGATION OF **SUM**.

**100.** The irregular verb **sum** is so important for the conjugation of all other verbs that its inflection is given at the outset.

### PRINCIPAL PARTS.

| Pres. Ind. | Pres. Inf. | Perf. Ind. | Fut. Partic.[1] |
|---|---|---|---|
| **sum** | **esse** | **fuī** | **futūrus** |

### INDICATIVE MOOD.

#### PRESENT TENSE.

| SINGULAR. | PLURAL. |
|---|---|
| sum, *I am*, | sumus, *we are*, |
| es, *thou art*, | estis, *you are*, |
| est, *he is*; | sunt, *they are*. |

#### IMPERFECT.

| | |
|---|---|
| eram, *I was*, | erāmus, *we were*, |
| erās, *thou wast*, | erātis, *you were*, |
| erat, *he was*; | erant, *they were*. |

#### FUTURE.

| | |
|---|---|
| erō, *I shall be*, | erimus, *we shall be*, |
| eris, *thou wilt be*, | eritis, *you will be*, |
| erit, *he will be*; | erunt, *they will be*. |

#### PERFECT.

| | |
|---|---|
| fuī, *I have been, I was*, | fuimus, *we have been, we were*, |
| fuistī, *thou hast been, thou wast*, | fuistis, *you have been, you were*, |
| fuit, *he has been, he was*; | fuērunt, fuēre, } *they have been, they were.* |

#### PLUPERFECT.

| | |
|---|---|
| fueram, *I had been*, | fuerāmus, *we had been*, |
| fuerās, *thou hadst been*, | fuerātis, *you had been*, |
| fuerat, *he had been*; | fuerant, *they had been*. |

#### FUTURE PERFECT.

| | |
|---|---|
| fuerō, *I shall have been*, | fuerimus, *we shall have been*, |
| fueris, *thou wilt have been*, | fueritis, *you will have been*, |
| fuerit, *he will have been*; | fuerint, *they will have been*. |

[1] The Perfect Participle is wanting in **sum**.

## SUBJUNCTIVE.[1]

### PRESENT.

| SINGULAR. | PLURAL. |
|---|---|
| sim, *may I be,* | sīmus, *let us be,* |
| sīs, *mayst thou be,* | sītis, *be ye, may you be,* |
| sit, *let him be, may he be;* | sint, *let them be.* |

### IMPERFECT.

| | |
|---|---|
| essem,[2] *I should be,* | essēmus, *we should be,* |
| essēs,[2] *thou wouldst be,* | essētis, *you would be,* |
| esset,[2] *he would be;* | essent,[2] *they would be.* |

### PERFECT.

| | |
|---|---|
| fuerim, *I may have been,* | fuerīmus, *we may have been,* |
| fuerīs, *thou mayst have been,* | fuerītis, *you may have been,* |
| fuerit, *he may have been;* | fuerint, *they may have been.* |

### PLUPERFECT.

| | |
|---|---|
| fuissem, *I should have been,* | fuissēmus, *we should have been,* |
| fuissēs, *thou wouldst have been,* | fuissētis, *you would have been,* |
| fuisset, *he would have been;* | fuissent, *they would have been.* |

## IMPERATIVE.

| | | |
|---|---|---|
| *Pres.* | es, *be thou;* | este, *be ye,* |
| *Fut.* | estō, *thou shalt be,* | estōte, *ye shall be,* |
| | estō, *he shall be;* | suntō, *they shall be.* |

## INFINITIVE.    PARTICIPLE.

| | |
|---|---|
| *Pres.* esse, *to be.* | |
| *Perf.* fuisse, *to have been.* | |
| *Fut.* futūrus esse,[3] *to be about to be.* | *Fut.* futūrus,[4] *about to be.* |

---

[1] The meanings of the different tenses of the Subjunctive are so many and so varied, particularly in subordinate clauses, that no attempt can be made to give them here. For fuller information the pupil is referred to the Syntax.

[2] For essem, essēs, esset, essent, the forms forem, forēs, foret, forent are sometimes used.

[3] For futūrus esse, the form fore is often used.

[4] Declined like bonus, -a, -um.

## FIRST (OR Ā–) CONJUGATION.

**101.** **Active Voice.** — Amō, *I love.*

### PRINCIPAL PARTS.

| PRES. IND. | PRES. INF. | PERF. IND. | PERF. PASS. PARTIC. |
|---|---|---|---|
| **amō** | **amāre** | **amāvī** | **amātus** |

### INDICATIVE MOOD.

#### PRESENT TENSE.

| SINGULAR. | PLURAL. |
|---|---|
| amō, *I love,* | amāmus, *we love,* |
| amās, *you love,* | amātis, *you love,* |
| amat, *he loves;* | amant, *they love.* |

#### IMPERFECT.

| | |
|---|---|
| amābam, *I was loving,*[1] | amābāmus, *we were loving,* |
| amābās, *you were loving,* | amābātis, *you were loving,* |
| amābat, *he was loving;* | amābant, *they were loving.* |

#### FUTURE.

| | |
|---|---|
| amābō, *I shall love,* | amābimus, *we shall love,* |
| amābis, *you will love,* | amābitis, *you will love,* |
| amābit, *he will love;* | amābunt, *they will love.* |

#### PERFECT.

| | |
|---|---|
| amāvī, *I have loved, I loved,* | amāvimus, *we have loved, we loved,* |
| amāvistī, *you have loved, you loved,* | amāvistis, *you have loved, you loved,* |
| amāvit, *he has loved, he loved;* | amāvērunt, -ēre, *they have loved, they loved.* |

#### PLUPERFECT.

| | |
|---|---|
| amāveram, *I had loved,* | amāverāmus, *we had loved,* |
| amāverās, *you had loved,* | amāverātis, *you had loved,* |
| amāverat, *he had loved;* | amāverant, *they had loved.* |

#### FUTURE PERFECT.

| | |
|---|---|
| amāverō, *I shall have loved,* | amāverimus, *we shall have loved,* |
| amāveris, *you will have loved,* | amāveritis, *you will have loved,* |
| amāverit, *he will have loved;* | amāverint, *they will have loved.* |

---

[1] The Imperfect also means *I loved.*

## SUBJUNCTIVE.

### PRESENT.

SINGULAR.

PLURAL.

amem, *may I love,*

amēmus, *let us love,*

amēs, *may you love,*

amētis, *may you love,*

amet, *let him love ;*

ament, *let them love.*

### IMPERFECT.

amārem, *I should love,*

amārēmus, *we should love,*

amārēs, *you would love,*

amārētis, *you would love,*

amāret, *he would love ;*

amārent, *they would love.*

### PERFECT.

amāverim, *I may have loved,*

amāverīmus, *we may have loved,*

amāverīs, *you may have loved,*

amāverītis, *you may have loved,*

amāverit, *he may have loved ;*

amāverint, *they may have loved.*

### PLUPERFECT.

amāvissem, *I should have loved,*

amāvissēmus, *we should have loved,*

amāvissēs, *you would have loved,*

amāvissētis, *you would have loved,*

amāvisset, *he would have loved ;*

amāvissent, *they would have loved.*

## IMPERATIVE.

*Pres.* amā, *love thou ;*

amāte, *love ye.*

*Fut.* amātō, *thou shalt love,*

amātōte, *ye shall love,*

amātō, *he shall love ;*

amantō, *they shall love.*

## INFINITIVE.

## PARTICIPLE.

*Pres.* amāre, *to love.*

*Pres.* amāns,[1] *loving.*

*Perf.* amāvisse, *to have loved.*

(Gen. amantis.)

*Fut.* amātūrus esse, *to be about to love.*

*Fut.* amātūrus, *about to love.*

## GERUND.

## SUPINE.

*Gen.* amandī, *of loving,*

*Dat.* amandō, *for loving,*

*Acc.* amandum, *loving,*

*Acc.* amātum, *to love,*

*Abl.* amandō, *by loving.*

*Abl.* amātū, *to love, be loved.*

[1] For declension of **amāns**, see § 70. 3.

## FIRST (OR Ā-) CONJUGATION.

**102.**          **Passive Voice.** — Amor, *I am loved.*

### PRINCIPAL PARTS.

| Pres. Ind. | Pres. Inf. | Perf. Ind. |
|---|---|---|
| amor | amārī | amātus **sum** |

### INDICATIVE MOOD.

#### PRESENT TENSE.

| SINGULAR. | *I am loved.* | PLURAL. |
|---|---|---|
| amor | | amāmur |
| amāris | | amāminī |
| amātur | | amantur |

#### IMPERFECT.
*I was loved.*

| | | |
|---|---|---|
| amābar | | amābāmur |
| amābāris, *or* -re | | amābāminī |
| amābātur | | amābantur |

#### FUTURE.
*I shall be loved.*

| | | |
|---|---|---|
| amābor | | amābimur |
| amāberis, *or* -re | | amābiminī |
| amābitur | | amābuntur |

#### PERFECT.
*I have been loved*, or *I was loved.*

| | |
|---|---|
| amātus (-a, -um) sum [1] | amātī (-ae, -a) sumus |
| amātus es | amātī estis |
| amātus est | amātī sunt |

#### PLUPERFECT.
*I had been loved.*

| | |
|---|---|
| amātus eram [1] | amātī erāmus |
| amātus erās | amātī erātis |
| amātus erat | amātī erant |

#### FUTURE PERFECT.
*I shall have been loved.*

| | |
|---|---|
| amātus erō [1] | amātī erimus |
| amātus eris | amātī eritis |
| amātus erit | amātī erunt |

---

[1] Fuī, fuistī, *etc.*, are sometimes used for sum, es, *etc.* So fueram, fuerās, *etc.*, for eram, *etc.;* fuerō, *etc.,* for erō, *etc.*

## SUBJUNCTIVE.

### PRESENT.

*May I be loved, let him be loved.*

| SINGULAR. | PLURAL. |
|---|---|
| amer | amēmur |
| amēris, *or* -re | amēminī |
| amētur | amentur |

### IMPERFECT.

*I should be loved, he would be loved.*

| | |
|---|---|
| amārer | amārēmur |
| amārēris, *or* -re | amārēminī |
| amārētur | amārentur |

### PERFECT.

*I may have been loved.*

| | |
|---|---|
| amātus sim [1] | amātī sīmus |
| amātus sīs | amātī sītis |
| amātus sit | amātī sint |

### PLUPERFECT.

*I should have been loved, he would have been loved.*

| | |
|---|---|
| amātus essem [1] | amātī essēmus |
| amātus essēs | amātī essētis |
| amātus esset | amātī essent |

## IMPERATIVE.

*Pres.* amāre,[2] *be thou loved;*   amāminī, *be ye loved.*

*Fut.* amātor, *thou shalt be loved,*

amātor, *he shall be loved;*   amantor, *they shall be loved*

| INFINITIVE. | PARTICIPLE. |
|---|---|

*Pres.* amārī, *to be loved.*

*Perf.* amātus esse, *to have been loved.*   *Perfect.* amātus, *loved, having been loved.*

*Fut.* amātum īrī, *to be about to be loved.*   *Gerundive.* amandus, *to be loved, deserving to be loved.*

---

[1] **Fuerim,** *etc.*, are sometimes used for **sim**; so **fuissem,** *etc.*, for **essem.**

[2] In actual usage passive imperatives occur only in deponents (§ 112).

## SECOND (OR Ē-) CONJUGATION.

**103.**     **Active Voice.** — Moneō, *I advise.*

### PRINCIPAL PARTS.

| PRES. IND. | PRES. INF. | PERF. IND. | PERF. PASS. PARTIC. |
|---|---|---|---|
| moneō | monēre | monuī | monitus |

### INDICATIVE MOOD.

#### PRESENT TENSE.

| SINGULAR. | *I advise.* | PLURAL. |
|---|---|---|
| moneō | | monēmus |
| monēs | | monētis |
| monet | | monent |

#### IMPERFECT.
*I was advising,* or *I advised.*

| | |
|---|---|
| monēbam | monēbāmus |
| monēbās | monēbātis |
| monēbat | monēbant |

#### FUTURE.
*I shall advise.*

| | |
|---|---|
| monēbō | monēbimus |
| monēbis | monēbitis |
| monēbit | monēbunt |

#### PERFECT.
*I have advised,* or *I advised.*

| | |
|---|---|
| monuī | monuimus |
| monuistī | monuistis |
| monuit | monuērunt, *or* -ēre |

#### PLUPERFECT.
*I had advised.*

| | |
|---|---|
| monueram | monuerāmus |
| monuerās | monuerātis |
| monuerat | monuerant |

#### FUTURE PERFECT.
*I shall have advised.*

| | |
|---|---|
| monuerō | monuerimus |
| monueris | monueritis |
| monuerit | monuerint |

## SUBJUNCTIVE.

PRESENT.

*May I advise, let him advise.*

| SINGULAR. | PLURAL. |
|---|---|
| moneam | moneāmus |
| moneās | moneātis |
| moneat | moneant |

IMPERFECT.

*I should advise, he would advise.*

| monērem | monērēmus |
|---|---|
| monērēs | monērētis |
| monēret | monērent |

PERFECT.

*I may have advised.*

| monuerim | monuerīmus |
|---|---|
| monuerīs | monuerītis |
| monuerit | monuerint |

PLUPERFECT.

*I should have advised, he would have advised.*

| monuissem | monuissēmu |
|---|---|
| monuissēs | monuissētis |
| monuisset | monuissent |

## IMPERATIVE.

*Pres.* monē, *advise thou;*    monēte, *advise ye.*
*Fut.* monētō, *thou shalt advise,*    monētōte, *ye shall advise,*
      monētō, *he shall advise;*    monentō, *they shall advise.*

## INFINITIVE.

*Pres.* monēre, *to advise.*
*Perf.* monuisse, *to have advised.*
*Fut.* monitūrus esse, *to be about to advise.*

## PARTICIPLE.

*Pres.* monēns, *advising.*
    (Gen. monentis.)
*Fut.* monitūrus, *about to advise.*

## GERUND.

*Gen.* monendī, *of advising,*
*Dat.* monendō, *for advising,*
*Acc.* monendum, *advising,*
*Abl.* monendō, *by advising.*

## SUPINE.

*Acc.* monitum, *to advise,*
*Abl.* monitū, *to advise, be advised.*

## SECOND (OR Ē-) CONJUGATION.

**104.**    **Passive Voice.** — Moneor, *I am advised.*

PRINCIPAL PARTS.

| PRES. IND. | PRES. INF. | PERF. IND. |
|---|---|---|
| moneor | monērī | monitus **sum** |

### INDICATIVE MOOD.

PRESENT TENSE.

SINGULAR.      *I am advised.*      PLURAL.

| | |
|---|---|
| moneor | monēmur |
| monēris | monēminī |
| monētur | monentur |

ɪMPERFECT.

*I was advised.*

| | |
|---|---|
| monēbar | monēbāmur |
| monēbāris, *or* -re | monēbāminī |
| monēbātur | monēbantur |

FUTURE.

*I shall be advised.*

| | |
|---|---|
| monēbor | monēbimur |
| monēberis, *or* -re | monēbiminī |
| monēbitur | monēbuntur |

PERFECT.

*I have been advised, I was advised.*

| | |
|---|---|
| monitus **sum** | monitī **sumus** |
| monitus **es** | monitī **estis** |
| monitus **est** | monitī **sunt** |

PLUPERFECT.

*I had been advised.*

| | |
|---|---|
| monitus **eram** | monitī **erāmus** |
| monitus **erās** | monitī **erātis** |
| monitus **erat** | monitī **erant** |

FUTURE PERFECT.

*I shall have been advised.*

| | |
|---|---|
| monitus **erō** | monitī **erimus** |
| monitus **eris** | monitī **eritis** |
| monitus **erit** | monitī **erunt** |

## SUBJUNCTIVE.

### PRESENT.

*May I be advised, let him be advised.*

| SINGULAR. | PLURAL. |
|---|---|
| monear | moneāmur |
| moneāris, *or* -re | moneāminī |
| moneātur | moneantur |

### IMPERFECT.

*I should be advised, he would be advised.*

| | |
|---|---|
| monērer | monērēmur |
| monērēris, *or* -re | monērēminī |
| monērētur | monērentur |

### PERFECT.

*I may have been advised.*

| | |
|---|---|
| monitus sim | monitī sīmus |
| monitus sīs | monitī sītis |
| monitus sit | monitī sint |

### PLUPERFECT.

*I should have been advised, he would have been advised.*

| | |
|---|---|
| monitus essem | monitī essēmus |
| monitus essēs | monitī essētis |
| monitus esset | monitī essent |

## IMPERATIVE.

*Pres.* monēre, *be thou advised;*    monēminī, *be ye advised.*
*Fut.* monētor, *thou shalt be advised,*
monētor, *he shall be advised.*    monentor, *they shall be advised.*

## INFINITIVE.

*Pres.* monērī, *to be advised.*
*Perf.* monitus esse, *to have been advised.*
*Fut.* monitum īrī, *to be about to be advised.*

## PARTICIPLE.

*Perfect.* monitus, *advised, having been advised.*
*Gerundive.* monendus, *to be advised, deserving to be advised.*

## THIRD (OR CONSONANT-) CONJUGATION.

**105.**  **Active Voice.** — Regō, *I rule.*

### PRINCIPAL PARTS.

| PRES. IND. | PRES. INF. | PERF. IND. | PERF. PASS. PARTIC. |
|---|---|---|---|
| regō | regere | rēxī | rēctus |

### INDICATIVE MOOD.

#### PRESENT TENSE.
*I rule.*

| SINGULAR. | PLURAL. |
|---|---|
| regō | regimus |
| regis | regitis |
| regit | regunt |

#### IMPERFECT.
*I was ruling,* or *I ruled.*

| | |
|---|---|
| regēbam | regēbāmus |
| regēbās | regēbātis |
| regēbat | regēbant |

#### FUTURE.
*I shall rule.*

| | |
|---|---|
| regam | regēmus |
| regēs | regētis |
| reget | regent |

#### PERFECT.
*I have ruled,* or *I ruled.*

| | |
|---|---|
| rēxī | rēximus |
| rēxistī | rēxistis |
| rēxit | rēxērunt, *or* -ēre |

#### PLUPERFECT.
*I had ruled.*

| | |
|---|---|
| rēxeram | rēxerāmus |
| rēxerās | rēxerātis |
| rēxerat | rēxerant |

#### FUTURE PERFECT.
*I shall have ruled.*

| | |
|---|---|
| rēxerō | rēxerimus |
| rēxeris | rēxeritis |
| rēxerit | rēxerint |

## SUBJUNCTIVE.

PRESENT.

*May I rule, let him rule.*

| SINGULAR. | PLURAL. |
|---|---|
| regam | regāmus |
| regās | regātis |
| regat | regant |

IMPERFECT.

*I should rule, he would rule.*

| | |
|---|---|
| regerem | regerēmus |
| regerēs | regerētis |
| regeret | regerent |

PERFECT.

*I may have ruled.*

| | |
|---|---|
| rēxerim | rēxerīmus |
| rēxerīs | rēxerītis |
| rēxerit | rēxerint |

PLUPERFECT.

*I should have ruled, he would have ruled.*

| | |
|---|---|
| rēxissem | rēxissēmus |
| rēxissēs | rēxissētis |
| rēxisset | rēxissent |

## IMPERATIVE.

| | | | |
|---|---|---|---|
| *Pres.* | rege, *rule thou ;* | regite, *rule ye.* | |
| *Fut.* | regitō, *thou shalt rule,* | regitōte, *ye shall rule,* | |
| | regitō, *he shall rule ;* | reguntō, *they shall rule.* | |

| INFINITIVE. | PARTICIPLE. |
|---|---|

| | | | |
|---|---|---|---|
| *Pres.* | regere, *to rule.* | *Pres.* | regēns, *ruling.* |
| *Perf.* | rēxisse, *to have ruled.* | | (Gen. regentis.) |
| *Fut.* | rēctūrus esse, *to be about to rule.* | *Fut.* | rēctūrus, *about to rule.* |

| GERUND. | SUPINE. |
|---|---|

| | | | |
|---|---|---|---|
| *Gen.* | regendī, *of ruling,* | | |
| *Dat.* | regendō, *for ruling,* | | |
| *Acc.* | regendum, *ruling,* | *Acc.* | rēctum, *to rule,* |
| *Abl.* | regendō, *by ruling.* | *Abl.* | rēctū, *to rule, be ruled.* |

## THIRD (OR CONSONANT-) CONJUGATION.

**106.**     **Passive Voice.** — Regor, *I am ruled.*

PRINCIPAL PARTS.

| ᴘʀᴇs. Iɴᴅ. | Pʀᴇs. Iɴꜰ. | Pᴇʀꜰ. Iɴᴅ. |
|---|---|---|
| regor | regī | rēctus sum |

### INDICATIVE MOOD.

Pʀᴇsᴇɴᴛ Tᴇɴsᴇ.

| ꜱɪɴɢᴜʟᴀʀ. | *I am ruled.* | ᴘʟᴜʀᴀʟ. |
|---|---|---|
| regor | | regimur |
| regeris | | regiminī |
| regitur | | reguntur |

Iᴍᴘᴇʀꜰᴇᴄᴛ.
*I was ruled.*

| regēbar | | regēbāmur |
| regēbāris, *or* -re | | regēbāminī |
| regēbātur | | regēbantur |

Fᴜᴛᴜʀᴇ.
*I shall be ruled.*

| regar | | regēmur |
| regēris, *or* -re | | regēminī |
| regētur | | regentur |

Pᴇʀꜰᴇᴄᴛ.
*I have been ruled,* or *I was ruled.*

| rēctus sum | | rēctī sumus |
| rēctus es | | rēctī estis |
| rēctus est | | rēctī sunt |

Pʟᴜᴘᴇʀꜰᴇᴄᴛ.
*I had been ruled.*

| rēctus eram | | rēctī erāmus |
| rēctus erās | | rēctī erātis |
| rēctus erat | | rēctī erant |

Fᴜᴛᴜʀᴇ Pᴇʀꜰᴇᴄᴛ.
*I shall have been ruled.*

| rēctus erð | | rēctī erimus |
| rēctus eris | | rēctī eritis |
| rēctus erit | | rēctī erunt |

## SUBJUNCTIVE.

### PRESENT.

*May I be ruled, let him be ruled.*

| SINGULAR. | PLURAL. |
|---|---|
| regar | regāmur |
| regāris, *or* -re | regāminī |
| regātur | regantur |

### IMPERFECT.

*I should be ruled, he would be ruled.*

| | |
|---|---|
| regerer | regerēmur |
| regerēris, *or* -re | regerēminī |
| regerētur | regerentur |

### PERFECT.

*I may have been ruled.*

| | |
|---|---|
| rēctus sim | rēctī sīmus |
| rēctus sīs | rēctī sītis |
| rēctus sit | rēctī sint |

### PLUPERFECT.

*I should have been ruled, he would have been ruled.*

| | |
|---|---|
| rēctus essem | rectī essēmus |
| rēctus essēs | rectī essētis |
| rēctus esset | rectī essent |

## IMPERATIVE.

*Pres.* regere, *be thou ruled;*     regiminī, *be ye ruled.*
*Fut.* regitor, *thou shalt be ruled,*
regitor, *he shall be ruled;*     reguntor, *they shall be ruled.*

## INFINITIVE.

*Pres.* regī, *to be ruled.*
*Perf.* rēctus esse, *to have been ruled.*
*Fut.* rēctum īrī, *to be about to be ruled.*

## PARTICIPLE.

*Perfect.* rēctus, *ruled, having been ruled.*
*Gerundive.* regendus, *to be ruled deserving to be ruled*

## FOURTH (OR Ī-) CONJUGATION.

**107.**　　　　　　**Active Voice.** — Audiō, *I hear.*

### PRINCIPAL PARTS.

| PRES. IND. | PRES. INF. | PERF. IND. | PERF. PASS. PARTIC. |
|---|---|---|---|
| audiō | audīre | audīvī | audītus |

### INDICATIVE MOOD.

#### PRESENT TENSE.

*I hear.*

| SINGULAR. | PLURAL. |
|---|---|
| audiō | audīmus |
| audīs | audītis |
| audit | audiunt |

#### IMPERFECT.

*I was hearing,* or *I heard.*

| | |
|---|---|
| audiēbam | audiēbāmus |
| audiēbās | audiēbātis |
| audiēbat | audiēbant |

#### FUTURE.

*I shall hear.*

| | |
|---|---|
| audiam | audiēmus |
| audiēs | audiētis |
| audiet | audient |

#### PERFECT.

*I have heard,* or *I heard.*

| | |
|---|---|
| audīvī | audīvimus |
| audīvistī | audīvistis |
| audīvit | audīvērunt, *or* -ēre |

#### PLUPERFECT.

*I had heard.*

| | |
|---|---|
| audīveram | audīverāmus |
| audīverās | audīverātis |
| audīverat | audīverant |

#### FUTURE PERFECT.

*I shall have heard.*

| | |
|---|---|
| audīverō | audīverimus |
| audīveris | audīveritis |
| audīverit | audīverint |

## SUBJUNCTIVE.
### PRESENT.
*May I hear, let him hear.*

| SINGULAR. | PLURAL. |
|---|---|
| audiam | audiāmus |
| audiās | audiātis |
| audiat | audiant |

### IMPERFECT.
*I should hear, he would hear.*

| | |
|---|---|
| audīrem | audīrēmus |
| audīrēs | audīrētis |
| audīret | audīrent |

### PERFECT.
*I may have heard.*

| | |
|---|---|
| audīverim | audīverīmus |
| audīverīs | audīverītis |
| audīverit | audīverint |

### PLUPERFECT.
*I should have heard, he would have heard.*

| | |
|---|---|
| audīvissem | audīvissēmus |
| audīvissēs | audīvissētis |
| audīvisset | audīvissent |

## IMPERATIVE.

| | | |
|---|---|---|
| *Pres.* | audī, *hear thou;* | audīte, *hear ye.* |
| *Fut.* | audītō, *thou shalt hear,* | audītōte, *ye shall hear,* |
| | audītō, *he shall hear;* | audiuntō, *they shall hear.* |

## INFINITIVE.

*Pres.* audīre, *to hear.*
*Perf.* audīvisse, *to have heard.*
*Fut.* audītūrus esse, *to be about to hear.*

## PARTICIPLE.

*Pres.* audiēns, *hearing.*
(Gen. audientis.)
*Fut.* audītūrus, *about to hear.*

## GERUND.

*Gen.* audiendī, *of hearing,*
*Dat.* audiendō, *for hearing,*
*Acc.* audiendum, *hearing,*
*Abl.* audiendō, *by hearing.*

## SUPINE.

*Acc.* audītum, *to hear,*
*Abl.* audītū, *to hear, be heard.*

## FOURTH (OR Ī-) CONJUGATION.

**108.** **Passive Voice.** — Audior, *I am heard.*

PRINCIPAL PARTS.

| PRES. IND. | PRES. INF. | PERF. IND. |
|---|---|---|
| audior | audīrī | audītus sum |

### INDICATIVE MOOD.

PRESENT TENSE.

| SINGULAR. | *I am heard.* | PLURAL. |
|---|---|---|
| audior | | audīmur |
| audīris | | audīminī |
| audītur | | audiuntur |

IMPERFECT.

*I was heard.*

| | | |
|---|---|---|
| audiēbar | | audiēbāmur |
| audiēbāris, *or* -re | | audiēbāminī |
| audiēbātur | | audiēbantur |

FUTURE.

*I shall be heard.*

| | | |
|---|---|---|
| audiar | | audiēmur |
| audiēris, *or* -re | | audiēminī |
| audiētur | | audientur |

PERFECT.

*I have been heard,* or *I was heard.*

| | | |
|---|---|---|
| audītus sum | | audītī sumus |
| audītus es | | audītī estis |
| audītus est | | audītī sunt |

PLUPERFECT.

*I had been heard.*

| | | |
|---|---|---|
| audītus eram | | audītī erāmus |
| audītus erās | | audītī erātis |
| audītus erat | | audītī erant |

FUTURE PERFECT.

*I shall have been heard.*

| | | |
|---|---|---|
| audītus erō | | audītī erimus |
| audītus eris | | audītī eritis |
| audītus erit | | audītī erunt |

## SUBJUNCTIVE.

### PRESENT.

*May I be heard, let him be heard.*

| SINGULAR. | PLURAL. |
|---|---|
| audiar | audiāmur |
| audiāris, *or* -re | audiāminī |
| audiātur | audiantur |

### IMPERFECT.

*I should be heard, he would be heard.*

| | |
|---|---|
| audīrer | audīrēmur |
| audīrēris, *or* -re | audīrēminī |
| audīrētur | audīrentur |

### PERFECT.

*I may have been heard.*

| | |
|---|---|
| audītus sim | audītī sīmus |
| audītus sīs | audītī sītis |
| audītus sit | audītī sint |

### PLUPERFECT.

*I should have been heard, he would have been heard.*

| | |
|---|---|
| audītus essem | audītī essēmus |
| audītus essēs | audītī essētis |
| audītus esset | audītī essent |

## IMPERATIVE.

*Pres.* audīre, *be thou heard;*    audīminī, *be ye heard.*
*Fut.* audītor, *thou shalt be heard,*
audītor, *he shall be heard;*    audiuntor, *they shall be heard.*

## INFINITIVE.

*Pres.* audīrī, *to be heard.*
*Perf.* audītus esse, *to have been heard.*
*Fut.* audītum īrī, *to be about to be heard.*

## PARTICIPLE.

*Perfect.* audītus, *heard, having been heard.*
*Gerundive.* audiendus, *to be heard, deserving to be heard.*

## VERBS IN –IŌ OF THE THIRD CONJUGATION.

**109.** 1. Verbs in -iō of the Third Conjugation take the endings of the Fourth Conjugation wherever the latter endings have two successive vowels. This occurs only in the Present System.

2. Here belong —

a) capiō, *to take*; cupiō, *to desire*; faciō, *to make*; fodiō, *to dig*; fugiō, *to flee*; jaciō, *to throw*; pariō, *to bear*; quatiō, *to shake*; rapiō, *to seize*; sapiō, *to taste*.

b) Compounds of laciō and speciō (both ante-classical); as, alliciō, *entice*; cōnspiciō, *behold*.

c) The deponents gradior, *to go*; morior, *to die*; patior, *to suffer*.

**110.**              **Active Voice.** — Capiō, *I take*.

### PRINCIPAL PARTS.

| Pres. Ind. | Pres. Inf. | Perf. Ind. | Perf. Pass. Partic. |
|---|---|---|---|
| capiō, | capere, | cēpī, | captus. |

### INDICATIVE MOOD.

SINGULAR.

**PRESENT TENSE.**

PLURAL.

capiō, capis, capit ;                capimus, capitis, capiunt.

IMPERFECT.

capiēbam, -iēbās, -iēbat ;                capiēbāmus, -iēbātis, -iēbant.

FUTURE.

capiam, -iēs, -iet ;                capiēmus, -iētis, -ient.

PERFECT.

cēpī, -istī, -it ;                cēpimus, -istis, -ērunt *or* -ēre.

PLUPERFECT.

cēperam, -erās, -erat ;                cēperāmus, -erātis, -erant.

FUTURE PERFECT.

cēperō, -eris, -erit '                cēperimus, -eritis, -erint.

## SUBJUNCTIVE.

SINGULAR.  **PRESENT.**  PLURAL.

capiam, -iās, -iat;   capiāmus, -iātis, -iant.

**IMPERFECT.**

caperem, -erēs, -eret;   caperēmus, -erētis, -erent.

**PERFECT.**

cēperim, -eris, -erit;   cēperīmus, -erītis, -erint.

**PLUPERFECT.**

cēpissem, -issēs, -isset;   cēpissēmus, -issētis, -issent.

## IMPERATIVE.

*Pres.* cape;   capite.
*Fut.* capitō,   capitōte,
capitō;   capiuntō.

## INFINITIVE.  PARTICIPLE.

*Pres.* capere   *Pres.* capiēns.
*Perf.* cēpisse.
*Fut.* captūrus esse.   *Fut.* captūrus.

## GERUND.  SUPINE.

*Gen.* capiendī,
*Dat.* capiendō,
*Acc.* capiendum,   *Acc.* captum,
*Abl.* capiendō.   *Abl.* captū.

**111.**   **Passive Voice.** — Capior, *I am taken.*

PRINCIPAL PARTS.

PRES. IND.   PRES. INF.   PERF. IND.
capior,   capī,   captus sum.

## INDICATIVE MOOD.

SINGULAR.   PRESENT TENSE.   PLURAL.
capior, caperis, capitur;   capimur, capiminī, capiuntur.

**IMPERFECT.**

capiēbar, -iēbāris, -iēbātur;   capiēbāmur, -iēbāminī, -iēbantur

**FUTURE.**

capiar, -iēris, -iētur;   capiēmur, -iēminī, -ientur.

| SINGULAR. | PERFECT. | PLURAL. |
|---|---|---|

captus sum, es, est;      captī sumus, estis, sunt.

PLUPERFECT.

captus eram, erās, erat;      captī erāmus, erātis, erant.

FUTURE PERFECT.

captus erō, eris, erit;      captī erimus, eritis, erunt.

## SUBJUNCTIVE.
### PRESENT.

capiar, -iāris, -iātur;      capiāmur, -iāminī, -iantur.

IMPERFECT.

caperer, -erēris, -erētur;      caperēmur, -erēminī, -erentur.

PERFECT.

captus sim, sīs, sit;      captī sīmus, sītis, sint.

PLUPERFECT.

captus essem, essēs, esset;      captī essēmus, essētis, essent.

## IMPERATIVE.

*Pres.* capere;      capiminī.
*Fut.* capitor,
       capitor;      capiuntor.

| INFINITIVE. | PARTICIPLE. |
|---|---|

*Pres.* capī.
*Perf.* captus esse.      *Perfect.* captus.
*Fut.* captum īrī.      *Gerundive.* capiendus.

## DEPONENT VERBS.

**112.** Deponent Verbs have in the main Passive *forms* with Active or Neuter *meaning*. But —

     *a.* They have the following Active forms: Future Infinitive, Present and Future Participles, Gerund, and Supine.

     *b.* They have the following Passive meanings: always in the Gerundive, and sometimes in the Perfect Passive Participle; as, —

       **sequendus,** *to be followed;* **adeptus,** *attained.*

**113.** Paradigms of Deponent Verbs are —
    I. Conj.   **mīror, mīrārī, mīrātus sum,** *admire.*
    II. Conj.   **vereor, verērī, veritus sum,** *fear.*
    III. Conj.   **sequor, sequī, secūtus sum,** *follow.*
    IV. Conj.   **largior, largīrī, largītus sum,** *give.*
    III. (in -ior)   **patior, patī, passus sum,** *suffer.*

### INDICATIVE MOOD.

| | I. | II. | III. | IV. | III (in -ior). |
|---|---|---|---|---|---|
| *Pres.* | mīror | vereor | sequor | largior | patior |
| | mīrāris | verēris | sequeris | largiris | pateris |
| | mīrātur | verētur | sequitur | largītur | patitur |
| | mīrāmur | verēmur | sequimur | largīmur | patimur |
| | mīrāminī | verēminī | sequiminī | largīminī | patiminī |
| | mīrantur | verentur | sequuntur | largiuntur | patiuntur |
| *Impf.* | mīrābar | verēbar | sequēbar | largiēbar | patiēbar |
| *Fut.* | mīrābor | verēbor | sequar | largiar | patiar |
| *Perf.* | mīrātus sum | veritus sum | secūtus sum | largītus sum | passus sum |
| *Plup.* | mīrātus eram | veritus eram | secūtus eram | largītus eram | passus eram |
| *F. P.* | mīrātus erō | veritus erō | secūtus erō | largītus erō | passus erō |

### SUBJUNCTIVE.

| | | | | | |
|---|---|---|---|---|---|
| *Pres.* | mīrer | verear | sequar | largiar | patiar |
| *Impf.* | mīrārer | verērer | sequerer | largīrer | paterer |
| *Perf.* | mīrātus sim | veritus sim | secūtus sim | largītus sim | passus sim |
| *Plup.* | mīrātus essem | veritus essem | secūtus essem | largītus essem | passus essem |

### IMPERATIVE.

| | | | | | |
|---|---|---|---|---|---|
| *Pres.* | mīrāre, *etc.* | verēre, *etc.* | sequere, *etc.* | largīre, *etc.* | patere. *etc.* |
| *Fut.* | mīrātor, *etc.* | verētor, *etc.* | sequitor, *etc.* | largītor, *etc.* | patitor, *etc.* |

### INFINITIVE.

| | | | | | |
|---|---|---|---|---|---|
| *Pres.* | mīrārī | verērī | sequī | largīrī | patī |
| *Perf.* | mīrātus esse | veritus esse | secūtus esse | largītus esse | passus esse |
| *Fut.* | mīrātūrus esse | veritūrus esse | secūtūrus esse | largītūrus esse | passūrus esse |

### PARTICIPLES.

| | | | | | |
|---|---|---|---|---|---|
| *Pres.* | mīrāns | verēns | sequēns | largiēns | patiēns |
| *Fut.* | mīrātūrus | veritūrus | secūtūrus | largītūrus | passūrus |
| *Perf.* | mīrātus | veritus | secūtus | largītus | passus |
| *Ger.* | mīrandus | verendus | sequendus | largiendus | patiendus |

### GERUND.

| | | | | | |
|---|---|---|---|---|---|
| | mīrandī | verendī | sequendī | largiendī | patiendī |
| | mīrandō, *etc.* | verendō, *etc.* | sequendō, *etc.* | largiendō, *etc.* | patiendō, *etc.* |

### SUPINE.

| | | | | | |
|---|---|---|---|---|---|
| | mīrātum, -tū | veritum, -tū | secūtum, -tū | largītum, -tū | passum. -sū |

## SEMI-DEPONENTS.

**114.** 1. Semi-Deponents are verbs which have the Present System in the Active Voice, but the Perfect System in the Passive without change of meaning.   Here belong —

| | | | |
|---|---|---|---|
| audeō, | audēre, | ausus sum, | *to dare.* |
| gaudeō, | gaudēre, | gāvīsus sum, | *to rejoice.* |
| soleō, | solēre, | solitus sum, | *to be wont.* |
| fīdō, | fīdere, | fīsus sum, | *to trust.* |

2. The following verbs have a Perfect Passive Participle with Active meaning : —

| | |
|---|---|
| adolēscō, *grow up;* | adultus, *having grown up.* |
| cēnāre, *dine;* | cēnātus, *having dined.* |
| placēre, *please;* | placitus, *having pleased, agreeable.* |
| prandēre, *lunch;* | prānsus, *having lunched.* |
| pōtāre, *drink;* | pōtus, *having drunk.* |
| jūrāre, *swear;* | jūrātus, *having sworn.* |

*a.* Jūrātus is used in a passive sense also.

3. **Revertor** and **dēvertor** both regularly form their Perfect in the Active Voice; *viz.* —

revertor, revertī (Inf.), revertī (Perf.), *to return.*
dēvertor, dēvertī (Inf.), dēvertī (Perf.), *to turn aside.*

## PERIPHRASTIC CONJUGATION.

**115.** There are two Periphrastic Conjugations, — the Active and the Passive.  The Active is formed by combining the Future Active Participle with the auxiliary **sum**, the Passive by combining the Gerundive with the same auxiliary.

### Active Periphrastic Conjugation.

#### INDICATIVE MOOD.

| | | |
|---|---|---|
| *Pres.* | amātūrus (-a, -um) sum, | *I am about to love.* |
| *Imp.* | amātūrus eram, | *I was about to love.* |
| *Fut.* | amātūrus erō, | *I shall be about to love.* |
| *Perf.* | amātūrus fuī, | *I have been (was) about to love.* |
| *Plup.* | amātūrus fueram, | *I had been about to love.* |
| *Fut. P.* | amātūrus fuerō, | *I shall have been about to love.* |

### SUBJUNCTIVE.

*Pres.* amātūrus sim, *may I be about to love.*
*Imp.* amātūrus essem, *I should be about to love.*
*Perf.* amātūrus fuerim, *I may have been about to love.*
*Plup.* amātūrus fuissem, *I should have been about to love.*

### INFINITIVE.

*Pres.* amātūrus esse, *to be about to love.*
*Perf.* amātūrus fuisse, *to have been about to love.*

## Passive Periphrastic Conjugation.

### INDICATIVE.

*Pres.* amandus (-a, -um) sum, *I am to be loved, must be loved.*
*Imp.* amandus eram, *I was to be loved.*
*Fut.* amandus erō, *I shall deserve to be loved.*
*Perf.* amandus fuī, *I was to be loved.*
*Plup.* amandus fueram, *I had deserved to be loved.*
*Fut. P.* amandus fuerō, *I shall have deserved to be loved.*

### SUBJUNCTIVE.

*Pres.* amandus sim, *may I deserve to be loved.*
*Imp.* amandus essem, *I should deserve to be loved.*
*Perf.* amandus fuerim, *I may have deserved to be loved.*
*Plup.* amandus fuissem, *I should have deserved to be loved.*

### INFINITIVE.

*Pres.* amandus esse, *to deserve to be loved.*
*Perf.* amandus fuisse, *to have deserved to be loved.*

## PECULIARITIES OF CONJUGATION.

**116.** 1. Perfects in -**āvī**, -**ēvī**, and -**īvī**, with the forms derived from them, often drop the **ve** or **vi** before endings beginning with **r** or **s**. So also **nōvī** (from **nōscō**) and the compounds of **mōvī** (from **moveō**). Thus: —

| | | | |
|---|---|---|---|
| amāvistī | amāstī | dēlēvistī | dēlēstī |
| amāvisse | amāsse | dēlēvisse | dēlēsse |
| amāvērunt | amārunt | dēlēvērunt | dēlērunt |
| amāverim | amārim | dēlēverim | dēlērim |
| amāveram | amāram | dēlēveram | dēlēram |
| amāverō | amārō | dēlēverō | dēlērō |
| nōvistī | nōstī | nōverim | nōrim |
| nōvisse | nōsse | nōveram | nōram |
| audīvistī | audīstī | audīvisse | audīsse |

2. In the Gerund and Gerundive of the Third and Fourth Conjugations, the endings **-undus, -undī**, often occur instead of **-endus** and **-endī**, as **faciundus, faciundī.**

3. **Dīcō, dūcō, faciō**, form the Imperatives, **dīc, dūc, fac.** But compounds of **faciō** form the Imperative in **-fice**, as **cōnfice.** Compounds of **dīcō, dūcō**, accent the ultima; as, **ēdūc, ēdīc.**

4. Archaic and Poetic forms: —

    *a.* The ending **-ier** in the Present Infinitive Passive; as, **amārier, monērier, dīcier**, for **amārī, monērī, dīcī.**

    *b.* The ending **-ībam** for **-iēbam** in Imperfects of the Fourth Conjugation, and **-ībō** for **-iam** in Futures; as, **scībam, scībō**, for **sciēbam, sciam.**

    *c.* Instead of the fuller forms, in such words as **dīxistī, scrīpsistis, surrēxisse**, we sometimes find **dīxtī, scrīpstis, surrēxe**, *etc.*

    *d.* The endings **-im, -īs**, *etc.* (for **-am, -ās**, *etc.*) occur in a few Subjunctive forms; as, **edim** (*eat*), **duint, perduint.**

5. In the Future Active and Perfect Passive Infinitive, the auxiliary **esse** is often omitted; as, **āctūrum** for **āctūrum esse**; **ējectus** for **ējectus esse.**

## FORMATION OF THE VERB STEMS.

### Formation of the Present Stem.

**117.** Many verbs employ the simple Verb Stem for the Present Stem;[1] as, **dīcere, amāre, monēre, audīre.** Others modify the Verb Stem to form the Present, as follows: —

1. By appending the vowels, **ā, ē, ī**; as, —

    **juvāre**, Present Stem **juvā-** (Verb Stem **juv-**).
    **augēre**, " " **augē-** ( " " **aug-**).
    **vincīre**, " " **vincī-** ( " " **vinc-**).

2. By adding **i**, as **capiō**, Present Stem **capi-** (Verb Stem **cap-**).

3. By the insertion of **n** (**m** before labial-mutes) before the final consonant of the Verb Stem; as, **fundō** (Stem **fud-**), **rumpō** (Stem **rup-**)

4. By appending **-n** to the Verb Stem; as, —

    **cern-ō**        **pell-ō** (for **pel-nō**).

[1] Strictly speaking, the Present Stem always ends in a Thematic Vowel (ĕ or ŏ); as, dīc-ĕ-, dīc-ŏ-; amā-ĕ-, amā-ŏ-. But the multitude of phonetic changes involved prevents a scientific treatment of the subject here. See the author's *Latin Language.*

5. By appending **t** to the Verb Stem; as, —

   **flect-ō.**

6. By appending **sc** to the Verb Stem; as, —

   **crēsc-ō,**            **scīsc-ō.**

7. By Reduplication, that is, by prefixing the initial consonant of the Verb Stem with **i**; as, —

   **gi-gn-ō** (root **gen-**),        **si-st-ō** (root **sta-**).

### Formation of the Perfect Stem.

**118.** The Perfect Stem is formed from the Verb Stem —

1. By adding **v** (in case of Vowel Stems); as, —

   **amāv-ī,**        **dēlēv-ī,**        **audīv-ī.**

2. By adding **u** (in case of some Consonant Stems); as, —

   **strepu-ī,**        **genu-ī,**        **alu-ī.**

3. By adding **s** (in case of most Consonant Stems); as, —

   **carp-ō,** Perfect **carps-ī.**

   **scrīb-ō,** " **scrīps-ī** (for **scrīb-sī**).
   **rīd-eō,** " **rīs-ī** (for **rīd-sī**).
   **sent-iō,** " **sēns-ī** (for **sent-sī**).
   **dīc-ō,** " **dīx-ī** (*i.e.* **dīc-sī**).

   *a.* Note that before the ending -**sī** a Dental Mute (**t, d**) is lost; a Guttural Mute (**c, g**) unites with **s** to form **x**; while the Labial **b** is changed to **p**.

4. Without addition. Of this formation there are three types: —

   *a)* The Verb Stem is reduplicated by prefixing the initial consonant with the following vowel or **e**; as, —

   **currō,** Perfect **cu-currī.**
   **poscō,** " **po-poscī.**
   **pellō,** " **pe-pulī.**

   NOTE 1. — Compounds, with the exception of **dō, stō, sistō, discō, poscō,** omit the reduplication. Thus: **com pulī,** but **re-poposcī.**

   NOTE 2. — Verbs beginning with **sp** or **st** retain both consonants in the reduplication, but drop **s** from the stem; as, **spondeō, spo-pondī; stō, stetī.**

   *b)* The short vowel of the Verb Stem is lengthened; as, **legō, lēgī; agō, ēgī.** Note that **ă** by this process becomes **ē.**

   *c)* The vowel of the Verb Stem is unchanged; as, **vertō, vertī; minuō, minuī.**

### Formation of the Participial Stem.

**119.** The Perfect Passive Participle, from which the Participial Stem is derived by dropping -us, is formed : —

1. By adding -tus (sometimes to the Present Stem, sometimes to the Verb Stem) ; as, —

amā-re, Participle amā-tus.

dēlē-re,    "    dēlē-tus.

audī-re,    "    audī-tus.

leg-ere,    "    lēc-tus.

scrīb-ere,    "    scrīp-tus.

sentī-re,    "    sēn-sus (for sent-tus).

caed-ere,    "    cae-sus (for caed-tus).

     *a.* Note that **g**, before **t**, becomes **c** (see § 8, 5) ; **b** becomes **p**; while **dt** or **tt** becomes **ss**, which is then often simplified to **s** (§ 8, 2).

2. After the analogy of Participles like **sēnsus** and **caesus**, where -sus arises by phonetic change, -sus for -tus is added to other Verb Stems ; as, —

lāb-ī,   Participle lāp-sus.

fīg-ere,    "    fī-xus.

     *a.* The same consonant changes occur in appending this ending -sus to the stem as in the case of the Perfect ending -sī (see § 118, 3, *a*).

3. A few Verbs form the Participle in -ĭtus ; as, —

domā-re,          dom-ĭtus.

monē-re,          mon-ĭtus.

4. The Future Active Participle is usually identical in its stem with the Perfect Passive Participle ; as, **amā-tus, amātūrus; moni-tus, monitūrus.** But —

| | | | | | | | |
|---|---|---|---|---|---|---|---|
| juvā-re, | Perf. Partic. | jūtus, | | has Fut. Act. Partic. | | | juvātūrus.[1] |
| lavā-re, | " | " | lautus, | " | " | " | " | lavātūrus. |
| par-ere, | " | " | partus, | " | " | " | " | paritūrus. |
| ru-ere, | " | " | -rutus, | " | " | " | " | ruitūrus. |
| secā-re, | " | " | sectus, | " | " | " | " | secātūrus. |
| fru-ī, | " | " | -frūctus, | " | " | " | " | fruitūrus. |
| mor-ī, | " | " | mortuus, | " | " | " | " | moritūrus. |
| orī-rī, | " | " | ortus, | " | " | " | " | oritūrus. |

---

[1] But the compounds of **Juvō** sometimes have *-jūtūrus;* as, *adjūtūrus.*

## LIST OF THE MOST IMPORTANT VERBS, WITH PRINCIPAL PARTS.

### First (Ā-) Conjugation.

**120.  I. PERFECT IN -VĪ.**

| | | | | |
|---|---|---|---|---|
| amō | amāre | amāvī | amātus | *love* |

All regular verbs of the First Conjugation follow this model.

| | | | | |
|---|---|---|---|---|
| pōtō | pōtāre | pōtāvī | pōtus (§ 114, 2) | *drink* |

**II. PERFECT IN -UĪ.**

| | | | | |
|---|---|---|---|---|
| crepō | crepāre | crepuī | crepitūrus | *rattle* |
| cubō | cubāre | cubuī | cubitūrus | *lie down* |
| domō | domāre | domuī | domitus | *tame* |
| fricō | fricāre | fricuī | frictus *and* fricātus | *rub* |
| micō | micāre | micuī | —— | *glitter* |
| dimicō | dīmicāre | dīmicāvī | dīmicātum (est)[1] | *fight* |
| ex-plicō | explicāre | explicāvī (-uī) | explicātus (-itus) | *unfold* |
| im-plicō | implicāre | implicāvī (-uī) | implicātus (-itus) | *entwine* |
| secō | secāre | secuī | sectus | *cut* |
| sonō | sonāre | sonuī | sonātūrus | *sound* |
| tonō | tonāre | tonuī | —— | *thunder* |
| vetō | vetāre | vetuī | vetitus | *forbid* |

**III. PERFECT IN -Ī WITH LENGTHENING OF THE STEM VOWEL.**

| | | | | |
|---|---|---|---|---|
| juvō | juvāre | jūvī | jūtus | *help* |
| lavō | lavāre | lāvī | lautus | *wash* |

**IV. PERFECT REDUPLICATED.**

| | | | |
|---|---|---|---|
| stō | stāre | stetī | stātūrus |

**V. DEPONENTS.**

These are all regular, and follow *mīror, mīrārī, mīrātus sum.*

### Second (Ē-) Conjugation.

**121.  I. PERFECT IN -VĪ.**

| | | | | |
|---|---|---|---|---|
| dēleō | dēlēre | dēlēvī | dēlētus | *destroy* |
| fleō | flēre | flēvī | flētus | *weep, lament* |
| com-pleō[2] | complēre | complēvī | complētus | *fill up* |
| aboleō | abolēre | abolēvī | abolitus | *destroy* |
| cieō[8] | ciēre | cīvī | citus | *set in motion* |

---

[1] Used only impersonally.      [2] So *impleō, expleō.*
[8] Compounds follow the Fourth Conjugation : *acciō, accīre, etc.*

## II. Perfect in -UĪ.

### a. Type -eō, -ēre, -uī, -itus.

| | | | | |
|---|---|---|---|---|
| arceō | arcēre | arcuī | | *keep off* |
| coerceō | coercēre | coercuī | coercitus | *hold in check* |
| exerceō | exercēre | exercuī | exercitus | *practise* |
| caleō | calēre | caluī | calitūrus | *be warm* |
| careō | carēre | caruī | caritūrus | *be without* |
| doleō | dolēre | doluī | dolitūrus | *grieve* |
| habeō | habēre | habuī | habitus | *have* |
| dēbeō | dēbēre | dēbuī | dēbitus | *owe* |
| praebeō | praebēre | praebuī | praebitus | *offer* |
| jaceō | jacēre | jacuī | jacitūrus | *lie* |
| mereō | merēre | meruī | meritus | *earn, deserve* |
| moneō | monēre | monuī | monitus | *advise* |
| noceō | nocēre | nocuī | nocitum (est) | *injure* |
| pāreō | pārēre | pāruī | pāritūrus | *obey* |
| placeō | placēre | placuī | placitūrus | *please* |
| taceō | tacēre | tacuī | tacitūrus | *be silent* |
| terreō | terrēre | terruī | territus | *frighten* |
| valeō | valēre | valuī | valitūrus | *be strong* |

Note 1. — The following lack the Participial Stem : —

| | | | | |
|---|---|---|---|---|
| egeō | egēre | eguī | —— | *want* |
| ēmineō | ēminēre | ēminuī | —— | *stand forth* |
| flōreō | flōrēre | flōruī | —— | *bloom* |
| horreō | horrēre | horruī | —— | *bristle* |
| lateō | latēre | latuī | —— | *lurk* |
| niteō | nitēre | nituī | —— | *gleam* |
| oleō | olēre | oluī | —— | *smell* |
| palleō | pallēre | palluī | —— | *be pale* |
| pateō | patēre | patuī | —— | *lie open* |
| rubeō | rubēre | rubuī | —— | *be rea* |
| sileō | silēre | siluī | —— | *be silent* |
| splendeō | splendēre | splenduī | —— | *gleam* |
| studeō | studēre | studuī | —— | *study* |
| stupeō | stupēre | stupuī | —— | *be amazed* |
| timeō | timēre | timuī | —— | *fear* |
| torpeō | torpēre | torpuī | —— | *be dull* |
| vigeō | vigēre | viguī | —— | *flourish* |
| vireō | virēre | viruī | —— | *be green* |

and others.

NOTE 2. — The following are used only in the Present System : —

| | | | | |
|---|---|---|---|---|
| aveō | avēre | —— | —— | *wish* |
| frīgeō | frīgēre | —— | —— | *be cold* |
| immineō | imminēre | —— | —— | *overhang* |
| maereō | maerēre | —— | —— | *mourn* |
| polleō | pollēre | —— | —— | *be strong* |

and others.

### b. Type -eō, -ēre, -uī, -tus (-sus).

| | | | | |
|---|---|---|---|---|
| cēnseō | cēnsēre | cēnsuī | cēnsus | *estimate* |
| doceō | docēre | docuī | doctus | *teach* |
| misceō | miscēre | miscuī | mixtus | *mix* |
| teneō | tenēre | tenuī | —— | *hold* |

So *contineō* and *sustineō* ; but —

| | | | | |
|---|---|---|---|---|
| retineō | retinēre | retinuī | retentus | *retain* |
| obtineō | obtinēre | obtinuī | obtentus | *maintain* |
| torreō | torrēre | torruī | tostus | *bake* |

### III. PERFECT IN -SĪ.

| | | | | |
|---|---|---|---|---|
| augeō | augēre | auxī | auctus | *increase* |
| torqueō | torquēre | torsī | tortus | *twist* |
| indulgeō | indulgēre | indulsī | —— | *indulge* |
| lūceō | lūcēre | lūxī | —— | *be light* |
| lūgeō | lūgēre | lūxī | —— | *mourn* |
| jubeō | jubēre | jussī | jussus | *order* |
| per-mulceō | permulcēre | permulsī | permulsus | *soothe* |
| rīdeō | rīdēre | rīsī | rīsum (est) | *laugh* |
| suādeō | suādēre | suāsī | suāsum (est) | *advise* |
| abs-tergeō | abstergēre | abstersī | abstersus | *wipe off* |
| ārdeō | ārdēre | ārsī | ārsūrus | *burn* |
| haereō | haerēre | haesī | haesūrus | *stick* |
| maneō | manēre | mānsī | mānsūrus | *stay* |
| algeō | algēre | alsī | —— | *be cold* |
| fulgeō | fulgēre | fulsī | —— | *gleam* |
| urgeō | urgēre | ursī | —— | *press* |

### IV. PERFECT IN -Ī WITH REDUPLICATION.

| | | | | |
|---|---|---|---|---|
| mordeō | mordēre | momordī | morsus | *bite* |
| spondeō | spondēre | spopondī | spōnsus | *promise* |
| tondeō | tondēre | totondī | tōnsus | *shear* |
| pendeō | pendēre | pependī | —— | *hang* |

## V. Perfect in -Ī with Lengthening of Stem Vowel.

| | | | | |
|---|---|---|---|---|
| caveō | cavēre | cāvī | cautūrus | *take care* |
| faveō | favēre | fāvī | fautūrus | *favor* |
| foveō | fovēre | fōvī | fōtus | *cherish* |
| moveō | movēre | mōvī | mōtus | *move* |
| paveō | pavēre | pāvī | —— | *fear* |
| sedeō | sedēre | sēdī | sessūrus | *sit* |
| videō | vidēre | vīdī | vīsus | *see* |
| voveō | vovēre | vōvī | vōtus | *vow* |

## VI. Perfect in -Ī without either Reduplication or Lengthening of Stem Vowel.

| | | | | |
|---|---|---|---|---|
| ferveō | fervēre | (fervī, ferbuī) —— | | *boil* |
| prandeō | prandēre | prandī | prānsus (§ 114, 2) | *lunch* |
| strīdeō | strīdēre | strīdī | —— | *creak* |

## VII. Deponents.

| | | | |
|---|---|---|---|
| liceor | licērī | licitus sum | *bid* |
| polliceor | pollicērī | pollicitus sum | *promise* |
| mereor | merērī | meritus sum | *earn* |
| misereor | miserērī | miseritus sum | *pity* |
| vereor | verērī | veritus sum | *fear* |
| fateor | fatērī | fassus sum | *confess* |
| cōnfiteor | cōnfitērī | cōnfessus sum | *confess* |
| reor | rērī | ratus sum | *think* |
| medeor | medērī | —— | *heal* |
| tueor | tuērī | —— | *protect* |

### Third (Consonant) Conjugation.

**122.** I. Verbs with Present Stem ending in a Consonant.

1. Perfect in -sī.

*a.* Type -ō, -ĕre, -sī, -tus.

| | | | | |
|---|---|---|---|---|
| carpō | carpere | carpsī | carptus | *pluck* |
| sculpō | sculpere | sculpsī | sculptus | *chisel* |
| rēpō | rēpere | rēpsī | —— | *creep* |
| serpō | serpere | serpsī | —— | *crawl* |
| scrībō | scrībere | scrīpsī | scrīptus | *write* |
| nūbō | nūbere | nūpsī | nūpta (woman only) | *marry* |
| regō | regere | rēxī | rēctus | *govern* |

| | | | | |
|---|---|---|---|---|
| tegō | tegere | tēxī | tēctus | *cover* |
| af-flīgō | afflīgere | afflīxī | afflīctus | *shatter* |
| dīcō | dīcere | dīxī | dictus | *say* |
| dūcō | dūcere | dūxī | ductus | *lead* |
| coquō | coquere | coxī | coctus | *cook* |
| trahō | trahere | trāxī | trāctus | *draw* |
| vehō | vehere | vexī | vectus | *carry* |
| cingō | cingere | cīnxī | cīnctus | *gird* |
| tingō | tingere | tīnxī | tīnctus | *dip* |
| jungō | jungere | jūnxi | jūnctus | *join* |
| fingō | fingere | fīnxī | fīctus | *mould* |
| pingō | pingere | pīnxī | pīctus | *paint* |
| stringō | stringere | strīnxī | strictus | *bind* |
| -stinguō [1] | -stinguere | -stīnxī | -stīnctus | *blot out* |
| unguō | unguere | ūnxī | ūnctus | *anoint* |
| vīvō | vīvere | vīxī | vīctum (est) | *live* |
| gerō | gerere | gessī | gestus | *carry* |
| ūrō | ūrere | ussī | ūstus | *burn* |
| temnō | temnere | con-tempsī | con-temptus | *despise* |

*b*. Type -ō, -ĕre, -sĭ, -sus.

| | | | | |
|---|---|---|---|---|
| fīgō | fīgere | fīxī | fīxus | *fasten* |
| mergō | mergere | mersī | mersus | *sink* |
| spargō | spargere | sparsī | sparsus | *scatter* |
| flectō | flectere | flexī | flexus | *bend* |
| nectō | nectere | nexuī (nexī) | nexus | *twine* |
| mittō | mittere | mīsī | missus | *send* |
| rādō | rādere | rāsī | rāsus | *shave* |
| rōdō | rōdere | rōsī | rōsus | *gnaw* |
| vādō | vādere | -vāsī [2] | -vāsum (est) [2] | *march, walk* |
| lūdō | lūdere | lūsī | lūsum (est) | *play* |
| trūdō | trūdere | trūsī | trūsus | *push* |
| laedō | laedere | laesī | laesus | *injure, hurt* |
| claudō | claudere | clausī | clausus | *close* |
| plaudō | plaudere | plausī | plausum (est) | *clap* |
| explōdō | explōdere | explōsī | explōsus | *hoot off* |
| cēdō | cēdere | cessī | cessum (est) | *withdraw* |
| dīvidō | dīvidere | dīvīsī | dīvīsus | *divide* |
| premō | premere | pressī | pressus | *press* |

[1] Fully conjugated only in the compounds : *exstinguō, restinguō, distinguō.*
[2] Only in the compounds : *ēvādō, invādō, pervādō.*

**2.  Perfect in -ī with Reduplication.**

| | | | | |
|---|---|---|---|---|
| ab-dō | abdere | abdidī | abditus | *conceal* |
| red-dō | red-dere | reddidī | redditus | *return* |

So *addō, condō, dēdō, perdō, prōdō, trādō, etc.*

| | | | | |
|---|---|---|---|---|
| cōn-sistō | cōnsistere | cōnstitī | —— | *take one's stand* |
| resistō | resistere | restitī | —— | *resist* |
| circumsistō | circumsistere | circumstetī | —— | *surround* |
| cadō | cadere | cecidī | cāsūrus | *fall* |
| caedō | caedere | cecīdī | caesus | *kill* |
| pendō | pendere | pependī | pēnsus | *weigh, pay* |
| tendō | tendere | tetendī | tentus | *stretch* |
| tundō | tundere | tutudī | tūsus, tūnsus | *beat* |
| fallō | fallere | fefellī | (falsus, as Adj.) | *deceive* |
| pellō | pellere | pepulī | pulsus | *drive out* |
| currō | currere | cucurrī | cursum (est) | *run* |
| parcō | parcere | pepercī | parsūrus | *spare* |
| canō | canere | cecinī | —— | *sing* |
| tangō | tangere | tetigī | tāctus | *touch* |
| pungō | pungere | pupugī | pūnctus | *prick* |

NOTE. — In the following verbs the perfects were originally reduplicated, but have lost the reduplicating syllable : —

| | | | | |
|---|---|---|---|---|
| per-cellō | percellere | perculī | perculsus | *strike down* |
| findō | findere | fidī | fissus | *split* |
| scindō | scindere | scidī | scissus | *tear apart* |
| tollō | tollere | sus-tulī | sublātus | *remove* |

**3.  Perfect in -ī with Lengthening of Stem Vowel.**

| | | | | |
|---|---|---|---|---|
| agō | agere | ēgī | āctus | *drive, do* |
| peragō | peragere | perēgī | perāctus | *finish* |
| subigō | subigere | subēgī | subāctus | *subdue* |
| cōgō | cōgere | coēgī | coāctus | *force, gather* |
| frangō | frangere | frēgī | frāctus | *break* |
| perfringō | perfringere | perfrēgī | perfrāctus | *break down* |
| legō | legere | lēgī | lēctus | *gather, read* |
| perlegō | perlegere | perlēgī | perlēctus | *read through* |
| colligō | colligere | collēgī | collēctus | *collect* |
| dēligō | dēligere | dēlēgī | dēlēctus | *choose* |
| dīligō | dīligere | dīlēxī | dīlēctus | *love* |
| intellegō | intellegere | intellēxī | intellēctus | *understand* |
| neglegō | neglegere | neglēxī | neglēctus | *neglect* |

| | | | | |
|---|---|---|---|---|
| emō | emere | ēmī | ēmptus | *buy* |
| coëmō | coëmere | coēmī | coēmptus | *buy up* |
| redimō | redimere | redēmī | redēmptus | *buy back* |
| dirimō | dirimere | dirēmī | dirēmptus | *destroy* |
| dēmō | dēmere | dēmpsī | dēmptus | *take away* |
| sūmō | sūmere | sūmpsī | sūmptus | *take* |
| prōmō | prōmere | prōmpsī | (prōmptus, as Adj.) | *take out* |
| vincō | vincere | vīcī | victus | *conquer* |
| re-linquō | relinquere | relīquī | relīctus | *leave* |
| rumpō | rumpere | rūpī | ruptus | *break* |
| edō | ēsse (§ 128) ēdī | | ēsus | *eat* |
| fundō | fundere | fūdī | fūsus | *pour* |

4. Perfect in -ī without either Reduplication or Lengthening of Stem Vowel.

| | | | | |
|---|---|---|---|---|
| excūdō | excūdere | excūdī | excūsus | *hammer* |
| cōnsīdō | cōnsīdere | cōnsēdī | —— | *take one's seat* |
| possīdō | possīdere | possēdī | possessus | *take possession* |
| accendō | accendere | accendī | accēnsus | *kindle* |
| a-scendō | ascendere | ascendī | ascēnsum (est) | *climb* |
| dē-fendō | dēfendere | dēfendī | dēfēnsus | *defend* |
| pre-hendō | prehendere | prehendī | prehēnsus | *seize* |
| īcō | īcere | īcī | ictus | *strike* |
| vellō | vellere | vellī | vulsus | *pluck* |
| vertō | vertere | vertī | versus | *turn* |
| pandō | pandere | pandī | passus | *spread* |
| solvō | solvere | solvī | solūtus | *loose* |
| vīsō | vīsere | vīsī | vīsus | *visit* |
| volvō | volvere | volvī | volūtus | *roll* |
| verrō | verrere | verrī | versus | *sweep* |

5. Perfect in -uī.

| | | | | |
|---|---|---|---|---|
| in-cumbō | incumbere | incubuī | incubitūrus | *lean on* |
| gignō | gignere | genuī | genitus | *bring forth* |
| molō | molere | moluī | molitus | *grind* |
| vomō | vomere | vomuī | vomitus | *vomit* |
| fremō | fremere | fremuī | —— | *snort* |
| gemō | gemere | gemuī | —— | *sigh* |
| metō | metere | messuī | messus | *reap* |

| tremō | tremere | tremuī | —— | *tremble* |
|---|---|---|---|---|
| strepō | strepere | strepuī | —— | *rattle* |
| alō | alere | aluī | altus (alitus) | *nourish* |
| colō | colere | coluī | cultus | *cultivate* |
| incolō | incolere | incoluī | —— | *inhabit* |
| excolō | excolere | excoluī | excultus | *perfect* |
| cōnsulō | cōnsulere | cōnsuluī | cōnsultus | *consult* |
| cōnserō | cōnserere | cōnseruī | cōnsertus | *join* |
| dēserō | dēserere | dēseruī | dēsertus | *desert* |
| disserō | disserere | disseruī | —— | *discourse* |
| texō | texere | texuī | textus | *weave* |

### 6. Perfect in -vī.

| sinō | sinere | sīvī | situs | *allow* |
|---|---|---|---|---|
| dēsinō | dēsinere | dēsiī | dēsitus | *cease* |
| pōnō | pōnere | posuī | positus | *place* |
| ob-linō | oblinere | oblēvī | oblitus | *smear* |
| serō | serere | sēvī | satus | *sow* |
| cōnserō | cōnserere | cōnsēvī | cōnsitus | *plant* |
| cernō | cernere | —— | —— | *separate* |
| discernō | discernere | discrēvī | discrētus | *distinguish* |
| dēcernō | dēcernere | dēcrēvī | dēcrētus | *decide* |
| spernō | spernere | sprēvī | sprētus | *scorn* |
| sternō | sternere | strāvī | strātus | *spread* |
| prō-sternō | prōsternere | prōstrāvī | prōstrātus | *overthrow* |
| petō | petere | petīvī (petiī) | petītus | *seek* |
| appetō | appetere | appetīvī | appetītus | *long for* |
| terō | terere | trīvī | trītus | *rub* |
| quaerō | quaerere | quaesīvī | quaesītus | *seek* |
| acquīrō | acquīrere | acquīsīvī | acquīsītus | *acquire* |
| arcessō | arcessere | arcessīvī | arcessītus | *summon* |
| capessō | capessere | capessīvī | capessītus | *seize* |
| lacessō | lacessere | lacessīvī | lacessītus | *provoke* |

### 7. Used only in Present System.

| angō | angere | —— | —— | *choke* |
|---|---|---|---|---|
| lambō | lambere | —— | —— | *lick* |
| claudō | claudere | —— | —— | *be lame* |
| furō | furere | —— | —— | *rave* |
| vergō | vergere | —— | ——. | *bend* |

and a few others.

## II. VERBS WITH PRESENT STEM ENDING IN -U.

| | | | | |
|---|---|---|---|---|
| induō | induere | induī | indūtus | *put on* |
| imbuō | imbuere | imbuī | imbūtus | *moisten* |
| luō | luere | luī | —— | *wash* |
| polluō | polluere | polluī | pollūtus | *defile* |
| minuō | minuere | minuī | minūtus | *lessen* |
| statuō | statuere | statuī | statūtus | *set up* |
| cōnstituō | cōnstituere | cōnstituī | cōnstitūtus | *determine* |
| suō | suere | suī | sūtus | *sew* |
| tribuō | tribuere | tribuī | tribūtus | *allot* |
| ruō | ruere | ruī | ruitūrus | *fall* |
| dīruō | dīruere | dīruī | dīrutus | *destroy* |
| obruō | obruere | obruī | obrutus | *overwhelm* |
| acuō | acuere | acuī | —— | *sharpen* |
| arguō | arguere | arguī | —— | *accuse* |
| congruō | congruere | congruī | —— | *agree* |
| metuō | metuere | metuī | —— | *fear* |
| ab-nuō | abnuere | abnuī | —— | *decline* |
| re-spuō | respuere | respuī | —— | *reject* |
| struō | struere | strūxī | strūctus | *build* |
| fluō | fluere | flūxī | (flūxus, as Adj.) | *flow* |

## III. VERBS WITH PRESENT STEM ENDING IN -I.

| | | | | |
|---|---|---|---|---|
| cupiō | cupere | cupīvī | cupītus | *wish* |
| sapiō | sapere | sapīvī | —— | *taste* |
| rapiō | rapere | rapuī | raptus | *snatch* |
| dīripiō | dīripere | dīripuī | dīreptus | *plunder* |
| cōnspiciō | cōnspicere | cōnspexī | cōnspectus | *gaze at* |
| aspiciō | aspicere | aspexī | aspectus | *behold* |
| illiciō | illicere | illexī | illectus | *allure* |
| pelliciō | pellicere | pellexī | pellectus | *allure* |
| ēliciō | ēlicere | ēlicuī | ēlicitus | *elicit* |
| quatiō | quatere | —— | quassus | *shake* |
| concutiō | concutere | concussī | concussus | *shake* |
| pariō | parere | peperī | partus | *bring forth* |
| capiō | capere | cēpī | captus | *take* |
| accipiō | accipere | accēpī | acceptus | *accept* |
| incipiō | incipere | incēpī | inceptus | *begin* |
| faciō | facere | fēcī | factus | *make* |
| afficiō | afficere | affēcī | affectus | *affect* |

*Passive,* afficior, afficī, affectus sum.

So other prepositional compounds, *perficiō, perficior ; interficiō. interficior;* *etc.* But—

| assuēfaciō | assuēfacere | assuēfēcī | assuēfactus | *accustom* |

*Passive*, assuēfīō, assuēfierī, assuēfactus sum.

So also *patefaciō, patefīō ; calefaciō, calefīō ;* and all non-prepositional compounds.

| jaciō | jacere | jēcī | jactus | *hurt* |
|---|---|---|---|---|
| abiciō | abicere | abjēcī | abjectus | *throw away* |
| fodiō | fodere | fōdī | fossus | *dig* |
| fugiō | fugere | fūgī | fugitūrus | *flee* |
| effugiō | effugere | effūgī | —— | *escape* |

## IV. Verbs in -SCŌ.

### 1. Verbs in -scō from Simple Roots.

| poscō | poscere | poposcī | —— | *demand* |
|---|---|---|---|---|
| discō | discere | didicī | —— | *learn* |
| pāscō | pāscere | pāvī | pāstus | *feed* |
| pāscor | pāscī | pāstus sum | | *graze* |
| crēscō | crēscere | crēvī | crētus | *grow* |
| cōnsuēscō | cōnsuēscere | cōnsuēvī | cōnsuētus | *accustom one's self* |
| quiēscō | quiēscere | quiēvī | quiētūrus | *be still* |
| adolēscō | adolēscere | adolēvī | adultus | *grow up* |
| obsolēscō | obsolēscerē | obsolēvī | —— | *grow old* |
| nōscō | nōscere | nōvī | —— | { *become acquainted with* |
| ignōscō | ignōscere | ignōvī | ignōtūrus | *pardon* |
| agnōscō | agnōscere | agnōvī | agnitus | *recognize* |
| cognōscō | cognōscere | cognōvī | cognitus | { *get acquainted with* |

### 2. Verbs in -scō formed from other Verbs.

These usually have Inchoative or Inceptive meaning (see § 155. 1). When they have the Perfect, it is the same as that of the Verbs from which they are derived.

| flōrēscō | flōrēscere | flōruī | *begin to bloom* | (flōreō) |
|---|---|---|---|---|
| scīscō | scīscere | scīvī | *enact* | (sciō) |
| ārēscō | ārēscere | āruī | *become dry* | (āreō) |
| calēscō | calēscere | caluī | *become hot* | (caleō) |
| cōnsenēscō | cōnsenēscere | cōnsenuī | *grow old* | (seneō) |
| extimēscō | extimēscere | extimuī | *fear greatly* | (timeō) |
| ingemīscō | ingemīscere | ingemuī | *sigh* | (gemō) |
| adhaerēscō | adhaerēscere | adhaesī | *stick* | (haereō) |

3. Verbs in -scō derived from Adjectives, usually with Inchoative meaning.

| | | | | |
|---|---|---|---|---|
| obdūrēscō | obdūrēscere | obdūruī | *grow hard* | (dūrus) |
| ēvānēscō | ēvānēscere | ēvānuī | *disappear* | (vānus) |
| percrēbrēscō | percrēbrēscere | percrēbruī | *grow fresh* | (crēber) |
| mātūrēscō | mātūrēscere | mātūruī | *grow ripe* | (mātūrus) |
| obmūtēscō | obmūtēscere | obmūtuī | *grow dumb* | (mūtus) |

## V. Deponents.

| | | | |
|---|---|---|---|
| fungor | fungī | fūnctus sum | *perform* |
| queror | querī | questus sum | *complain* |
| loquor | loquī | locūtus sum | *speak* |
| sequor | sequī | secūtus sum | *follow* |
| fruor | fruī | fruitūrus | *enjoy* |
| perfruor | perfruī | perfrūctus sum | *thoroughly enjoy* |
| lābor | lābī | lāpsus sum | *glide* |
| amplector | amplectī | amplexus sum | *embrace* |
| nītor | nītī | nīsus sum, nīxus sum | *strive* |
| gradior | gradī | gressus sum | *walk* |
| patior | patī | passus sum | *suffer* |
| perpetior | perpetī | perpessus sum | *endure* |
| ūtor | ūtī | ūsus sum | *use* |
| morior | morī | mortuus sum | *die* |
| adipīscor | adipīscī | adeptus sum | *acquire* |
| commīnīscor | commīnīscī | commentus sum | *invent* |
| reminīscor | reminīscī | —— | *remember* |
| nancīscor | nancīscī | nanctus (nactus) sum | *acquire* |
| nāscor | nāscī | nātus sum | *be born* |
| oblīvīscor | oblīvīscī | oblītus sum | *forget* |
| pacīscor | pacīscī | pactus sum | *covenant* |
| proficīscor | proficīscī | profectus sum | *set out* |
| ulcīscor | ulcīscī | ultus sum | *avenge* |
| īrāscor | īrāscī | (īrātus, as Adj.) | *be angry* |
| vescor | vescī | —— | *eat* |

## Fourth Conjugation.

**123.** I. Perfect ends in -vī.

| | | | | |
|---|---|---|---|---|
| audiō | audīre | audīvī | audītus | *hear* |

So all regular Verbs of the Fourth Conjugation.

| | | | | |
|---|---|---|---|---|
| sepeliō | sepelīre | sepelīvī | sepultus | *bury* |

## II. Perfect ends in -UĪ.

| aperiō | aperīre | aperuī | apertus | *open* |
| operiō | operīre | operuī | opertus | *cover* |
| saliō | salīre | saluī | —— | *leap* |

## III. Perfect ends in -SĪ.

| saepiō | saepīre | saepsī | saeptus | *hedge in* |
| sanciō | sancīre | sānxī | sānctus | *ratify* |
| vinciō | vincīre | vinxī | vinctus | *bind* |
| amiciō | amicīre | —— | amictus | *envelop* |
| fulciō | fulcīre | fulsī | fultus | *prop up* |
| referciō | refercīre | refersī | refertus | *fill* |
| sarciō | sarcīre | sarsī | sartus | *patch* |
| hauriō | haurīre | hausī | haustus | *draw* |
| sentiō | sentīre | sēnsī | sēnsus | *feel* |

## IV. Perfect in -Ī with Lengthening of Stem Vowel.

| veniō | venīre | vēnī | ventum (est) | *come* |
| adveniō | advenīre | advēnī | adventum (est) | *arrive* |
| inveniō | invenīre | invēnī | inventus | *find* |

## V. Perfect with Loss of Reduplication.

| reperiō | reperīre | repperī | repertus | *find* |
| comperiō | comperīre | comperī | compertus | *learn* |

## VI. Used only in the Present.

| feriō | ferīre | —— | —— | *strike* |
| ēsuriō | ēsurīre | —— | —— | *be hungry* |

## VII. Deponents.

| largior | largīrī | largītus sum | *bestow* |

So many others.

| experior | experīrī | expertus sum | *try* |
| opperior | opperīrī | oppertus sum | *await* |
| ōrdior | ōrdīrī | ōrsus sum | *begin* |
| orior | orīrī | ortus sum | *arise* |

*Orior* usually follows the Third Conjugation in its inflection ; as, *oreris, orĭtur, orĭmur; orerer* (Imp. Subj.) ; *orere* (Imper.).

| mētior | mētīrī | mēnsus sum | *measure* |
| assentior | assentīrī | assēnsus sum | *assent* |

## IRREGULAR VERBS.

**124.** A number of Verbs are called Irregular. The most important are **sum, dō, edō, ferō, volō, nōlō, mālō, eō, fīō.** The peculiarity of these Verbs is that they append the personal endings in many forms directly to the stem, instead of employing a connecting vowel, as **fer-s** (2d Sing. of **fer-ō**), instead of **fer-i-s.** They are but the relics of what was once in Latin a large class of Verbs.

**125.** The Inflection of **sum** has already been given. Its various compounds are inflected in the same way. They are —

| absum | abesse | āfuī | *am absent* |
|---|---|---|---|

*Pres. Partic.* absēns (absentis), *absent.*

| adsum | adesse | adfuī | *am present* |
|---|---|---|---|
| dēsum | deesse | dēfuī | *am lacking* |
| insum | inesse | īnfuī | *am in* |
| intersum | interesse | interfuī | *am among* |
| praesum | praeesse | praefuī | *am in charge of* |

*Pres. Partic.* praesēns (praesentis), *present.*

| obsum | obesse | obfuī | *hinder* |
|---|---|---|---|
| prōsum | prōdesse | prōfuī | *am of advantage* |
| subsum | subesse | subfuī | *am underneath* |
| supersum | superesse | superfuī | *am left* |

NOTE. — **Prōsum** is compounded of **prōd** (earlier form of **prō**) and **sum**; the **d** disappears before consonants, as **prōsumus**; but **prōdestis.**

**126. Possum.** In its Present System **possum** is a compound of **pot** (for **pote,** *able*) and **sum**; **potuī** is from an obsolete **potēre.**

### PRINCIPAL PARTS.

**possum,** **posse,** **potuī,** *to be able.*

### INDICATIVE MOOD.

| | SINGULAR. | PLURAL. |
|---|---|---|
| *Pres.* | possum, potes, potest ; | possumus, potestis, **possunt.** |
| *Imp.* | poteram ; | poterāmus. |
| *Fut.* | poterō ; | poterimus. |
| *Perf.* | potuī ; | potuimus. |
| *Plup.* | potueram ; | potuerāmus. |
| *Fut. P.* | potuerō ; | potuerimus. |

## SUBJUNCTIVE.

| | SINGULAR. | PLURAL. |
|---|---|---|
| *Pres.* | possim, possīs, possit ; | possīmus, possītis, possint. |
| *Imp.* | possem ; | possēmus. |
| *Perf.* | potuerim ; | potuerīmus. |
| *Plup.* | potuissem ; | potuissēmus. |

| INFINITIVE. | | PARTICIPLE. |
|---|---|---|
| *Pres.* posse. | *Pres.* | potēns (*as an adjective*). |
| *Perf.* potuisse. | | |

**127.**                     Dō, *I give.*

### PRINCIPAL PARTS.

dō,          dăre,          dedī,          dătus.

### Active Voice.

#### INDICATIVE MOOD.

| | SINGULAR. | PLURAL. |
|---|---|---|
| *Pres.* | dō, dās, dat ; | dămus, dătis, dant. |
| *Imp.* | dăbam, *etc.* ; | dăbāmus. |
| *Fut.* | dăbō, *etc.* ; | dăbimus. |
| *Perf.* | dedī ; | dedimus. |
| *Plup.* | dederam ; | dederāmus. |
| *Fut. P.* | dederō ; | dederimus. |

#### SUBJUNCTIVE.

| | | |
|---|---|---|
| *Pres.* | dem ; | dēmus. |
| *Imp.* | dărem ; | dărēmus. |
| *Perf.* | dederim ; | dederīmus. |
| *Plup.* | dedissem ; | dedissēmus. |

#### IMPERATIVE.

| | | |
|---|---|---|
| *Pres.* | dā ; | dăte. |
| *Fut.* | dătō ; | dătōte. |
| | dătō. | dantō. |

| INFINITIVE. | PARTICIPLE. |
|---|---|
| *Pres.* dăre. | dāns. |
| *Perf.* dedisse. | |
| *Fut.* dătūrus esse. | dătūrus. |

| GERUND. | SUPINE. |
|---|---|
| dandī, *etc.* | dătum, dătū. |

1. The Passive is inflected regularly with the short vowel. Thus: **dărī, dătur, dăbātur, dărētur,** *etc.*

2. The archaic and poetic Present Subjunctive forms **duim, duint, perduit, perduint,** *etc.*, are not from the root **da-,** but from **du-,** a collateral root of similar meaning.

**128.**                     **Edō,** *I eat.*

PRINCIPAL PARTS.

**edō,**          **ēsse,**          **ēdī,**          **ēsus.**

### Active Voice.

#### INDICATIVE MOOD.

*Pres.*  edō,                         edimus,
         ēs,                          ēstis,
         ēst;                         edunt.

#### SUBJUNCTIVE.

*Imp.*  ēssem,                       ēssēmus,
        ēssēs,                       ēssētis,
        ēsset;                       ēssent.

#### IMPERATIVE.

*Pres.* és;                          ēste.
*Fut.*  ēstō;                        ēstōte.
        ēstō;                        eduntō·

#### INFINITIVE.

*Pres.* ēsse.

### Passive Voice.

#### INDICATIVE MOOD.

*Pres. 3d Sing.* ēstur.

#### SUBJUNCTIVE.

*Imp. 3d Sing.* ēssētur.

1. Observe the long vowel of the forms in **ēs-,** which alone distinguishes them from the corresponding forms of **esse,** *to be.*

2. Note **comedō, comēsse, comēdī, comēsus** or **comēstus,** *consume.*

3. The Present Subjunctive has **edim, -īs, -it,** *etc.*, less often **edam, -ās,** *etc.*

**129.**                          Ferō, *I bear.*

PRINCIPAL PARTS.

**ferō,**             **ferre,**             **tulī,**             **lātus.**

### Active Voice.

### INDICATIVE MOOD.

| SINGULAR. | | PLURAL. |
|---|---|---|
| *Pres.* | ferō, fers, fert ; | ferimus, fertis, ferunt. |
| *Imp.* | ferēbam ; | ferēbāmus. |
| *Fut.* | feram ; | ferēmus. |
| *Perf.* | tulī ; | tulimus. |
| *Plup.* | tuleram ; | tulerāmus. |
| *Fut. P.* | tulerō ; | tulerimus. |

### SUBJUNCTIVE.

| | | |
|---|---|---|
| *Pres.* | feram ; | ferāmus. |
| *Imp.* | ferrem ; | ferrēmus. |
| *Perf.* | tulerim ; | tulerīmus. |
| *Plup.* | tulissem ; | tulissēmus. |

### IMPERATIVE.

| | | |
|---|---|---|
| *Pres.* | fer ; | ferte. |
| *Fut.* | fertō ; | fertōte. |
| | fertō ; | feruntō. |

| INFINITIVE. | | PARTICIPLE. |
|---|---|---|
| *Pres.* | ferre. | *Pres.* ferēns. |
| *Perf.* | tulisse. | |
| *Fut.* | lātūrus esse. | *Fut.* lātūrus. |

| GERUND. | | SUPINE. |
|---|---|---|
| *Gen.* | ferendī. | |
| *Dat.* | ferendō. | |
| *Acc.* | ferendum. | *Acc.* lātum. |
| *Abl.* | ferendō. | *Abl.* lātū. |

---

[1] It will be observed that not all the forms of **ferō** lack the connecting vowel. Some of them, as **ferimus, ferunt,** follow the regular inflection of verbs of the Third Conjugation.

### Passive Voice.

| feror, | ferrī, | lātus sum, | *to be borne.* |

## INDICATIVE MOOD.

| | SINGULAR. | PLURAL. |
|---|---|---|
| *Pres.* | feror, ferris, fertur; | ferimur, feriminī, feruntur. |
| *Imp.* | ferēbar; | ferēbāmur. |
| *Fut.* | ferar; | ferēmur. |
| *Perf.* | lātus sum; | lātī sumus. |
| *Plup.* | lātus eram; | lātī erāmus. |
| *Fut. P.* | lātus erō; | iātī erimus. |

## SUBJUNCTIVE.

| *Pres.* | ferar; | ferāmur. |
|---|---|---|
| *Imp.* | ferrer; | ferrēmur. |
| *Perf.* | lātus sim; | lātī sīmus. |
| *Plup.* | lātus essem; | lātī essēmus. |

## IMPERATIVE.

| *Pres.* | ferre; | feriminī. |
|---|---|---|
| *Fut.* | fertor; | —— |
| | fertor; | feruntor. |

## INFINITIVE.          PARTICIPLE.

| *Pres.* | ferrī. | | |
|---|---|---|---|
| *Perf.* | lātus esse. | *Perf.* | lātus. |
| *Fut.* | lātum īrī. | *Ger.* | ferendus. |

So also the Compounds —

| afferō | afferre | attulī | allātus | *bring toward* |
|---|---|---|---|---|
| auferō | auferre | abstulī | ablātus | *take away* |
| cōnferō | cōnferre | contulī | collātus | *compare* |
| differō | differre | distulī | dīlātus | *put off* |
| efferō | efferre | extulī | ēlātus | *carry out* |
| īnferō | īnferre | intulī | illātus | *bring against* |
| offerō | offerre | obtulī | oblātus | *present* |
| referō | referre | rettulī | relātus | *bring back* |

NOTE. — The forms **sustulī** and **sublātus** belong to **tollō**.

**130.**        **Volō, nōlō, mālō.**

### PRINCIPAL PARTS.

| volō, | velle, | voluī, | *to wish.* |
| nōlō, | nōlle, | nōluī, | *to be unwilling.* |
| mālō, | mālle, | māluī, | *to prefer.* |

### INDICATIVE MOOD.

| | | | |
|---|---|---|---|
| *Pres.* | volō, | nōlō, | mālō, |
| | vīs, | nōn vīs, | māvīs, |
| | vult; | nōn vult; | māvult; |
| | volumus, | nōlumus, | mālumus, |
| | vultis, | nōn vultis, | māvultis, |
| | volunt. | nōlunt. | mālunt. |
| *Imp.* | volēbam. | nōlēbam. | mālēbam. |
| *Fut.* | volam. | nōlam. | mālam. |
| *Perf.* | voluī. | nōluī. | māluī. |
| *Plup.* | volueram. | nōlueram. | mālueram. |
| *Fut. P.* | voluerō. | nōluerō. | māluerō. |

### SUBJUNCTIVE.

| | | | |
|---|---|---|---|
| *Pres.* | velim, -īs, -it, *etc.* | nōlim. | mālim. |
| *Imp.* | vellem, -ēs, -et, *etc.* | nōllem. | māllem. |
| *Perf.* | voluerim. | nōluerim. | māluerim. |
| *Plup.* | voluissem. | nōluissem. | māluissem. |

### IMPERATIVE.

| | | |
|---|---|---|
| *Pres.* | nōlī; | nōlīte. |
| *Fut.* | nōlītō; | nōlītōte. |
| | nōlītō; | nōluntō. |

### INFINITIVE.

| | | | |
|---|---|---|---|
| *Pres.* | velle. | nōlle. | mālle. |
| *Perf.* | voluisse. | nōluisse. | māluisse. |

### PARTICIPLE.

| | | |
|---|---|---|
| *Pres.* | volēns. | nōlēns. | —— |

## 131. Fīō.

PRINCIPAL PARTS.

fīō, fierī, factus sum, *to become, be made.*

### INDICATIVE MOOD.

| | SINGULAR. | PLURAL. |
|---|---|---|
| *Pres.* | fīō, fīs, fit; | fīmus, fītis, fīunt. |
| *Imp.* | fīēbam; | fīēbāmus. |
| *Fut.* | fīam; | fīēmus. |
| *Perf.* | factus sum; | factī sumus. |
| *Plup.* | factus eram; | factī erāmus. |
| *Fut. P.* | factus erō; | factī erimus. |

### SUBJUNCTIVE.

| | | |
|---|---|---|
| *Pres.* | fīam; | fīāmus. |
| *Imp.* | fierem; | fierēmus. |
| *Perf.* | factus sim; | factī sīmus. |
| *Plup.* | factus essem; | factī essēmus. |

### IMPERATIVE.

| | | |
|---|---|---|
| *Pres.* | fī; | fīte. |

### INFINITIVE.            PARTICIPLE.

| | | | |
|---|---|---|---|
| *Pres.* | fierī. | | |
| *Perf.* | factus esse. | *Perf.* | factus. |
| *Fut.* | factum īrī. | *Ger.* | faciendus. |

NOTE. — A few isolated forms of compounds of fīō occur; as, dēfit, *lacks*; īnfit, *begins*.

## 132. Eō.

PRINCIPAL PARTS.

eō, īre, īvī, itum (est), *to go.*

### INDICATIVE MOOD.

| | SINGULAR. | PLURAL. |
|---|---|---|
| *Pres.* | eō, īs, it; | īmus, ītis, eunt. |
| *Imp.* | ībam; | ībāmus. |
| *Fut.* | ībō; | ībimus. |
| *Perf.* | īvī (iī); | īvimus (iimus). |
| *Plup.* | īveram (ieram); | īverāmus (ierāmus). |
| *Fut. P.* | īverō (ierō); | īverimus (ierimus). |

### SUBJUNCTIVE.

| SINGULAR. | PLURAL. |
|---|---|
| *Pres.* eam ; | eāmus. |
| *Imp.* īrem ; | īrēmus. |
| *Perf.* īverim (ierim) ; | īverīmus (ierīmus). |
| *Plup.* īvissem (iissem, īssem) ; | īvissēmus (iissēmus, īssēmus). |

### IMPERATIVE.

| *Pres.* | ī ; | īte. |
|---|---|---|
| *Fut.* | ītō ; | ītōte, |
| | ītō ; | euntō. |

### INFINITIVE.                    PARTICIPLE.

| *Pres.* | īre. | *Pres.* | iēns. |
|---|---|---|---|
| *Perf.* | īvisse (īsse). | *(Gen.* | euntis.) |
| *Fut.* | itūrus esse. | *Fut.* | itūrus.    *Gerundive,* eundum. |

### GERUND.                    SUPINE.

eundī, *etc.*                    itum, itū.

1. Transitive compounds of **eō** admit the full Passive inflection; as, **adeor, adīris, adītur,** *etc.*

## DEFECTIVE VERBS.

Defective Verbs lack certain forms. The following are the most important : —

**133.** Used Mainly in the Perfect System.

**Coepī,** *I have begun.*       **Meminī,** *I remember.*       **Ōdī,** *I hate.*

### INDICATIVE MOOD.

| *Perf.* | coepī. | meminī. | ōdī. |
|---|---|---|---|
| *Plup.* | coeperam. | memineram. | ōderam. |
| *Fut. P.* | coeperō. | meminerō. | ōderō. |

### SUBJUNCTIVE.

| *Perf.* | coeperim. | meminerim. | ōderim. |
|---|---|---|---|
| *Plup.* | coepissem. | meminissem. | ōdissem. |

### IMPERATIVE.

*Sing.* mementō ; *Plur.* mementōte.

## INFINITIVE.

*Perf.* coepisse.           meminisse.           ōdisse.
*Fut.*  coeptūrus esse.                          ōsūrus esse.

## PARTICIPLE.

*Perf.* coeptus, *begun.*                        ōsus.
*Fut.*  coeptūrus.                               ōsūrus.

1. When **coepī** governs a Passive Infinitive it usually takes the form **coeptus est**; as, **amārī coeptus est,** *he began to be loved.*

2. Note that **meminī** and **ōdī**, though Perfect in form, are Present in sense. Similarly the Pluperfect and Future Perfect have the force of the Imperfect and Future; as, **memineram,** *I remembered;* **ōderō,** *I shall hate.*

**134.** **Inquam,** *I say* (inserted between words of a direct quotation)

## INDICATIVE MOOD.

| SINGULAR. | PLURAL. |
|---|---|
| *Pres.* inquam, | —— |
| inquis, | —— |
| inquit ; | inquiunt. |
| *Fut.* —— | —— |
| inquiēs, | —— |
| inquiet. | —— |

*Perf.* 3d Sing. inquit.

**135.**                    **Ajō,** *I say.*

## INDICATIVE MOOD.

| SINGULAR. | PLURAL |
|---|---|
| *Pres.* ajō, | —— |
| aīs, | —— |
| aıt ; | ajunt. |
| *Imp.* ajēbam, | ajēbāmus, |
| ajēbās, | ajēbātis, |
| ajēbat ; | ajēbant. |

*Perf.* 3d Sing. aīt.

## SUBJUNCTIVE.

*Pres* 3d Sing. ajat.

NOTE. — For **aïsne.** *do you mean?* **aīn** is common

**136.**                    **Fārī**, *to speak.*

This is inflected regularly in the perfect tenses.   In the Present
System it has —

### INDICATIVE MOOD.

|  | SINGULAR. | PLURAL. |
|---|---|---|
| *Pres.* | —— | —— |
|  | fātur. | —— |
| *Fut.* | fābor, | —— |
|  | fābitur. | —— |
| *Impv.* | fāre. | |
| *Inf.* | fārī. | |
| *Pres. Partic.* | fantis, fantī, *etc.* | |
| *Gerund, G.,* | fandī ; *D. and Abl.*, fandō. | |
| *Gerundive,* | fandus. | |

NOTE. — Forms of **fārī** are rare.   More frequent are its compounds; as, —
**affātur**, *he addresses;* **praefāmur**, *we say in advance.*

**137.** OTHER DEFECTIVE FORMS.

1. **Queō, quīre, quīvī,** *to be able,* and **nequeō, nequīre, nequīvī,**
*to be unable,* are inflected like **eō,** but occur chiefly in the Present Tense,
and there only in special forms.

2. **Quaesō,** *I entreat;* **quaesumus,** *we entreat.*

3. **Cedo** (2d sing. Impv.), **cette** (2d plu.) ; *give me, tell me.*

4. **Salvē, salvēte,** *hail.*   Also Infinitive, **salvēre.**

5. **Havē (avē), havēte,** *hail.*   Also Infinitive, **havēre.**

### IMPERSONAL VERBS.

**138.** Impersonal Verbs correspond to the English, *it
snows, it seems, etc.*   They have no personal subject, but
may take an Infinitive, a Clause, or a Neuter Pronoun;
as, **mē pudet hōc fēcisse,** lit. *it shames me to have done this;*
**hōc decet,** *this is fitting.*   Here belong —

I. Verbs denoting operations of the weather; as, —

| | | |
|---|---|---|
| fulget | fulsit | *it lightens* |
| tonat | tonuit | *it thunders* |

| | | |
|---|---|---|
| grandinat | —— | *it hails* |
| ningit | ninxit | *it snows* |
| pluit | pluit | *it rains* |

## II. Special Verbs.

| | | | |
|---|---|---|---|
| paenitet | paenitēre | paenituit | *it repents* |
| piget | pigēre | piguit | *it grieves* |
| pudet | pudēre | puduit | *it causes shame* |
| taedet | taedēre | taeduit | *it disgusts* |
| miseret | miserēre | miseruit | *it causes pity* |
| libet | libēre | libuit | *it pleases* |
| licet | licēre | licuit | *it is lawful* |
| oportet | oportēre | oportuit | *it is fitting* |
| decet | decēre | decuit | *it is becoming* |
| dēdecet | dēdecēre | dēdecuit | *it is unbecoming* |
| rēfert | rēferre | rētulit | *it concerns* |

## III. Verbs Impersonal only in Special Senses.

| | | | |
|---|---|---|---|
| cōnstat | cōnstāre | cōnstitit | *it is evident* |
| praestat | praestāre | praestitit | *it is better* |
| juvat | juvāre | jūvit | *it delights* |
| appāret | appārēre | appāruit | *it appears* |
| placet | placēre | placuit (placitum est) | *it pleases* |
| accēdit | accēdere | accessit | *it is added* |
| accidit | accidere | accidit | *it happens* |
| contingit | contingere | contigit | *it happens* |
| ēvenit | ēvenīre | ēvēnit | *it turns out* |
| interest | interesse | interfuit | *it concerns* |

## IV. The Passive of Intransitive Verbs; as, —

| | | |
|---|---|---|
| ītur | lit. *it is gone* | *i.e. some one goes* |
| curritur | lit. *it is run* | *i.e. some one runs* |
| ventum est | lit. *it has been come* | *i.e. some one has come* |
| veniendum est | lit. *it must be come* | *i.e. somebody must come* |
| pugnārī potest | lit. *it can be fought* | *i.e. somebody can fight* |

# Part III.

◆

## PARTICLES.

◆

**139.** Particles are the four Parts of Speech that do not admit of inflection; *viz.* Adverbs, Prepositions, Conjunctions, Interjections.

### ADVERBS.

**140.** Adverbs denote manner, place, time, or degree. Most adverbs are in origin case-forms which have become stereotyped by usage. The common adverbial terminations have already been given above (§ 76). The following TABLE OF CORRELATIVES is important: —

| RELATIVE AND INTERROGATIVE. | DEMONSTRATIVE. | INDEFINITE. |
|---|---|---|
| ubi, *where; where?* | hīc, *here.* <br> ibi, illīc, istīc, *there.* | alicubī, ūsquam, ūs-piam, *somewhere.* |
| quō, *whither; whither?* | hūc, *hither.* <br> eō, istūc, illūc, *thither.* | aliquō, *to some place.* |
| unde, *whence; whence?* | hinc, *hence.* <br> inde, istinc, illinc, *thence.* | alicunde, *from some-where.* |
| quā, *where; where?* | hāc, *by this way.* <br> eā, istāc, illāc, *by that way.* | aliquā, *by some way.* |
| cum, *when.* <br> quandō, *when?* | nunc, *now.* <br> tum, tunc, *then.* | aliquandō, umquam, *sometime, ever.* |
| quotiēns, *as often as; how often?* | totiēns, *so often.* | aliquotiēns, *some number of times.* |
| quam, *as much as; how much?* | tam, *so much.* | aliquantum, *somewhat.* |

## PREPOSITIONS.

**141.** Prepositions show relations of words. The following Prepositions govern the Accusative : —

| | | |
|---|---|---|
| **ad,** *to.* | **contrā,** *against.* | **post,** *after.* |
| **adversus,** *against.* | **ergā,** *toward.* | **praeter,** *past.* |
| **adversum,** *toward,* | **extrā,** *outside.* | **prope,** *near.* |
| *against.* | **īnfrā,** *below.* | **propter,** *on account of.* |
| **ante,** *before.* | **inter,** *between.* | **secundum,** *after.* |
| **apud,** *with, near.* | **intrā,** *within.* | **subter,** *beneath.* |
| **circā,** *around.* | **jūxtā,** *near.* | **super,** *over.* |
| **circiter,** *about.* | **ob,** *on account of.* | **suprā,** *above.* |
| **circum,** *around.* | **penes,** *in the hands of.* | **trāns,** *across.* |
| **cis,** *this side of.* | **per,** *through.* | **ultrā,** *beyond.* |
| **citrā,** *this side of.* | **pōne,** *behind.* | **versus,** *toward.* |

1. **Ūsque** is often prefixed to **ad**, in the sense of *even*; as, —

   **ūsque ad urbem,** *even to the city.*

2. **Versus** always follows its case; as, —

   **Rōmam versus,** *toward Rome.*

   It may be combined with a preceding Preposition; as, —

   **ad urbem versus,** *toward the city.*

3. Like **prope,** the Comparatives **propior, propius,** and the Superlatives **proximus, proximē,** sometimes govern the Accusative; as, —

   **Ubiī proximē Rhēnum incolunt,** *the Ubii dwell next to the Rhine;* **propius castra hostium,** *nearer the camp of the enemy.*

**142.** The following Prepositions govern the Ablative : —

| | | |
|---|---|---|
| **ā, ab, abs,** *from, by.* | **cum,** *with.* | **prō,** *in front of,* |
| **absque,** *without.* | **dē,** *from, concerning.* | *for.* |
| **cōram,** *in the presence* | **ē, ex,** *from, out of.* | **sine,** *without.* |
| *of.* | **prae,** *before.* | **tenus,** *up to.* |

1. **Ā, ab, abs.** Before vowels or **h**, **ab** must be used; before consonants we find sometimes **ā**, sometimes **ab** (the latter usually not before the labials **b, p, f, v, m**; nor before **c, g, q,** or **t**); **abs** occurs only before **tē**, and **ā** is admissible even there.

2. **Ē, ex.** Before vowels or **h**, **ex** must be used; before consonants. we find sometimes **ē**, sometimes **ex**.

3. **Tenus** regularly follows its case, as, **pectoribus tenus,** *up to the breast.* It sometimes governs the Genitive, as, **labrōrum tenus,** *as far as the lips.*

4. **Cum** is appended to the Pronouns of the First and Second Persons, and to the Reflexive Pronoun; usually also to the Relative and Interrogative. Thus: —

| mēcum | nōbīscum | quōcum *or* cum quō |
| tēcum | vōbīscum | quācum *or* cum quā |
| sēcum |          | quibuscum *or* cum quibus |

On quīcum, see § 89, Footnote 1.

**143**. Two Prepositions, **in**, *in, into*, and **sub**, *under*, govern both the Accusative and the Ablative. With the Accusative they denote **motion**; with the Ablative, **rest**; as, —

  **in urbem,** *into the city;*   **in urbe,** *in the city.*

1. **Subter** and **super** are also occasionally construed with the Ablative.

**144**. RELATION OF ADVERBS AND PREPOSITIONS.

1. Prepositions were originally Adverbs, and many of them still retain their adverbial meaning; as, **post,** *afterwards;* **ante,** *previously;* **contrā,** *on the other hand, etc.*

2. Conversely several words, usually adverbs, are occasionally employed as prepositions; as, —

  **clam, prīdiē,** with the Accusative.
  **procul, simul, palam,** with the Ablative.

3. **Anástrophe.** A Preposition sometimes follows its case. This is called Anástrophe; as, —

  **eī, quōs inter erat,** *those among whom he was.*

Anastrophe occurs chiefly with dissyllabic prepositions.

### CONJUNCTIONS AND INTERJECTIONS.

**145**. 1. Conjunctions are used to connect ideas. For Coördinate Conjunctions, see §§ 341 ff. Subordinate Conjunctions are treated in connection with Subordinate Clauses.

2. Interjections express emotion Thus: —

  1. Surprise; as, **ēn, ecce, ō.**
  2. Joy; as, **iō, euoe.**
  3. Sorrow and Pain; as, **heu, ēheu, vae, prō.**
  4. Calling; as, **heus, eho.**

# Part IV.

————◆————

## WORD-FORMATION.

————◆————

### I. DERIVATIVES.

**146.** Derivatives are formed by appending certain terminations called Suffixes to stems of verbs, nouns, or
adjectives.

### *A.* NOUNS.

#### 1. Nouns derived from Verbs.

**147.** 1. The suffix -tor (-sor), Fem. -trīx, denotes *the agent*; as, –

victor, victrīx, *victor*;     dēfēnsor, *defender*.

NOTE. — The suffix -tor is occasionally appended to noun stems; as, —
gladiātor, *gladiator* (from gladius).

2. The suffix -or (originally -ōs) denotes *an activity or a condition*; as, —

amor, *love*;     timor, *fear*;     dolor, *pain*.

3. The suffixes -tiō (-siō), Gen. -ōnis, and -tus (-sus), Gen. -ūs,
denote *an action as in process*; as, —

vēnātiō, *hunting*; obsessiō, *blockade*; gemitus, *sighing*; cursus,
*running*.

NOTE. — Rarer endings with the same force are: —

*a*) -tūra, -sūra; as, —
sepultūra, *burial;* mēnsūra, *measuring.*

*b*) -ium; as, —
gaudium, *rejoicing.*

*c*) -īdō; as, —
cupīdō, *desire.*

4. The suffixes -men, -mentum, -crum, -trum, -bulum, -culum, denote *the means* or *place* of an action; as, —

| | |
|---|---|
| lūmen (lūc-s-men), *light;* | vocābulum, *word;* |
| ōrnāmentum, *ornament;* | documentum, *proof;* |
| sepulcrum, *grave;* | arātrum, *plough;* |

vehiculum, *carriage.*

## 2. Nouns derived from Nouns.

**148.** 1. Diminutives end in —

| | | |
|---|---|---|
| -ulus, | (-ula, | -ulum) |
| -olus, | (-ola, | -olum), after a vowel |
| -culus, | (-cula, | -culum) |
| -ellus, | (-ella, | -ellum) |
| -illus, | (-illa, | -illum) |

as, —

| | | |
|---|---|---|
| nīdulus | *little nest* | (nīdus); |
| virgula, | *wand* | (virga); |
| oppidulum, | *little town* | (oppidum); |
| fīliolus, | *little son* | (fīlius); |
| opusculum, | *little work* | (opus); |
| tabella, | *tablet* | (tabula); |
| lapillus, | *pebble* | (lapis). |

NOTE 1. — It will be observed that in gender the Diminutives follow the gender of the words from which they are derived.

NOTE 2. — The endings -ellus, -illus contain the primitive form of the diminutive suffix, *viz.*, -lo-. Thus: —

| | | | |
|---|---|---|---|
| agellus, | *field,* | for | ager-lus; |
| lapillus, | *pebble,* | for | lapid-lus. |

2. The suffix -ium appended to nouns denoting persons designates either *a collection* of such persons or *their function;* as, —

collēgium, *a corporation, body of colleagues* (collēga);
sacerdōtium, *priestly function* (sacerdōs).

3. The suffixes -ārium, -ētum, -īle designate a place where objects *are kept* or *are found in abundance;* as, —

| | | |
|---|---|---|
| columbārium, | *dove-cote* | (columba); |
| olīvētum, | *olive-orchard* | (olīva); |
| ovīle, | *sheep-fold* | (ovis). |

4. The suffix -ātus denotes *official position* or *honor;* as, — cōnsulātus, *consulship* (cōnsul).

5. The suffix -īna appended to nouns denoting persons designates *a vocation* or *the place where it is carried on;* as, —

doctrīna, *teaching* (doctor, *teacher*) ;
medicīna, *the art of healing* (medicus, *physician*);
sūtrīna, *cobbler's shop* (sūtor, *cobbler*).

6. Patronymics are Greek proper names denoting *son of . . ., daughter of . . . .* They have the following suffixes : —

*a*) Masculines: -idēs, -adēs, -īdēs; as, Priamidēs, *son of Priam;* Aeneadēs, *son of Aeneas;* Pēlīdēs, *son of Peleus.*
*b*) Feminines: -ēis, -is, -ias; as, Nērēis, *daughter of Nereus;* Atlantis, *daughter of Atlas;* Thaumantias, *daughter of Thaumas.*

### 3. Nouns derived from Adjectives.

**149**. The suffixes -tās (-itās), -tūdō (-itūdō), -ia, -itia are used for the formation of abstract nouns *denoting qualities;* as, —
bonitās, *goodness;* celeritās, *swiftness;* magnitūdō, *greatness,* audācia, *boldness;* amīcitia, *friendship.*

## *B.* ADJECTIVES.

### 1. Adjectives derived from Verbs.

**150**. 1. The suffixes -bundus and -cundus give nearly the force of a present participle; as, —
tremebundus, *trembling;* jūcundus (juvō), *pleasing.*

2. The suffixes -āx and -ulus denote *an inclination* or *tendency,* mostly a faulty one; as, —
loquāx, *loquacious;* crēdulus, *credulous.*

3. The suffix -idus denotes *a state;* as, —
calidus, *hot;* timidus, *timid;* cupidus, *eager.*

4. The suffixes -ilis and -bilis denote *capacity* or *ability,* usually in a passive sense; as, —
fragilis, *fragile* (*i.e.* capable of being broken) ;
docilis, *docile.*

## 2. Adjectives derived from Nouns.

### a) *From Common Nouns.*

**151.** 1. The suffixes **-eus** and **-inus** are appended to names of substances or materials; as, —

    **aureus,** *of gold;*    **ferreus,** *of iron;*    **fāginus,** *of beech.*

2. The suffixes **-ius, -icus, -īlis, -ālis, -āris, -ārius, -nus, -ānus, -īnus, -īvus, -ēnsis** signify *belonging to, connected with;* as, —

    **ōrātōrius,** *oratorical;*      **legiōnārius,** *legionary;*
    **bellicus,** *pertaining to war;*    **paternus,** *paternal;*
    **cīvīlis,** *civil;*      **urbānus,** *of the city;*
    **rēgālis,** *regal;*      **marīnus,** *marine;*
    **cōnsulāris,** *consular;*    **aestīvus,** *pertaining to summer;*
    **circēnsis,** *belonging to the circus.*

3. The suffixes **-ōsus** and **-lentus** denote *fullness;* as, —

    **perīculōsus,** *full of danger,*    **glōriōsus,** *glorious;*
    *dangerous;*      **opulentus,** *wealthy.*

4. The suffix **-tus** has the force of *provided with;* as, —

    **barbātus,** *bearded;*    **stellātus,** *set with stars.*

### b) *From Proper Names.*

**152.** 1. Names of *persons* take the suffixes: **-ānus, -iānus, -īnus;** as, —

    **Catōniānus,** *belonging to Cato;*  **Plautīnus,** *belonging to Plautus.*

2. Names of *nations* take the suffixes **-icus, -ius;** as, —

    **Germānicus,** *German;*    **Thrācius,** *Thracian.*

3. Names of *places* take the suffixes **-ānus, -īnus, -ēnsis, -aeus, -ius;** as, —

    **Rōmānus,** *Roman;*    **Athēniēnsis,** *Athenian;*
    **Amerīnus,** *of Ameria;*    **Smyrnaeus,** *of Smyrna;*
    **Corinthius,** *Corinthian.*

NOTE. —**-ānus** and **-ēnsis,** appended to names of countries, designate something *stationed in* the country or *connected with* it, but not indigenous; as, —

    **bellum Āfricānum,** *a war (of Romans with Romans) in Africa.*
    **bellum Hispāniēnse,** *a war carried on in Spain.*
    **legiōnēs Gallicānae,** *(Roman) legions stationed in Gaul.*

### 3. Adjectives derived from Adjectives.

**153.** Diminutives in -lus sometimes occur; as, —

> parvolus, *little;*
> misellus (passer), *poor little (sparrow)*;
> pauperculus, *needy.*

### 4. Adjectives derived from Adverbs.

**154.** These end in -ernus, -ternus, -tīnus, -tĭnus; as, —

| | | |
|---|---|---|
| hodiernus, | *of to-day* | (hodiē); |
| hesternus, | *of yesterday* | (herī); |
| intestīnus, | *internal* | (intus); |
| diūtinus, | *long-lasting* | (diū). |

## *C.* VERBS.

### 1. Verbs derived from Verbs.

**155.** 1. INCEPTIVES OR INCHOATIVES. These end in -scō, and are formed from Present Stems. They denote *the beginning of an action*; as, —

| | | |
|---|---|---|
| labāscō, | *begin to totter* | (from labō); |
| horrēscō, | *grow rough* | (from horreō); |
| tremēscō, | *begin to tremble* | (from tremō); |
| obdormīscō, | *fall asleep* | (from dormiō). |

2. FREQUENTATIVES OR INTENSIVES. These denote *a repeated or energetic action.* They are formed from the Participial Stem, and end in -tō or -sō. Those derived from verbs of the First Conjugation end in -itō (not -ātō, as we should expect). Examples of Frequentatives are —

| | | |
|---|---|---|
| jactō, | *toss about, brandish* | (from jaciō, *hurl*); |
| cursō, | *run hither and thither* | (from currō, *run*); |
| volitō, | *flit about* | (from volō, *fly*). |

*a.* Some double Frequentatives occur; as, —

| | | |
|---|---|---|
| cantitō, | *sing over and over* | (cantō); |
| cursitō, | *keep running about* | (cursō); |
| ventitō, | *keep coming.* | |

*b.* **agitō**, *set in motion*, is formed from the Present Stem

3. DESIDERATIVES. These denote *a desire to do something.* **They** are formed from the Participial Stem, and end in -**uriō**; as, —

> **ēsuriō,**   *desire to eat, am hungry*     (**edō**);
> **parturiō,** *want to bring forth, am in labor* (**pariō**).

### 2. Verbs derived from Nouns and Adjectives (Denominatives).

**156.** Denominatives of the First Conjugation are mostly transitive, those of the Second exclusively intransitive. Those of the Third and Fourth Conjugations are partly transitive, partly intransitive. Examples are—

> *a*) From Nouns : —

| | | |
|---|---|---|
| **fraudō,** | *defraud* | (**fraus**); |
| **vestiō,** | *clothe* | (**vestis**); |
| **flōreō,** | *bloom* | (**flōs**). |

> *b*) From Adjectives : —

| | | |
|---|---|---|
| **līberō,** | *free* | (**līber**); |
| **saeviō,** | *be fierce* | (**saevus**). |

### *D.* ADVERBS.

**157.** 1. Adverbs derived from verbs are formed from the Participial Stem by means of the suffix -**im**; as, —

| | | |
|---|---|---|
| **certātim,** | *emulously* | (**certō**); |
| **cursim,** | *in haste* | (**currō**); |
| **statim,** | *immediately* | (**stō**). |

2. Adverbs derived from nouns and adjectives are formed : —

> *a*) With the suffixes -**tim** (-**sim**), -**ātim**; as, —
>
>> **gradātim,** *step by step;*
>> **paulātim,** *gradually;*
>> **virītim,** *man by man.*

> *b*) With the suffix -**tus**; as, —
>
>> **antīquitus,** *of old;*
>> **rādīcitus,** *from the roots.*

> *c*) With the suffix -**ter**; as, —
>
>> **breviter,** *briefly.*

## II. COMPOUNDS.

**158.** 1. Compounds are formed by the union of simple words. The second member usually contains the *essential meaning* of the compound; the first member expresses *some modification* of this.

2. Vowel changes often occur in the process of composition. Thus: —

 a. In the second member of compounds. (See § 7. 1.)

 b. The final vowel of the stem of the first member of the compound often appears as ĭ where we should expect ŏ or ă; sometimes it is dropped altogether, and in case of consonant stems ĭ is often inserted; as, —

  signifer, *standard-bearer*;
  tubicen, *trumpeter*;
  magnanimus, *high-minded*;
  mātricīda, *matricide*.

**159.** EXAMPLES OF COMPOUNDS.

1. Nouns: —

 a) Preposition + Noun; as, —

  dē-decus, *disgrace*;
  pro-avus, *great-grandfather*.

 b) Noun + Verb Stem; as, —

  agri-cola, *farmer*;
  frātri-cīda, *fratricide*.

2. Adjectives: —

 a) Preposition + Adjective (or Noun); as, —

  per-magnus, *very great*;
  sub-obscūrus, *rather obscure*;
  ā-mēns, *frantic*.

 b) Adjective + Noun; as, —

  magn-animus, *great-hearted*;
  celeri-pēs, *swift-footed*.

 c) Noun + Verb Stem; as, —

  parti-ceps, *sharing*;
  morti-fer, *death-dealing*.

3. Verbs : —

The second member is always a verb.   The first may be —

   *a*)  A Noun ; as, —

        **aedi-ficō**, *build.*

   *b*)  An Adjective ; as, —

        **ampli-ficō**, *enlarge.*

   *c*)  An Adverb ; as, —

        **male-dīcō**, *rail at.*

   *d*)  Another Verb ; as, —

        **cale-faciō**, *make warm.*

   *e*)  A Preposition ; as, —

        **ab-jungō**, *detach ;*
        **re-ferō**, *bring back ;*
        **dis-cernō**, *distinguish ;*
        **ex-spectō**, *await.*

NOTE. — Here belong the so-called INSEPARABLE PREPOSITIONS : —

        **ambi- (amb-)**, *around ;*
        **dis- (dir-, dī-)**, *apart, asunder ;*
        **por-**, *forward ;*
        **red- (re-)**, *back ;*
        **sēd- (sē-)**, *apart from ;*
        **vē-**, *without.*

4. Adverbs : —

These are of various types ; as, —

        **anteā**, *before ;*
        **īlicō (in locō)**, *on the spot ;*
        **imprīmīs**, *especially ;*
        **obviam**, *in the way.*

# Part V.

---

## SYNTAX.

---

**160.** Syntax treats of the use of words in sentences.

### Chapter I. — *Sentences.*

#### CLASSIFICATION OF SENTENCES.

**161.** Sentences may be classified as follows: —

1. Declarative, which state something; as, —
   puer scrībit, *the boy is writing.*

2. Interrogative, which ask a question; as, —
   quid puer scrībit, *what is the boy writing?*

3. Exclamatory, which are in the form of an exclamation; as, —
   quot librōs scrībit, *how many books he writes!*

4. Imperative, which express a command or an admonition; as, —
   scrībe, *write!*

#### FORM OF INTERROGATIVE SENTENCES.

**162.** Questions may be either Word-Questions or Sentence-Questions.

1. **Word-Questions.** These are introduced by the various interrogative pronouns and adverbs; such as — quis, quī, quālis, quantus, quot, quotiēns, quō, quā, *etc.* Thus: —
   quis venit, *who comes?*
   quam diū manēbit, *how long will he stay?*

2. **Sentence-Questions.**   These are introduced —

  *a*)  By **nōnne** implying the answer '*yes*'; as, —
  **nōnne vidētis,** *do you not see?*

  *b*)  By **num** implying the answer '*no*'; as, —
  **num exspectās,** *do you expect? (i.e. you don't expect, do you?)*

  *c*)  By the enclitic -**ne,** appended to the emphatic word (which
  usually stands first), and simply asking for information; as, —
  **vidēsne,** *do you see?*

    A question introduced by -**ne** may receive a special impli-
    cation from the context; as, —
    **sēnsistīne,** *did you not perceive?*

  *d*)  Sometimes by no special word, particularly in expressions of
  *surprise or indignation*; as, —
    **tū in jūdicum cōnspectum venīre audēs,** *do you dare to
    come into the presence of the judges?*

3. **Rhetorical Questions.**   These are questions merely in
form, being employed to express an emphatic assertion;
as, **quis dubitat,** *who doubts?* ( = *no one doubts*).

4. **Double Questions.**   Double Questions are introduced
by the following particles : —

utrum . . . an;

-ne . . . . . an;

—— . . . . an.

If the second member is negative, **annōn** (less often **necne**) is used.
Examples : —

  utrum honestum est an turpe,  ⎫
  honestumne est an turpe,      ⎬ *is it honorable or base?*
  honestum est an turpe,        ⎭
  suntne dī annōn, *are there gods or not?*

  *a.*  **An** was not originally confined to double questions, but introduced single questions, having the force of -**ne, nōnne,**
  or **num.**   Traces of this use survive in classical Latin; as, —
    **Ā rēbus gerendīs abstrahit senectūs. Quibus? An
    eīs quae juventūte geruntur et vīribus?** *Old age (it is
    alleged) withdraws men from active pursuits. From what
    pursuits? Is it not merely from those which are carried on
    by the strength of youth?*

**5.** Answers.

> *a.* The answer YES is expressed by **ita, etiam, vērō, sānē,** or by repetition of the verb; as, —
>
> > 'vīsne locum mūtēmus?' 'sānē.' '*Shall we change the place?*' '*Certainly.*'
> > 'estisne vōs lēgātī?' 'sumus.' '*Are you envoys?*' '*Yes.*'
>
> *b.* The answer No is expressed by **nōn, minimē, minimē vērō,** or by repeating the verb with a negative; as, —
>
> > 'jam ea praeteriit?' 'nōn.' '*Has it passed?*' '*No.*'
> > 'estne frāter intus?' 'nōn est.' '*Is your brother within?*'
> > '*No.*'

## SUBJECT AND PREDICATE.

**163.** The two essential parts of a sentence are the SUB-JECT and PREDICATE.

The SUBJECT is that *concerning which something is said, asked, etc.* The PREDICATE is that *which is said, asked, etc., concerning* the SUBJECT.

## SIMPLE AND COMPOUND SENTENCES.

**164.** Sentences containing but one Subject and one Predicate are called SIMPLE SENTENCES, those containing more are called COMPOUND SENTENCES. Thus **puer librōs legit,** *the boy reads books,* is a Simple Sentence; but **puer librōs legit et epistulās scrībit,** *the boy reads books and writes letters,* is a Compound Sentence. The different members of a Compound Sentence are called Clauses.

**165.** COÖRDINATE AND SUBORDINATE CLAUSES. Clauses which stand upon an equality are called COÖRDINATE; a Clause dependent upon another is called SUBORDINATE. Thus in **puer librōs legit et epistulās scrībit** the two clauses are Coördinate; but in **puer librōs legit quōs pater scrībit,** *the boy reads the books which his father writes,* the second clause is Subordinate to the first.

## Chapter II. — *Syntax of Nouns.*

### SUBJECT.

**166.** The Subject of a Finite Verb (*i.e.* any form of the Indicative, Subjunctive, or Imperative) is in the Nominative Case.

1. The Subject may be —

   *a*) A Noun or Pronoun; as, —

   **puer scrībit**, *the boy writes* ;
   **hīc scrībit**, *this man writes.*

   *b*) An Infinitive; as, —

   **decōrum est prō patriā morī**, *to die for one's country is a noble thing.*

   *c*) A Clause; as, —

   **opportūnē accidit quod vīdistī**, *it happened opportunely that you saw.*

2. A Personal Pronoun as Subject is usually implied in the Verb, and is not separately expressed; as, —

   **scrībō**, *I write* ;          **videt**, *he sees.*

   *a.* But for the purpose of emphasis or contrast the Pronoun is expressed; as, —

   **ego scrībō et tū legis**, *I write. and you read.*

3. The verb is sometimes omitted when it can be easily supplied from the context, especially the auxiliary **sum**; as, —

**rēctē ille** (*sc.* **facit**), *he does rightly* ; **cōnsul profectus** (*sc.* **est**), *the consul set out.*

### PREDICATE NOUNS.

**167.** A Predicate Noun is one connected with the Subject by some form of the verb **Sum** or a similar verb.

**168.** A Predicate Noun agrees with its Subject in Case ;[1] as, —

---

[1] For the Predicate Genitive, see §§ 198, 3; 203, 5.

**Cicerō ōrātor fuit,** *Cicero was an orator ;*
**Numa creātus est rēx,** *Numa was elected king.*

1. When possible, the Predicate Noun usually agrees with its Sub‹
ject in Gender also ; as, —
**philosophia est vītae magistra,** *philosophy is the guide of life.*

2. Besides **sum,** the verbs most frequently accompanied by a Predi‹
cate Noun are —

  *a*) **fīō, ēvādō, exsistō ; maneō ; videor ;** as, —
  **Croesus nōn semper mānsit rēx,** *Croesus did not always
  remain king.*

  *b*) Passive verbs of *making, calling, regarding, etc.* ; as, **creor,
  appellor, habeor ;** as, —
  **Rōmulus rēx appellātus est,** *Romulus was called king ;*
  **habitus est deus,** *he was regarded as a god.*

### APPOSITIVES.

**169.** 1. An Appositive is a Noun explaining or defin‹
ing another Noun denoting the same person or thing ; as, —

> **Cicerō cōnsul,** *Cicero, the Consul ;*
> **urbs Rōma,** *the city Rome.*

2. An Appositive agrees with its Subject in Case ; as, —

**opera Cicerōnis ōrātōris,** *the works of Cicero, the orator ;*
**apud Hērodotum, patrem historiae,** *in the works of Herodotus, the
father of history.*

3. When possible, the Appositive agrees with its Subject in Gen‹
der also ; as, —

**assentātiō adjūtrīx vitiōrum,** *flattery, the promoter of evils.*

4. A Locative may take in Apposition the Ablative of **urbs or
oppidum,** with or without a preposition ; as, —

**Corinthī, Achāiae urbe,** or **in Achāiae urbe,** *at Corinth, a city of
Greece.*

5. PARTITIVE APPOSITION. A Noun denoting a whole is frequently
followed by an Appositive denoting a part ; as, —

**mīlitēs, fortissimus quisque, hostibus restitērunt,** *the soldiers, all
the bravest of them, resisted the enemy.*

## THE CASES.

### THE NOMINATIVE.

**170.** The Nominative is confined to its use as Subject, Appositive, or Predicate Noun, as already explained. See §§ 166–169.

### THE VOCATIVE

**171.** The Vocative is the Case of direct address; as, —

crēdite mihi, jūdicēs, *believe me, judges.*

1. By a species of attraction, the Nominative is occasionally used for the Vocative, especially in poetry and formal prose; as, **audī tū, populus Albānus,** *hear ye, Alban people!*

2. Similarly the Appositive of a Vocative may, in poetry, stand in the Nominative; as, **nāte, mea magna potentia sōlus,** *O son, alone the source of my great power.*

### THE ACCUSATIVE.

**172.** The Accusative is the Case of the Direct Object.

**173.** The Direct Object may express either of the two following relations : —

*A.* The PERSON OR THING AFFECTED by the action; as, —

cōnsulem interfēcit, *he slew the consul;*
legō librum, *I read the book.*

*B.* The RESULT PRODUCED by the action; as, —

librum scrīpsī, *I wrote a book* (*i.e.* produced one);
templum struit, *he constructs a temple.*

**174.** Verbs that admit a Direct Object of either of these two types are TRANSITIVE VERBS.

   *a.* Verbs that regularly take a Direct Object are sometimes used without it. They are then said to be employed *absolutely*; as, —

rūmor est meum gnātum amāre, *it is rumored that my son is in love.*

### Accusative of the Person or Thing Affected.

**175.** 1. This is the most frequent use of the Accusative; as in —

> parentēs amāmus, *we love our parents;*
> mare aspicit, *he gazes at the sea.*

2. The following classes of Verbs taking an Accusative of this kind are worthy of note : —

*a*) Many Intransitive Verbs, when compounded with a Preposition, become Transitive. Thus: —

> 1) Compounds of **circum, praeter, trāns**; as, —
> hostēs circumstāre, *to surround the enemy;*
> urbem praeterīre, *to pass by the city;*
> mūrōs trānscendere, *to climb over the walls.*

> 2) Less frequently, compounds of **ad, per, in, sub**; as, —
> adīre urbem, *to visit the city;*
> peragrāre Italiam, *to travel through Italy;*
> inīre magistrātum, *to take office;*
> subīre perīculum, *to undergo danger.*

*b*) Many Verbs expressing emotions, regularly Intransitive, have also a Transitive use; as, —

> queror fātum, *I lament my fate;*
> doleō ejus mortem, *I grieve at his death;*
> rīdeō tuam stultitiam, *I laugh at your folly.*

So also **lūgeō, maereō,** *mourn;* **gemō,** *bemoan;* **horreō,** *shudder,* and others.

*c*) The impersonals **decet,** *it becomes;* **dēdecet,** *it is unbecoming;* **juvat,** *it pleases,* take the Accusative of the Person Affected; as, —

> mē decet haec dīcere, *it becomes me to say this.*

*d*) In poetry many Passive Verbs, in imitation of Greek usage, are employed as Middles (§ 256, 1; 2), and take the Accusative as Object; as, —

> galeam induitur, *he puts on his helmet;*
> cīnctus tempora hederā, *having bound his temples with ivy;*
> nōdō sinus collēcta, *having gathered her dress in a knot.*

### Accusative of the Result Produced.

**176.** 1. The ordinary type of this Accusative is seen in such expressions as —

>   librum scrībō, *I write a book;*
>   domum aedificō, *I build a house.*

2. Many Verbs usually Intransitive take a *Neuter Pronoun, or Adjective,* as an Accusative of Result. Thus : —

>   *a)* A Neuter Pronoun; as, —
>
>>   haec gemēbat, *he made these moans;*
>>   idem glōriārī, *to make the same boast;*
>>   eadem peccat, *he makes the same mistakes.*
>
>   *b)* A Neuter Adjective, — particularly *Adjectives of number or amount,* — multum, multa, pauca, *etc.;* also nihil; as, —
>
>>   multa egeō, *I have many needs;*
>>   pauca studet, *he has few interests;*
>>   multum valet, *he has great strength;*
>>   nihil peccat, *he makes no mistake.*

NOTE. — In poetry other Adjectives are freely used in this construction; as, —

>>   minitantem vāna, *making vain threats;*
>>   acerba tuēns, *giving a fierce look;*
>>   dulce loquentem, *sweetly talking.*

3. The adverbial use of several Neuter Pronouns and Adjectives grows out of this Accusative; as, —

multum sunt in vēnātiōne, *they are much engaged in hunting.*

>   *a.* So also plūrimum, *very greatly;* plērumque, *generally;* aliquid, *somewhat;* quid, *why?* nihil, *not at all;* etc.

4. Sometimes an Intransitive Verb takes an Accusative of Result which is of kindred etymology with the Verb. This is called a COGNATE ACCUSATIVE, and is usually modified by an Adjective; as, —

sempiternam servitūtem serviat, *let him serve an everlasting slavery;*
vītam dūram vīxī, *I have lived a hard life.*

>   *a.* Sometimes the Cognate Accusative is not of kindred etymology, but merely of kindred meaning; as, —
>
>>   stadium currit, *he runs a race;*
>>   Olympia vincit, *he wins an Olympic victory.*

5. The Accusative of Result occurs also after Verbs of *tasting* and *smelling*; as, —

**piscis mare sapit,** *the fish tastes of the sea* ;
**ōrātiōnēs antīquitātem redolent,** *the speeches smack of the past.*

### Two Accusatives — Direct Object and Predicate Accusative.

**177.** 1. Many Verbs of *Making, Choosing, Calling, Showing,* and the like, take two Accusatives, one of the Person or Thing Affected, the other a Predicate Accusative; as, —

**mē hērēdem fēcit,** *he made me heir.*

Here **mē** is Direct Object, **hērēdēm** Predicate Accusative.
So also —

**eum jūdicem cēpēre,** *they took him as judge* ;
**urbem Rōmam vocāvit,** *he called the city Rome* ;
**sē virum praestitit,** *he showed himself a man.*

2. The Predicate Accusative may be an Adjective as well as a Noun ; as, —

**hominēs caecōs reddit cupiditās,** *covetousness renders men blind* ;
**Apollō Sōcratem sapientissimum jūdicāvit,** *Apollo adjudged Socrates the wisest man.*

    *a.* Some Verbs, as **reddō**, usually admit only an Adjective as the Predicate Accusative.

3. In the Passive the Direct Object becomes the Subject, and the Predicate Accusative becomes Predicate Nominative (§ 168. 2. *b*) ; as, —

**urbs Rōma vocāta est,** *the city was called Rome.*

    *a.* Not all Verbs admit the Passive construction ; **reddō** and **efficiō**, for example, never take it.

### Two Accusatives — Person and Thing.

**178.** 1. Some Verbs take two Accusatives, one of the Person Affected, the other of the Result Produced. Thus : —

    *a)* Verbs of *requesting* and *demanding*; as, —

        **ōtium dīvōs rogat,** *he asks the gods for rest* ;
        **mē duās ōrātiōnēs postulās,** *you demand two speeches of me*

# 126

SYNTAX.

So also **ōrō, poscō, reposcō, exposcō, flāgitō**, though some of these prefer the Ablative with **ab** to the Accusative of the Person; as, —

**opem ā tē poscō**, *I demand aid of you.*

*b*) Verbs of *teaching* (**doceō** and its compounds); as, —

**tē litterās doceō**, *I teach you your letters.*

*c*) Verbs of *inquiring*; as, —

**tē haec rogō**, *I ask you this;*
**tē sententiam rogō**, *I ask you your opinion.*

*a*) Several Special Verbs; *viz.* **moneō, admoneō, commoneō, cōgō, accūsō, arguō**, and a few others. These admit only a Neuter Pronoun or Adjective as Accusative of the Thing; as, —

**hōc tē moneō**, *I give you this advice;*
**mē id accūsās**, *you bring this accusation against me;*
**id cōgit nōs nātūra**, *nature compels us (to) this.*

*e*) One Verb of *concealing*, **cēlō**; as, —

**nōn tē cēlāvī sermōnem**, *I have not concealed the conversation from you.*

2. In the Passive construction the Accusative of the Person becomes the Subject, and the Accusative of the Thing is retained; as, —

**omnēs artēs ēdoctus est**, *he was taught all accomplishments;*
**rogātus sum sententiam**, *I was asked my opinion;*
**multa admonēmur**, *we are given many admonitions.*

*a.* Only a few Verbs admit the Passive construction.

### Two Accusatives with Compounds.

**179.** 1. Transitive compounds of **trāns** may take two Accusatives, one dependent upon the Verb, the other upon the Preposition; as, —

**mīlitēs flūmen trānsportat**, *he leads his soldiers across the river.*

2. With other compounds this construction is rare.

3. In the Passive the Accusative dependent upon the preposition is retained; as, —

**mīlitēs flūmen trādūcēbantur**, *the soldiers were led across the river.*

*Acc. of specification.*

## Synecdochical (or Greek) Accusative.

**180.** 1. The Synecdochical (or Greek) Accusative denotes the *part* to which an action or quality refers ; as, —

> **tremit artūs**, literally, *he trembles as to his limbs*, *i.e.* his limbs tremble;
> **nūda genū**, lit. *bare as to the knee*, *i.e.* with knee bare;
> **manūs revinctus**, lit. *tied as to the hands. i.e.* with hands tied.

2. Note that this construction —

    *a)* Is borrowed from the Greek.
    *b)* Is chiefly confined to poetry.
    *c)* Usually refers to a part of the body.
    *d)* Is used with Adjectives as well as Verbs.

### Accusative of Time and Space.

**181.** 1. *Duration of Time* and *Extent of Space* are denoted by the Accusative ; as, —

**quadrāgintā annōs vīxit**, *he lived forty years ;*
**hīc locus passūs sescentōs aberat**, *this place was six hundred paces away ;*
**arborēs quīnquāgintā pedēs altae**, *trees fifty feet high*
**abhinc septem annōs**, *seven years ago.*

2. Emphasis is sometimes added by using the Preposition **per** ; as,

> **per biennium labōrāvī**, *I toiled throughout two years.*

### Accusative of Limit of Motion.

**182.** 1. The Accusative of Limit of Motion is used —

    *a)* With names of *Towns, Small Islands*, and *Peninsulas* ; as, –

> **Rōmam vēnī**, *I came to Rome ;*
> **Athēnās proficīscitur**, *he sets out for Athens ;*
> **Dēlum pervēnī**, *I arrived at Delos.*

    *b)* With **domum, domōs, rūs** ; as, —

> **domum revertitur**, *he returns home ;*
> **rūs ībō**, *I shall go to the country.*

NOTE. — When **domus** means *house* (*i.e.* building), it takes a prep osition ; as. —

> **in domum veterem remigrāre**, *to move back to an old house.*

2. Other designations of place than those above mentioned require
a Preposition to denote Limit of Motion ; as, —

> **ad Italiam vēnit,** *he came to Italy.*

> *a.* The Preposition is also customary with the Accusatives
> **urbem** or **oppidum** when they stand in apposition with the
> name of a town ; as, —
>
> **Thalam, in oppidum magnum,** *to Thala, a large town;*
> **Genavam ad oppidum,** *to the town Geneva.*

> *b.* The name of a town denoting limit of motion may be com-
> bined with the name of a country or other word dependent
> upon a preposition ; as, —
>
> **Thūriōs in Italiam pervectus,** *carried to Thurii in Italy;*
> **cum Acēn ad exercitum vēnisset,** *when he had come to*
> *the army at Ace.*

3. To denote *toward, to the vicinity of, in the vicinity of,* **ad** is used ;
as, —

> **ad Tarentum vēnī,** *I came to the vicinity of Tarentum ;*
> **ad Cannās pugna facta est,** *a battle was fought near Cannae.*

4. In poetry the Accusative of any noun denoting a place may be
used without a preposition to express the limit of motion ; as, —

> **Italiam vēnit,** *he came to Italy.*

5. The *goal* notion seems to represent the original function of the
Accusative Case. Traces of this primitive force are recognizable in the
phrase **īnfitiās īre,** *to deny* (lit. *to go to a denial*), and a few other
similar expressions.

### Accusative in Exclamations.

**183.** The Accusative, generally modified by an Adjective, is used in Exclamations ; as, —

> **mē miserum,** *ah, wretched me!*
> **Ō fallācem spem,** *oh, deceptive hope!*

### Accusative as Subject of the Infinitive.

**184.** The Subject of the Infinitive is put in the Accusative ; as, —

> **videō hominem abīre.** *I see that the man is going away.*

### Other Uses of the Accusative.

**185.** Here belong —

1. Some Accusatives which were originally Appositives; *viz*. —

    **id genus,** *of that kind*; as, **hominēs id genus,** *men of that kind*
    (originally **hominēs, id genus hominum,** *men, that kind
    of men*);
    **virīle secus, muliebre secus,** *of the male sex, of the female sex*;
    **meam vicem, tuam vicem,** *etc., for my part, etc.*;
    **bonam partem, magnam partem,** *in large part*;
    **maximam partem,** *for the most part.*

2. Some phrases of doubtful origin; as, —

    **id temporis,** *at that time*;        **quod sī,** *but if*;
    **id aetātis,** *at that time*;          **cētera,** *in other respects.*

### THE DATIVE.

**186.** The Dative case, in general, expresses relations
which are designated in English by the prepositions **to**
and **for.**

### Dative of Indirect Object.

**187.** The commonest use of the Dative is to denote the
person *to whom* something is *given, said,* or *done.* Thus : —
I. With transitive verbs in connection with the Accusative; as, —

    **hanc pecūniam mihi dat,** *he gives me this money*;
    **haec nōbīs dīxit,** *he said this to us.*

   *a.* Some verbs which take this construction (particularly
   **dōnō** and **circumdō**) admit also the Accusative of the person along with the Ablative of the thing.   Thus : —
   Either **Themistoclī mūnera dōnāvit,** *he presented gifts to
   Themistocles,* or
   **Themistoclem mūneribus dōnāvit,** *he presented Themistocles with gifts* ;
   **urbī mūrōs circumdat,** *he builds walls around the city,* or
   **urbem mūrīs circumdat,** *ne surrounds the city with wall⸱*

## II. With many intransitive verbs; as, —

nūllī labōrī cēdit, *he yields to no labor.*

*a.* Here belong many verbs signifying *favor,*[1] *help, injure, please, displease, trust, distrust, command, obey, serve, resist, indulge, spare, pardon, envy, threaten, be angry, believe, persuade,* and the like; as, —

Caesar populāribus favet, *Caesar favors (i.e. is favorable to) the popular party;*

amīcīs cōnfīdō, *I trust (to) my friends;*

Orgetorīx Helvētiīs persuāsit, *Orgetorix persuaded (made it acceptable to) the Helvetians;*

bonīs nocet quī malīs parcit, *he injures (does harm to) the good, who spares the bad.*

NOTE. — It is to be borne in mind that these verbs do not take the Dative by virtue of their apparent English equivalence, but simply because they are *intransitive,* and adapted to an indirect object. Some verbs of the same apparent English equivalence are *transitive* and govern the Accusative; as, juvō, laedō, dēlectō. Thus: audentēs deus juvat, *God helps the bold;* nēminem laesit, *he injured no one.*

*b.* Verbs of this class are used in the passive only impersonally; as, —

tibi parcitur, *you are spared;*

mihi persuādētur, *I am being persuaded;*

eī invidētur, *he is envied.*

*c.* Some of the foregoing verbs admit also a Direct Object in connection with the Dative; as, —

mihi mortem minitātur, *he threatens me with death (threatens death to me).*

## III. With many verbs compounded with the prepositions: ad, ante, circum, com,[2] in, inter, ob, post, prae. prō, sub, super.

These verbs fall into two main classes, —

1. Many simple verbs which cannot take a Dative of the indirect object become capable of doing so when compounded with a preposition; as, —

afflīctīs succurrit, *he helps the afflicted;*

exercituī praefuit, *he was in command of the army;*

intersum cōnsiliīs, *I share in the deliberations.*

---

[1] Many such verbs were originally intransitive in English also, and once governed the Dative.  [2] This was the original form of the preposition cum.

2. Many transitive verbs which take only a direct object become capable, when compounded, of taking a dative also as indirect object; as, —

pecūniae pudōrem antepōnit, *he puts honor before money*;
inicere spem amīcīs, *to inspire hope in one's friends*;
mūnītiōnī Labiēnum praefēcit, *he put Labienus in charge of the fortifications*.

### Dative of Reference.

**188**. 1. The Dative of Reference denotes the person *to whom a statement refers, of whom it is true*, or *to whom it is of interest;* as, —

mihi ante oculōs versāris, *you hover before my eyes* (lit. *hover before the eyes to me*);
illī sevēritās amōrem nōn dēminuit, *in his case severity did not diminish love* (lit. *to him severity did not diminish*);
interclūdere inimīcīs commeātum, *to cut off the supplies of the enemy.*

> *a.* Note the phrase alicui interdīcere aquā et īgnī, *to interdict one from fire and water.*

NOTE. — The Dative of Reference, unlike the Dative of Indirect Object, does not modify the verb, but rather the sentence as a whole. It is often used where, according to the English idiom, we should expect a Genitive; so in the first and third of the above examples.

2. Special varieties of the Dative of Reference are —

*a)* **Dative of the Local Standpoint.** This is regularly a participle; as, —

> oppidum prīmum Thessaliae venientibus ab Ēpīrō, *the first town of Thessaly as you come from Epirus* (lit. *to those coming from Epirus*).

*b)* **Ethical Dative.** This name is given to those Dative constructions of the personal pronouns in which the connection of the Dative with the rest of the sentence is of the very slightest sort; as, —

> tū mihi istīus audāciam dēfendis? *tell me, do you defend that man's audacity?*
> quid mihi Celsus agit? *what is my Celsus doing?*

*c*) **Dative of Person Judging**; as, —

**erit ille mihi semper deus,** *he will always be a god to me*
(*i.e.* in my opinion) ;

**quae ista servitūs tam clārō hominī,** *how can that be
slavery to so illustrious a man* (*i.e.* to his mind)!

*d*) **Dative of Separation.** Some verbs of *taking away*,
especially compounds of **ab, dē, ex, ad,** govern a Dative of
the person, less often of the thing ; as, —

**honōrem dētrāxērunt hominī,** *they took away the honor
from the man;*

**Caesar rēgī tetrarchiam ēripuit,** *Caesar took the tetrarchy
away from the king;*

**silicī scintillam excūdit,** *he struck a spark from the flint.*

### Dative of Agency.

**189.** The Dative is used to denote *agency* —

1. Regularly with the Gerundive ; as, —

**haec nōbīs agenda sunt,** *these things must be done by us;*
**mihi eundum est,** *I must go* (lit. *it must be gone by me*).

    *a.* To avoid ambiguity, **ā** with the Ablative is sometimes used with the
Gerundive ; as, —

        **hostibus ā nōbīs parcendum est,** *the enemy must be spared by us.*

2. Much less frequently with the compound tenses of the passive
voice and the perfect passive participle ; as, —

**disputātiō quae mihi nūper habita est,** *the discussion which was
recently conducted by me.*

3. Rarely with the uncompounded tenses of the passive ; as, —

**honesta bonīs virīs quaeruntur,** *noble ends are sought by good men.*

### Dative of Possession.

**190.** The Dative of Possession occurs with the verb **esse**
in such expressions as : —

    **mihi est liber,** *I have a book;*
    **mihi nōmen est Mārcus,** *I have the name Marcus.*

1. But with **nōmen est** the name is more commonly attracted into
the Dative ; as, **mihi Mārcō nōmen est.**

## Dative of Purpose or Tendency.

**191.** The Dative of Purpose or Tendency designates *the end toward which an action is directed* or *the direction in which it tends.* It is used —

1. Unaccompanied by another Dative; as, —

**castrīs locum dēligere,** *to choose a place for a camp;*
**legiōnēs praesidiō relinquere,** *to leave the legions as a guard* (lit. *for a guard*);
**receptuī canere,** *to sound the signal for a retreat.*

2. Much more frequently in connection with another Dative of the person : —

    *a*) Especially with some form of **esse** ; as, —

        **fortūnae tuae mihi cūrae sunt,** *your fortunes are a care to me* (lit. *for a ccre*) ;
        **quibus sunt odiō,** *to whom they are an object of hatred;*
        **cui bonō?** *to whom is it of advantage?*

    *b*) With other verbs; as, —

        **hōs tibi mūnerī mīsit,** *he has sent these to you for a present;*
        **Pausaniās Atticīs vēnit auxiliō,** *Pausanias came to the aid of the Athenians* (lit. *to the Athenians for aid*).

3. In connection with the Gerundive ; as, —

**decemvirī lēgibus scrībundīs,** *decemvirs for codifying the laws;*
**mē gerendō bellō ducem creāvēre,** *me they have made leader for carrying on the war.*

NOTE. — This construction with the gerundive is not common till Livy.

## Dative with Adjectives.

**192.** The use of the Dative with Adjectives corresponds very closely to its use with verbs. Thus : —

1. Corresponding to the Dative of Indirect Object it occurs with adjectives signifying: *friendly, unfriendly, similar, dissimilar, equal, near, related to, etc.* ; as, —

    **mihi inimīcus,** *hostile to me* ;
    **sunt proximī Germānīs,** *they are next to the Germans* ;
    **noxiae poena pār estō,** *let the penalty be equal to the damage.*

*a.* For **propior** and **proximus** with the Accusative, see § 141, 3.

**2.** Corresponding to the Dative of Purpose, the Dative occurs with adjectives signifying: *suitable, adapted, fit*; as, —

> **castrīs idōneus locus,** *a place fit for a camp*;
> **apta diēs sacrificiō,** *a day suitable for a sacrifice.*

NOTE. — Adjectives of this last class often take the Accusative with **ad.**

### Dative of Direction.

**193.** In the poets the Dative is occasionally used to denote the *direction of motion*; as, —

> **it clāmor caelō,** *the shout goes heavenward*;
> **cinerēs rīvō fluentī jace,** *cast the ashes toward a flowing stream.*

**1.** By an extension of this construction the poets sometimes use the Dative to denote the *limit of motion*; as, —

> **dum Latiō deōs īnferret,** *till he should bring his gods to Latium.*

### THE GENITIVE.

**194.** The Genitive is used with Nouns, Adjectives, and Verbs.

### GENITIVE WITH NOUNS.

**195.** With Nouns the Genitive is *the case which defines the meaning of the limited noun more closely.* This relation is generally indicated in English by the preposition **of**. There are the following varieties of the Genitive with Nouns: —

| | |
|---|---|
| Genitive of Origin, | Objective Genitive, |
| Genitive of Material, | Genitive of the Whole, |
| Genitive of Possession, | Appositional Genitive, |
| Subjective Genitive, | Genitive of Quality. |

**196.** Genitive of Origin; as, —

> **Mārcī fīlius,** *the son of Marcus.*

**197.** Genitive of Material; as, —

> **talentum aurī,** *a talent of gold*;
> **acervus frūmentī,** *a pile of grain.*

**198. Genitive of Possession or Ownership**; as, —
domus Cicerōnis, *Cicero's house.*

1. Here belongs the Genitive with **causā** and **grātiā**. The Genitive always precedes; as, —

hominum causā, *for the sake of men*;
meōrum amīcōrum grātiā, *for the sake of my friends.*

2. The Possessive Genitive is often used predicatively, especially with **esse** and **fierī**; as, —

domus est rēgis, *the house is the king's*;
stultī est in errōre manēre, *it is (the part) of a fool to remain in error*;
dē bellō jūdicium imperātōris est, nōn mīlitum, *the decision concerning war belongs to the general, not to the soldiers.*

   *a.* For the difference in force between the Possessive Genitive and the Dative of Possession, see § 359, 1.

**199. Subjective Genitive.** This denotes *the person who makes or produces something or who has a feeling*; as, —

dicta Platōnis, *the utterances of Plato*;
timōrēs līberōrum, *the fears of the children.*

**200. Objective Genitive.** This denotes *the object of an action or feeling*; as, —

metus deōrum, *the fear of the gods*;
amor lībertātis, *love of liberty*;
cōnsuētūdō bonōrum hominum, *intercourse with good men.*

1. This relation is often expressed by means of prepositions; as, —
amor ergā parentēs, *love toward one's parents.*

**201. Genitive of the Whole.** This designates the *whole* of which a part is taken. It is used —

1. With Nouns, Pronouns, Comparatives, Superlatives, and Ordinal Numerals; as, —

magna pars hominum, *a great part of mankind*;
duo mīlia peditum, *two thousand foot-soldiers*;
quis mortālium, *who of mortals?*
major frātrum, *the elder of the brothers*;
gēns maxima Germānōrum, *the largest tribe of the Germans*
prīmus omnium, *the first of all.*

*a.* Yet instead of the Genitive of the Whole we often find **ex** or **dē** with the Ablative, regularly so with Cardinal numbers and **quĭdam**; as, —

**fĭdēlissimus dē servīs,** *the most trusty of the slaves;*
**quĭdam ex amīcĭs,** *certain of his friends;*
**ūnus ex mīlitibus,** *one of the soldiers.*

*b.* In English we often use *of* where there is no relation of whole to part. In such cases the Latin is more exact, and does not use the Genitive; as, —

**quot vōs estis,** *how many of you are there?*
**trecentī conjūrāvimus,** *three hundred of us have conspired* (*i.e.* we, three hundred in number).

**2.** The Genitive of the Whole is used also with the Nominative or Accusative Singular Neuter of Pronouns, or of Adjectives used substantively; also with the Adverbs **parum, satis,** and **partim** when used substantively; as, —

**quid cōnsilī,** *what purpose?*
**tantum cibī,** *so much food;*
**plūs auctōritātis,** *more authority;*
**minus labōris,** *less labor;*
**satis pecūniae,** *enough money;*
**parum industriae,** *too little industry.*

*a.* An Adjective of the second declension used substantively may be employed as a Genitive of the Whole; as, **nihil bonī,** *nothing good.*
*b.* But Adjectives of the third declension agree directly with the noun they limit; as, **nihil dulcius,** *nothing sweeter.*

**3.** Occasionally we find the Genitive of the Whole dependent upon Adverbs of place; as, —

**ubi terrārum? ubi gentium?** *where in the world?*

*a.* By an extension of this usage the Genitive sometimes occurs in dependence upon **prīdiē** and **postrīdiē,** but only in the phrases **prīdiē ejus diēī,** *on the day before that;* **postrīdiē ejus diēī,** *on the day after that.*

**202. Appositional Genitive.** The Genitive sometimes has the force of an appositive; as, —

**nōmen rēgis,** *the name of king;*
**poena mortis,** *the penalty of death;*
**ars scrībendī,** *the art of writing.*

**203. Genitive of Quality.** The Genitive modified by an Adjective is used to denote quality. This construction presents several varieties. Thus it is used —

1. To denote some internal or permanent characteristic of a person or thing; as, —

> **vir magnae virtūtis,** *a man of great virtue;*
> **ratiōnēs ejus modī,** *considerations of that sort.*

> *a.* Only a limited number of Adjectives occur in this construction, chiefly **magnus, maximus, summus, tantus,** along with **ejus.**

2. To denote measure (*breadth, length, etc.*) ; as, —

> **fossa quīndecim pedum,** *a trench fifteen feet wide* (or *deep*) ;
> **exsilium decem annōrum,** *an exile of ten years.*

3. Equivalent to the Genitive of Quality (though probably of different origin) are the Genitives **tantī, quantī, parvī, magnī, minōris, plūris, minimī, plūrimī, maximī.** These are used predicatively to denote *indefinite value;* as, —

> **nūlla studia tantī sunt,** *no studies are of so much value;*
> **magnī opera ejus exīstimāta est,** *his assistance was highly esteemed.*

4. By an extension of the notion of *value,* **quantī, tantī, plūris,** and **minōris** are also used with verbs of *buying* and *selling,* to denote *indefinite price;* as, —

> **quantī aedēs ēmistī,** *at how high a price did you purchase the house?*

5. Any of the above varieties of the Genitive of Quality may be used predicatively; as, —

> **tantae mōlis erat Rōmānam condere gentem,** *of so great difficulty was it to found the Roman race.*

## GENITIVE WITH ADJECTIVES.

**204.** The Genitive is used with many Adjectives *to limit the extent of their application.* Thus : —

1. With adjectives signifying *desire, knowledge, familiarity, memory, participation, power, fullness,* and their opposites ; as, —

> **studiōsus discendī,** *desirous of learning;*
> **perītus bellī,** *skilled in war ;*
> **īnsuētus labōris,** *unused to toil;*
> **immemor mandātī tuī,** *unmindful of your commission ;*
> **plēna perīculōrum est vīta,** *life is full of dangers.*

> *a.* Some participles used adjectively also take the Genitive; as, —
>> **dīligēns vēritātis,** *fond of truth ;*
>> **amāns patriae,** *devoted to one's country.*

2. Sometimes with **proprius** and **commūnis**; as, —

**virī propria est fortitūdō,** *bravery is characteristic of a man.*
**memoria est commūnis ɔmnium artium,** *memory is common to al!*
*professions.*

    *a.* **proprius** and **commūnis** are also construed with the Dative.

3. With **similis** the Genitive is the commoner construction in Cicero, when the reference is to living objects; as, —

      **fīlius patris simillimus est,** *the sɔɔ is exactly like his father;*
      **meī similis,** *like me;* **vestrī similis,** *like you.*

When the reference is to things, both Genitive and Dative occur : as, —

      **mors somnō** (or **somnī**) **similis est,** *death is like sleep.*

    4. In the poets and later prose writers the use of the Genitive with Adjectives is extended far beyond earlier limits; as, **atrōx animī,** *fierce of temper ;* **incertus cōnsilī,** *undecided in purpose.*

## GENITIVE WITH VERBS.

**205.** The Genitive is used with the following classes of Verbs : —

### *Meminī, Reminīscor, Oblīvīscor.*

**206.** 1. WHEN REFERRING TO PERSONS —

    *a.* **meminī** always takes the Genitive of personal or reflexive pronouns ; as, —

    **meī mineminerīs,** *remember me !*
    **nostrī meminit,** *he remembers us.*

With other words denoting persons **meminī** takes tne Accusative, rarely the Genitive ; as, —

      **Sullam meminī,** *I recall Sulla ;*
      **vīvōrum meminī,** *I remember the living.*

    *b.* **oblīvīscor** regularly takes the Genitive ; as, —
      **Epicūrī nōn licet oblīvīscī,** *we mustn't forget Epicurus.*

    2. WHEN REFERRING TO THINGS, **meminī, reminīscor, oblīvīscor** take sometimes the Genitive, sometimes the Accusative, without difference of meaning ; as, —

    **animus praeteritōrum meminit,** *the mind remembers the past ;*
    **meministīne nōmina,** *do you remember the names ?*
    **reminīscere veteris incommodī,** *remember the former disaster :*
    **reminīscēns acerbitātem,** *remembering the bitterness.*

*a.* But neuter pronouns, and adjectives used substantively, regularly stand in the Accusative; as, —

haec meminī, *I remember this;*
multa reminīscor, *I remember many things.*

3. The phrase mihi (tibi, *etc.*) in mentem venit, following the analogy of meminī, takes the Genitive; as, —

mihi patriae veniēbat in mentem, *I remembered my country.*

### Admoneō, Commoneō, Commonefaciō.

**207.** These verbs, in addition to an Accusative of the person, occasionally take a Genitive of the thing; as, —

tē veteris amīcitiae commonefaciō, *I remind you of our old friendship.*

*a.* But more frequently (in Cicero almost invariably) these verbs take dē with the Ablative; as, —

mē admonēs dē sorōre, *you remind me of your sister.*

*b.* A neuter pronoun or adjective used substantively regularly stands in the Accusative (178. 1. *d*); as, —

tē hōc admoneō, *I give you this warning.*

### Verbs of Judicial Action.

**208.** 1. Verbs of *Accusing, Convicting, Acquitting* take the Genitive of the *charge;* as, —

mē fūrtī accūsat, *he accuses me of theft;*
Verrem avāritiae coarguit, *he convicts Verres of avarice;*
impietātis absolūtus est, *he was acquitted of blasphemy.*

2. Verbs of *Condemning* take —

*a.* The Genitive of the *charge;* as, —

pecūniae pūblicae condemnātus, *condemned (on the charge) of embezzlement* (lit. *public money*);
capitis damnātus, *condemned on a capital charge* (lit. *on a charge involving his head*).

*b.* The Ablative of the *penalty;* as, —

capite damnātus est, *he was condemned to death;*
mīlle nummīs damnātus est, *he was condemned (to pay) a thousand sesterces* (lit. *by a thousand sesterces,* Abl. of Means).

3. Note the phrases : —

vōtī damnātus, vōtī reus, *having attained one's prayer* (lit. *condemned on the score of one's vow*) ;

dē vī, (*accused, convicted, etc.*) *of assault;*

inter sīcāriōs, (*accused, convicted, etc.*) *of murder.*

### Genitive with Impersonal Verbs.

**209.** ʟ. The Impersonals **pudet, paenitet, miseret, taedet, piget** take the Accusative of *the person affected*, along with the Genitive *of the person or thing toward whom the feeling is directed ;* as, —

pudet mē tuī, *I am ashamed of you* (lit. *it shames me of you*) ;
paenitet mē hūjus factī, *I repent of this act ;*
eum taedet vītae, *he is weary of life ;*
pauperum tē miseret, *you pity the poor.*

> *a.* Instead of the Genitive of the thing we often find an Infinitive or Neuter Pronoun used as subject of the verb. Thus : —
>
> mē paenitet hōc fēcisse, *I repent of having done this ;*
> mē hōc pudet, *I am ashamed of this.*

2. **Misereor** and **miserēscō** also govern the Genitive ; as, —
   miserēminī sociōrum, *pity the allies.*

### *Interest, Rēfert.*

**210.** With **interest**, *it concerns*, three points enter into consideration ; *viz.* —

*a*) the *person concerned ;*
*b*) the *thing about which* he is concerned ;
*c*) the *extent* of his concern.

**211.** I. The *person concerned* is regularly denoted by the Genitive ; as, —

patris interest, *it concerns the father.*

> *a.* But instead of the Genitive of the personal pronouns, **meī, tuī, nostri, vestrī,** the Latin uses the Ablative Singular Feminine of the Possessive, *viz.* : **meā, tuā,** *etc.* ; as, —
> meā interest, *it concerns me.*

2. The *thing about which* a person is concerned is denoted —

    *a*) by a Neuter Pronoun as subject; as, —

        **hōc reī pūblicae interest,** *this concerns the state.*

    *b*) by an Infinitive; as, —

        **omnium interest valēre,** *it concerns all to keep well.*

    *c*) by an Indirect Question; as, —

        **meā interest quandō veniās,** *I am concerned as to when you are coming.*

3. The *degree of concern* is denoted —

    *a*) by the Genitive (cf. § 203, 3): **magnī, parvī,** *etc.*; as, —

        **meā magnī interest,** *it concerns me greatly.*

    *b*) by the Adverbs, **magnopere, magis, maximē,** *etc.*; as, —

        **cīvium minimē interest,** *it concerns the citizens very little.*

    *c*) by the Neuters, **multum, plūs, minus,** *etc.*; as, —

        **multum vestrā interest,** *it concerns you much.*

4. **Rēfert** follows **interest** in its construction, except that it rarely takes the Genitive of the person. Thus: —

                **meā rēfert,** *it concerns me;*

but rarely **illīus rēfert,** *it concerns him.*

### Genitive with Other Verbs.

**212.** 1. Verbs of *Plenty* and *Want* sometimes govern the Genitive; as, —

        **pecūniae indigēs,** *you need money.*

    *a.* These verbs more commonly take the Ablative (§ 214, 1); **indigeō** is the only verb which has a preference for the Genitive.

2. **Potior,** though usually followed by the Ablative, sometimes takes the Genitive, almost always so in Sallust; and regularly in the phrase: **potīrī rērum,** *to get control of affairs.*

    3. In poetry some verbs take the Genitive in imitation of the Greek; as, —

        **dēsine querellārum,** *cease your complaints;*

        **operum solūtī,** *freed from their tasks.*

## THE ABLATIVE.

**213.** The Latin Ablative unites in itself three cases which were originally distinct both **in form** and **in meaning**; *viz.* —

> The Ablative or **from**-case.
> The Instrumental or **with**-case.
> The Locative or **where**-case.

The uses of the Latin Ablative accordingly fall into Genuine Ablative uses, Instrumental uses, and Locative uses.

### GENUINE ABLATIVE USES.

#### Ablative of Separation.

**214.** The Ablative of Separation is construed sometimes with, sometimes without, a preposition.

1. The following words regularly take the Ablative without a preposition: —

*a*) The Verbs of *freeing*: **līberō, solvō, levō**;

*b*) The Verbs of *depriving*: **prīvō, spoliō, exuō, fraudō, nūdō**;

*c*) The Verbs of *lacking*: **egeō, careō, vacō**;

*d*) The corresponding Adjectives, **līber, inānis, vacuus, nūdus**, and some others of similar meaning.

> Thus: —
>
> **cūrīs līberātus**, *freed from cares*:
> **Caesar hostēs armīs exuit**, *Caesar stripped the enemy of their arms*;
> **caret sēnsū commūnī**, *he lacks common sense*;
> **auxiliō eget**, *he needs help*;
> **bonōrum vīta vacua est metū**, *the life of the good is free from fear*.

NOTE 1. — Yet Adjectives and **līberō** may take the preposition **ab**, — regularly so with the Ablative of persons; as, —

> **urbem ā tyrannō līberārunt**, *they freed the city from the tyrant.*

NOTE 2. — **Indigeō** usually takes the Genitive. See § 212, 1, *a*.

2. Of Verbs signifying *to keep from, to remove, to withdraw*, some take the preposition, others omit it. The same Verb often admits both constructions. Examples: —

**abstinēre cibō**, *to abstain from food;*
**hostēs fīnibus prohibuērunt**, *they kept the enemy from their borders;*
**praedōnēs ab īnsulā prohibuit**, *he kept the pirates from the island.*

3. Other Verbs of separation usually take the Ablative with a Preposition, particularly compounds of **dis-** and **sē-**; as, —

> **dissentiō ā tē**, *I dissent from you;*
> **sēcernantur ā nōbīs**, *let them be separated from us.*

4. The Preposition is freely omitted in poetry.

### Ablative of Source.

**215.** The Ablative of Source is used with the participles **nātus** and **ortus** (in poetry also with **ēditus, satus**, and some others), to designate *parentage* or *station;* as, —

**Jove nātus**, *son of Jupiter;*
**summō locō nātus**, *high-born* (lit. *born from a very high place*);
**nōbilī genere ortus**, *born of a noble family.*

1. Pronouns regularly (nouns rarely) take **ex**; as,

> **ex mē nātus**, *sprung from me.*

2. To denote remoter descent, **ortus ab**, or **oriundus** (with or without **ab**), is used; as, —

> **ab Ulixe oriundus**, *descended from Ulysses.*

### Ablative of Agent.

**216.** The Ablative accompanied by **ā (ab)** is used with passive verbs to denote the *personal agent;* as, —

> **ā Caesare accūsātus est**, *he was arraigned by Caesar.*

1. Collective nouns referring to persons, and abstract nouns when personified, may be construed as the personal agent. Thus : —

**hostēs ā fortūnā dēserēbantur**, *the enemy were deserted by Fortune;*
**ā multitūdine hostium montēs tenēbantur**, *the mountains were held by a multitude of the enemy.*

2. Names of animals sometimes admit the same construction. Thus: —
> **ā canibus laniātus est**, *he was torn to pieces by dogs.*

### Ablative of Comparison.

**217.** 1. The Ablative is often used with Comparatives in the sense of *than;* as, —

**melle dulcior,** *sweeter than honey;*
**patria mihi vītā cārior est,** *my country is dearer to me than life.*

2. This construction, as a rule, occurs only as a substitute for **quam** (*than*) with the Nominative or Accusative. In other cases **quam** must be used; as, —

**tuī studiōsior sum quam illīus,** *I am fonder of you than of him.*

     **Studiōsior illō** would have meant, *I am fonder of you than he is.*

     **Plūs, minus, amplius, longius** are often employed as the equivalents of **plūs quam, minus quam,** *etc.* Thus : —

**amplius vīgintī urbēs incenduntur,** *more than twenty cities are fired;*
**minus quīnque mīlia prōcessit,** *he advanced less than five miles.*

     3. Note the use of **opīniōne** with Comparatives; as, —
**opīniōne celerius venit,** *he comes more quickly than expected* (lit. *than opinion*).

## INSTRUMENTAL USES OF THE ABLATIVE.

### Ablative of Means.

**218.** The Ablative is used to denote *means* or *instrument;* as, —

**Alexander sagittā vulnerātus est,** *Alexander was wounded by an arrow.*

There are the following special varieties of this Ablative : —

1. **Ūtor, fruor, fungor, potior, vescor,** and their compounds take the Ablative; as, —

**dīvitiīs ūtitur,** *he uses his wealth* (lit. *he benefits himself by his wealth*);
**vītā fruitur,** *he enjoys life* (lit. *he enjoys himself by life*);
**mūnere fungor,** *I perform my duty* (lit. *I busy myself with duty*);
**carne vescuntur,** *they eat flesh* (lit. *feed themselves by means of*);
**castrīs potītus est,** *he got possession of the camp* (lit. *made himself powerful by the camp*).

     *a.* **Potior** sometimes governs the Genitive. See § 212. *a.*

2. With **opus est** (rarely **ūsus est**), *there is need*; as, —
   **duce nōbīs opus est,** *we need a leader*.

   *a.* A Neuter Pronoun or Adjective often stands as subject with
   **opus** as predicate. Thus: —
   **hōc mihi opus est,** *this is necessary for me*.

   *b.* An ordinary substantive rarely stands as subject. Thus **dux
   nōbīs opus est** is a rare form of expression.

   *c.* Note the occasional use of a perfect passive participle with **opus est**;
   as, —
   **opus est properātō,** *there is need of haste*.

3. With **nītor, innīxus,** and **frētus**; as, —
   **nītitur hastā,** *he rests on a spear* (lit. *supports himself by a spear*);
   **frētus virtūte,** *relying on virtue* (lit. *supported by virtue*).

4. With **continērī, cōnsistere, cōnstāre,** *consist of*; as, —
   **nervīs et ossibus continentur,** *they consist of sinews and bones* (lit.
   *they are held together by sinews and bones*);
   **mortālī cōnsistit corpore mundus,** *the world consists of mortal substance* (lit. *holds together by means of, etc.*).

6. In expressions of the following type: —
   **quid hōc homine faciās,** *what can you do with this man?*
   **quid meā Tulliolā fīet,** *what will become of my dear Tullia?* (lit. *what
   will be done with my dear Tullia?*)

7. In the following special phrases at variance with the ordinary
   English idiom: —
   **proeliō contendere, vincere,** *to contend, conquer in battle;*
   **proeliō lacessere,** *to provoke to battle;*
   **currū vehī,** *to ride in a chariot;*
   **pedibus īre,** *to go on foot;*
   **castrīs sē tenēre,** *to keep in camp*.

8. With Verbs of *filling* and Adjectives of *plenty*; as, —
   **fossās virgultīs complērunt,** *they filled the trenches with brush*.

   *a.* But **plēnus** more commonly takes the Genitive. See § 204, 1.

9. Under 'Means' belongs also the Ablative of the Way by
   Which; as, —
   **vīnum Tiberī dēvectum,** *wine brought down (by) the Tiber.*

10. The means may be a person as well as a thing. Thus: —

**mīlitibus ā lacū Lemannō ad montem Jūram mūrum perdūcit,** *with* (*i.e.* by means of) *his troops he runs a wall from Lake Geneva to Mt. Jura.*

### Ablative of Cause.

**219.** The Ablative is used to denote *cause ;* as, —

**multa glōriae cupiditāte fēcit,** *he did many things on account of his love of glory.*

1. So especially with verbs denoting mental states ; as, **dēlector, gāudeō, laetor, glōrior, fīdō, cōnfīdō.** Also with **contentus ;** as, —

**fortūnā amīcī gaudeō,** *I rejoice at the fortune of my friend (i.e. on account of it)* ;

**victōriā suā glōriantur,** *they exult over their victory* ;

**nātūrā locī cōnfīdēbant,** *they trusted in the character of their country* (lit. *were confident on account of the character*).

   *a.* **fīdō** and **cōnfīdō** always take the Dative of the person (§ 187. II. *a*) ; sometimes the Dative of the thing.

2. As Ablatives of Cause are to be reckoned also such Ablatives as **jussū,** *by order of,* **injussū,** *without the order,* **rogātū,** *etc.*

### Ablative of Manner.

**220.** The Ablative with **cum** is used to denote *manner ;* as, —

   **cum gravitāte loquitur,** *he speaks with dignity.*

1. The preposition may be absent when the Ablative is modified by an adjective ; as, —

   **magnā gravitāte loquitur,** *he speaks with great dignity.*

2. The preposition is regularly absent in the expressions **jūre, injūriā, jocō, vī, fraude, voluntāte, fūrtō, silentiō.**

3. A special variety of the Ablative of Manner denotes that *in accordance with which* or *in pursuance of which* anything is or is done. It is generally used without a preposition. Thus : —

   **meā sententiā,** *according to my opinion* ;
   **suīs mōribus,** *in accordance with their custom* ;
   **suā sponte,** *voluntarily, of his (their) own accord* ;
   **eā condiciōne,** *on these terms.*

### Ablative of Attendant Circumstance.

**221.** The Ablative is often used to denote an *attendant circumstance* of an action or an event; as, —

bonīs auspiciīs, *under good auspices*;

nūlla est altercātiō clāmōribus umquam habita majōribus, *no debate was ever held under circumstances of greater applause*;

exstinguitur ingentī lūctū prōvinciae, *he dies under circumstances of great grief on the part of the province*;

longō intervāllō sequitur, *he follows at a great distance.*

### Ablative of Accompaniment.

**222.** The Ablative with **cum** is used with verbs of motion to denote *accompaniment*; as, —

cum comitibus profectus est, *he set out with his attendants*;

cum febrī domum rediit, *he returned home with a fever.*

1. In military expressions the Ablative may stand without **cum** when modified by any adjective except a numeral; as, —

omnibus cōpiīs, ingentī exercitū, magnā manū; but usually **cum exercitū, cum duābus legiōnibus.**

### Ablative of Association.

**222 A.** The Ablative is often used with verbs of *joining, mixing, clinging, exchanging*; also with assuēscō, cōnsuēscō, assuēfaciō, and some others to denote *association*; as, —

improbitās scelere jūncta, *badness joined with crime*;

āēr calōre admixtus, *air mixed with heat*;

assuētus labōre, *accustomed to* (lit. *familiarized with*) *toil*;

pācem bellō permūtant, *they change peace for* (lit. *with*) *war.*

### Ablative of Degree of Difference.

**223.** The Ablative is used with comparatives and words involving comparison (as **post, ante, īnfrā, suprā**) to denote the *degree of difference*; as, —

dīmidiō minor, *smaller by a half*;

tribus pedibus altior, *three feet higher*;

paulō post, *a little afterwards*;

quō plūrā habēmus, eō cupimus ampliōra, *the more we have, the more we want.*

### Ablative of Quality.

**224.** The Ablative, modified by an adjective, is used to denote *quality;* as, —

> puella eximiā fōrmā, *a girl of exceptional beauty ;*
> vir singulārī industriā, *a man of singular industry.*

1. The Ablative of Quality may also be used predicatively; as, —
    est magnā prūdentiā, *he is (a man) of great wisdom ;*
    bonō animō sunt, *they are of good courage.*

2. In place of the Adjective we sometimes find a limiting Genitive ; as, —
sunt speciē et colōre taurī, *they are of the appearance and color of a bull.*

3. In poetry the Ablative of Quality sometimes denotes *material ;* as, —
    scopulīs pendentibus antrum, *a cave of arching rocks.*

### Ablative of Price.

**225.** With verbs of *buying* and *selling*, price is designated by the Ablative ; as —
servum quīnque minīs ēmit, *he bought the slave for five minae.*

1. The Ablatives magnō, plūrimō, parvō, minimō (by omission of pretiō) are used to denote *indefinite price ;* as, —
    aedēs magnō vēndidit, *he sold the house for a high price.*

2. For the Genitive of Indefinite Price, see § 203. 4.

### Ablative of Specification.

**226.** The Ablative of Specification is used to denote that *in respect to which* something is or is done ; as, —
Helvētiī omnibus Gallīs virtūte praestābant, *the Helvetians surpassed all the Gauls in valor ;*
pede claudus, *lame in his foot.*

1. Note the phrases : —
    major nātū, *older* (lit. *greater as to age*) ;
    minor nātū, *younger.*

2. Here belongs the use of the Ablative with dignus, *worthy,* indignus, *unworthy,* and dignor, *deem worthy of ;* as, —
    dignī honōre, *worthy of honor (i.e. in point of honor) ;*
    fidē indignī, *unworthy of confidence ;*
    mē dignor honōre, *I deem myself worthy of honor.*

### Ablative Absolute.

**227.** The Ablative Absolute is grammatically independent of the rest of the sentence. In its commonest form it consists of a noun or pronoun limited by a participle ; as, —

**urbe captā, Aenēās fūgit,** *when the city had been captured, Aeneas fled* (lit. *the city having been captured*).

1. Instead of a participle we often find an adjective or noun; as, —

**vīvō Caesare rēs pūblica salva erat,** *while Caesar was alive the state was safe* (lit. *Caesar being alive*) ;

**Tarquiniō rēge, Pȳthagorās in Italiam vēnit,** *in the reign of Tarquin Pythagoras came into Italy* (lit. *Tarquin being king*) ;

**Cn. Pompejō, M. Crassō cōnsulibus,** *in the consulship of Gnaeus Pompey and Marcus Crassus* (lit. *P. and C. being consuls*).

2. The Ablative Absolute is generally used in Latin where in English we employ subordinate clauses. Thus the Ablative Absolute may correspond to a clause denoting —

*a*) Time, as in the foregoing examples.

*b*) Condition; as, —
**omnēs virtūtēs jacent, voluptāte dominante,** *all virtues lie prostrate, if pleasure is master.*

*c*) Opposition; as, —
**perditīs omnibus rēbus, virtūs sē sustentāre potest,** *though everything else is lost, yet Virtue can maintain herself.*

*d*) Cause; as, —
**nūllō adversante rēgnum obtinuit,** *since no one opposed him, he secured the throne.*

*e*) Attendant circumstance; as, —
**passīs palmīs pācem petīvērunt,** *with hands outstretched, they sued for peace.*

3. An Infinitive or clause sometimes occurs in the Ablative Absolute construction, especially in Livy and later writers ; as, —
**audītō eum fūgisse,** *when it was heard that he had fled.*

4. A noun or pronoun stands in the Ablative Absolute construction only when it denotes a different person or thing from any in the clause in which it stands. Exceptions to this principle are extremely rare.

## LOCATIVE USES OF THE ABLATIVE.

### Ablative of Place.

*A. Place where.*

**228.** The place where is regularly denoted by the *Ab lative with a preposition ;* as, —

> **in urbe habitat,** *he dwells in the city.*

1. But certain words stand in the Ablative without a preposition; *viz.* —

    *a*) Names of towns, — except Singulars of the First and Second Declensions (see § 232. 1) ; as, —

> **Carthāginī,** *at Carthage ;*
> **Athēnīs,** *at Athens ;*
> **Vejīs,** *at Veii.*

    *b*) The general words **locō, locīs, parte**; also many words modified by **tōtus** or even by other Adjectives; as, —

> **hōc locō,** *at this place ;*
> **tōtīs castrīs,** *in the whole camp.*

    *c*) The special words : **forīs,** *out of doors ;* **rūrī,** *in the country ;* **terrā marīque,** *on land and sea.*

    *d*) The poets freely omit the preposition with any word denoting place ; as, —

> **stant lītore puppēs,** *the sterns rest on the beach.*

*B. Place from which.*[1]

**229.** Place from which is regularly denoted by the *Ablative with a preposition :* as, —

> **ab Italiā profectus est,** *he set out from Italy ;*
> **ex urbe rediit,** *he returned from the city.*

1. But certain words stand in the Ablative without a preposition; *viz.* —

    *a*) Names of towns and small islands ; as, —
> **Rōmā profectus est,** *he set out from Rome ;*
> **Rhodō revertit,** *he returned from Rhodes.*

---

[1] Place from which, though strictly a Genuine Ablative use, is treated here for sake of convenience.

*b*) **domō**, *from home;* **rūre**, *from the country.*

*c*) Freely in poetry; as, —

    **Italiā dēcessit,** *he withdrew from Italy.*

2. With names of towns, **ab** is used to mean *from the vicinity of,* or to denote the point *whence distance is measured;* as, —

    **ā Gergoviā discessit,** *he withdrew from the vicinity of Gergovia;*
    **ā Rōmā X mīlia aberat,** *he was ten miles distant from Rome.*

**Urbe** and **oppidō**, when standing in apposition with a town name, are accompanied by a preposition; as, —

    **Curibus ex oppidō Sabīnōrum,** *from Cures, a town of the Sabines.*

### Ablative of Time.

#### A. Time at which.

**230.** The Ablative is used to denote the time *at which;* as, —

**quārtā hōrā mortuus est,** *he died at the fourth hour;*
**annō septuāgēsimō cōnsul creātus,** *elected consul in his seventieth year.*

1. Any word denoting a period of time may stand in this construction, particularly **annus, vēr, aestās, hiems, diēs, nox, hōra, comitia** (*Election Day*), **lūdī** (*the Games*), *etc.*

2. Words not denoting time require the preposition **in**, unless accompanied by a modifier. Thus: —

        **in pāce,** *in peace;*         **in bellō,** *in war;*
but       **secundō bellō Pūnicō,** *in the second Punic War.*

3. Expressions like **in eō tempore, in summā senectūte**, take the preposition because they denote *situation* rather than *time.*

#### B. Time within which.

**231.** Time *within which* is denoted by the Ablative either *with* or *without a preposition;* as, —

**stella Sāturnī trīgintā annīs cursum cōnficit,** *the planet Saturn completes its orbit within thirty years;*
**ter in annō,** *thrice in the course of the year.*

1. Occasionally the Ablative denotes *duration of time;* as, —
**bienniō prōsperās rēs habuit,** *for two years he had a prosperous administration.*

## THE LOCATIVE.

**232**. The Locative case occurs chiefly in the following words : —

1. Regularly in the Singular of names of towns and small islands of the first and second declensions, to denote the place *in which* ; as, —

> **Rōmae**, *at Rome;*　　　**Corinthī**, *at Corinth;*
> **Rhodī**, *at Rhodes.*

2. In the following special forms : —

> **domī**, *at home;*　　　**humī**, *on the ground;*
> **bellī**, *in war;*　　　**mīlitiae**, *in war;*
> **vesperī**, *at evening;*　　**herī**, *yesterday.*

3. Note the phrase **pendēre animī**, lit. *to be in suspense in one's mind.*

4. For **urbs** and **oppidum** in apposition with a Locative, see § 169. 4.

——◆——

## CHAPTER III. — *Syntax of Adjectives.*

**233**. 1. The word with which an Adjective agrees is called its Subject.

2. **Attributive and Predicate Adjectives.** An Attributive Adjective is one that limits its subject directly ; as, —

> **vir sapiēns,** *a wise man.*

A Predicate Adjective is one that limits its subject through the medium of a verb (usually **esse**) ; as, —

> **vir est sapiēns**, *the man is wise;*
> **vir vidēbātur sapiēns**, *the man seemed wise;*
> **vir jūdicātus est sapiēns**, *the man was judged wise;*
> **hunc virum sapientem jūdicāvimus**, *we adjudged this man wise.*

3. Participles and Adjective Pronouns have the construction of Adjectives.

## AGREEMENT OF ADJECTIVES.

**234.** **Agreement with One Noun.** When an Adjective limits one noun it agrees with it in Gender, Number, and Case.

1. Two Adjectives in the Singular may limit a noun in the Plural; as, **prīma et vīcēsima legiōnēs,** *the first and twentieth legions.*

2. A Predicate Adjective may stand in the Neuter when its Subject is Masculine or Feminine and denotes a thing; as, —

**omnium rērum mors est extrēmum,** *death is the end of all things.*

**235.** **Agreement with Two or More Nouns.**

### *A.* AGREEMENT AS TO NUMBER.

1. When the Adjective is Attributive, it regularly agrees in number with the nearest noun; as, —

> **pater tuus et māter,** *your father and mother;*
> **eadem alacritās et studium,** *the same eagerness and zeal.*

2. When the Adjective is Predicative, it is regularly Plural; as, —

**pāx et concordia sunt pulchrae,** *peace and concord are glorious.*

### *B.* AGREEMENT AS TO GENDER.

1. When the Adjective is Attributive, it regularly agrees in gender with the nearest noun; as, —

**rēs operae multae ac labōris,** *a matter of much effort and labor.*

2. When the Adjective is Predicative —

> *a)* If the nouns are of the same gender, the Adjective agrees with them in gender; as, —
> **pater et fīlius captī sunt,** *father and son were captured.*
>
> Yet with feminine abstract nouns, the Adjective is more frequently Neuter; as, —
> **stultitia et timidītās fugienda sunt,** *folly and cowardice must be shunned.*

*b*) If the nouns are of different gender; then, —

    *α*) In case they denote persons. the Adjective is Masculine: as, —

**pater et māter mortuī sunt,** *the father and mother have died.*

    *β*) In case they denote things, the Adjective is Neuter; as, —

**honōrēs et victōriae fortuīta sunt,** *honors and victories are accidental.*

    *γ*) In case they include both persons and things, the Adjective is, —

        *αα*) Sometimes Masculine; as, —

**domus, uxor, līberī inventī sunt,** *home, wife, and children are secured.*

        *ββ*) Sometimes Neuter; as, —

**parentēs, līberōs, domōs vīlia habēre,** *to hold parents, children, houses cheap..*

        *γγ*) Sometimes it agrees with the nearest noun; as, —

**populī prōvinciaeque līberātae sunt,** *nations and provinces were liberated.*

*c*) **Construction according to Sense.** Sometimes an Adjective does not agree with a noun according to strict grammatical form, but according to sense; as, —

**pars bēstiīs objectī sunt,** *part (of the men) were thrown to beasts.*

### ADJECTIVES USED SUBSTANTIVELY.

**236.** I. PLURAL ADJECTIVES USED SUBSTANTIVELY. Adjectives are quite freely used as Substantives in the Plural. The Masculine denotes persons; the Neuter denotes things; as, —

| | |
|---|---|
| **doctī,** *scholars;* | **parva,** *small things;* |
| **malī,** *the wicked;* | **magna,** *great things;* |
| **Graecī,** *the Greeks;* | **ūtilia,** *useful things;* |
| | **nostrī,** *our men.* |

2. Neuter Plural Adjectives thus used are confined mainly to the Nominative and Accusative cases. Such forms as **magnōrum, om·nium**; **magnīs, omnibus**, would ordinarily lead to ambiguity; yet where there is no ambiguity, they sometimes occur; as, —

**parvīs compōnere magna,** *to compare great things with small.*

Otherwise the Latin says: **magnārum rērum, magnīs rēbus,** *etc.*

**237.** SINGULAR ADJECTIVES USED SUBSTANTIVELY. Adjectives are less freely used as Substantives in the Singular than in the Plural.

1. Masculine Adjectives occur only occasionally in this use; as, — **probus invidet nēminī,** *the honest man envies nobody.*

> *a.* Usually **vir, homō,** or some similar word is employed; as, —
>> **homō doctus,** *a scholar;*
>> **vir Rōmānus,** *a Roman.*

> *b.* But when limited by a pronoun any adjective may be so used; as, —
>> **hīc doctus,** *this scholar;*
>> **doctus quīdam,** *a certain scholar.*

2. Neuters are likewise infrequent; as, —
>> **vērum,** *truth;*
>> **jūstum,** *justice;*
>> **honestum,** *virtue.*

> *a.* This substantive use of Neuter Singulars is commonest in the construction of the Genitive of the Whole, and after Prepositions; as, —
>> **aliquid vērī,** *something true;*
>> **nihil novī,** *nothing new;*
>> **in mediō,** *in the midst.*

**238.** From Adjectives which, like the above, occasionally admit the substantive use, must be carefully distinguished certain others which have become nouns; as, —

| | |
|---|---|
| **adversārius,** *cpponent*; | **hīberna,** *winter quarters*; |
| **aequālis,** *contemporary*; | **propinquus,** *relative*: |
| **amīcus,** *friend*; | **socius,** *partner*; |
| **cognātus,** *kinsman*; | **sodālis,** *comrade*; |

**vīcīnus,** *neighbor; etc.*

## ADJECTIVES WITH THE FORCE OF ADVERBS.

**239.** The Latin often uses an Adjective where the English idiom employs an Adverb or an adverbial phrase; as, —

senātus frequēns convēnit, *the senate assembled in great numbers;* fuit assiduus mēcum, *he was constantly with me.*

### COMPARATIVES AND SUPERLATIVES.

**240.** 1. The Comparative often corresponds to the English Positive with '*rather*,' '*somewhat*,' '*too*'; as, —

senectūs est loquācior, *old age is rather talkative.*

2. So the Superlative often corresponds to the Positive with '*very*'; as, —

vir fortissimus, *a very brave man.*

3. **Strengthening Words.** Vel and quam are often used with the Superlative as strengthening particles, vel with the force of '*very*,' and quam with the force of '*as possible*'; as, —

vel maximus, *the very greatest;*
quam maximae cōpiae, *as great forces as possible.*

4. Phrases of the type '*more rich than brave*' regularly take the Comparative in both members; as, —

exercitus erat dītior quam fortior, *the army was more rich than brave.*

### OTHER PECULIARITIES.

**241.** 1. Certain Adjectives may be used to denote *a part of an object,* chiefly prīmus, extrēmus, summus, medius, īnfimus, īmus; as, —

summus mōns, *the top of the mountain;*
extrēmā hieme, *in the last part of the winter.*

2. Prior, prīmus, ultimus, and postrēmus are frequently equivalent to a relative clause; as, —

prīmus eam vīdī, *I was the first who saw her;*
ultimus dēcessit, *he was the last who withdrew.*

3. When multus and another adjective both limit the same noun, et is generally used; as, —

multae et magnae cōgitātiōnēs, *many (and) great thoughts.*

## Chapter IV. — *Syntax of Pronouns.*

### PERSONAL PRONOUNS.

**242.** 1. The Personal Pronouns as subjects of verbs are, as a rule, not expressed except for the purpose of *emphasis, contrast,* or *clearness.* Thus ordinarily : —

> **videō,** *I see ;* **amat,** *he loves.*

But **ego tē videō, et tū mē vidēs,** *I see you, and you see me.*

2. The Genitives **meī, tuī, nostrī, vestrī** are used only as Objective Genitives ; **nostrum** and **vestrum** as Genitives of the Whole. Thus : —

> **memor tuī,** *mindful of you ;*
> **dēsīderium vestrī,** *longing for you ;*
> **nēmō vestrum,** *no one of you.*

> *a.* But **nostrum** and **vestrum** are regularly used in the place of the Possessive in the phrases **omnium nostrum, omnium vestrum.**

3. The First Plural is often used for the First Singular of Pronouns and Verbs. Compare the Eng. editorial 'we.'

4. When two Verbs govern the same object, the Latin does not use a pronoun with the second, as is the rule in English. Thus : —

> **virtūs amīcitiās conciliat et cōnservat,** *virtue establishes friendships and maintains them* (not **eās cōnservat**).

### POSSESSIVE PRONOUNS.

**243.** 1. The Possessive Pronouns, as a rule, are not employed except for the purpose of *clearness.* Thus :—

> **patrem amō,** *I love my father ;*
> **dē fīliī morte flēbās,** *you wept for the death of your son.*

But —

> **dē morte fīliī meī flēbās,** *you wept for the death of my son.*

> *a.* When expressed merely for the sake of clearness, the possessive usually stands after its noun ; but in order to indicate emphasis or contrast, it precedes ; as, —
>
> > **suā manū līberōs occīdit,** *with his own hand he slew his children ;*
> > **meā quidem sententiā,** *in my opinion at least.*

2. Sometimes the Possessive Pronouns are used with the force of an Objective Genitive; as, —

> metus vester, *fear of you*;
> dēsīderium tuum, *longing for you.*

3. For special emphasis, the Latin employs ipsīus or ipsōrum, in apposition with the Genitive idea implied in the Possessive; as, —

> meā ipsīus operā, *by my own help*;
> nostrā ipsōrum operā, *by our own help*;

    *a.* So sometimes other Genitives; as, —

> meā ūnīus operā, *by the assistance of me alone.*

### REFLEXIVE PRONOUNS.

**244.** 1. The Reflexive Pronoun sē and the Possessive Reflexive suus have a double use: —

I. They may refer to the subject of the clause (either principal or subordinate) in which they stand, — 'Direct Reflexives'; as, —

> sē amant, *they love themselves*;
> suōs amīcōs adjuvāt, *he helps his own friends*;
> eum ōrāvī, ut sē servāret, *I besought him to save himself.*

II. They may stand in a subordinate clause and refer to the subject of the principal clause, — 'Indirect Reflexives'; as, —

mē ōrāvit ut sē dēfenderem, *he besought me to defend him* (lit. *that I defend himself*);

mē ōrāvērunt, ut fortūnārum suārum dēfēnsiōnem susciperem, *they besought me to undertake the defense of their fortunes.*

    *a.* The Indirect Reflexive is mainly restricted to those clauses which express the thought, not of the author, but of the subject of the principal clause.

2. The Genitive suī is regularly employed, like meī and tuī, as an Objective Genitive, *e.g.* oblītus suī, *forgetful of himself*; but it occasionally occurs — particularly in post-Augustan writers — in place of the Possessive suus; as, fruitur fāmā suī, *he enjoys his own fame.*

3. Sē and suus are sometimes used in the sense, *one's self, one's own*, where the reference is not to any particular person; as, —

> sē amāre, *to love one's self*;
> suum genium propitiāre, *to propitiate one's own genius.*

4. **Suus** sometimes occurs in the meaning *his own, their own, etc.*, referring not to the subject but to an oblique case ; as, —

**Hannibalem suī cīvēs ē cīvitāte ējēcērunt,** *his own fellow-citizens drove out Hannibal.*

> *a.* This usage is particularly frequent in combination with **quisque** ; as, —
>
> **suus quemque error vexat,** *his own error troubles each.*

5. The Reflexives for the first and second persons are supplied by the oblique cases of **ego** and **tū** (§ 85) ; as, —

> **vōs dēfenditis,** *you defend yourselves.*

## RECIPROCAL PRONOUNS.

**245**. 1. The Latin has no special reciprocal pronoun (*'each other'*), but expresses the reciprocal notion by the phrases : **inter nōs, inter vōs, inter sē** ; as, —

**Belgae obsidēs inter sē dedērunt,** *the Belgae gave each other hostages* (lit. *among themselves*);

**amāmus inter nōs,** *we love each other ;*

**Gallī inter sē cohortātī sunt,** *the Gauls exhorted each other.*

> *a.* Note that the Object is not expressed in sentences of this type.

## DEMONSTRATIVE PRONOUNS.

### Hīc, Ille, Iste.

**246**. 1. Where **hīc** and **ille** are used in contrast, **hīc** usually refers to the latter of two objects, and **ille** to the former.

2. **Hīc** and **ille** are often used in the sense of '*the following*' ; as, —

**Themistoclēs hīs verbīs epistulam mīsit,** *Themistocles sent a letter (couched) in the following words ;*

**illud intellegō, omnium ōra in mē conversa esse,** *I understand this, that the faces of all are turned toward me.*

3. **Ille** often means *the famous* ; as, **Solōn ille,** *the famous Solon.*

4. **Iste** frequently involves contempt ; as, **iste homō,** *that fellow !*

5. The above pronouns, along with **is**, are usually attracted to the gender of a predicate noun ; as, **hīc est honor, meminisse officium suum,** *this is an honor, to be mindful of one's duty.*

## Is.

**247.** 1. **Is** often serves as the antecedent of the relative **quī**. Thus: —

**Maximum, eum quī Tarentum recēpit, dīlēxī,** *I loved Maximus, the man who retook Tarentum.*

> *a.* Closely akin to this usage is **is** in the sense of *such* ( = **tālis**) ; as, —
>
>> **nōn sum is quī terrear,** *I am not such a person as to be frightened.*
>
> *b.* Note the phrase **id quod**, where **id** stands in apposition with an entire clause ; as, —
>
>> **nōn suspicābātur (id quod nunc sentiet) satis multōs testēs nōbīs reliquōs esse,** *he did not suspect (a thing which he will now perceive) that we had witnesses enough left.*
>
> Yet **quod** alone, without preceding **id**, sometimes occurs in this use.

2. **Is** also in all cases serves as the personal pronoun of the third person, '*he*,' '*she*,' '*it*,' '*they*,' '*them*.'

3. When the English uses '*that of*,' '*those of*,' to avoid repetition of the noun, the Latin omits the pronoun ; as, —

**in exercitū Sullae et posteā in Crassī fuerat,** *he had been in the army of Sulla and afterward in that of Crassus ;*

**nūllae mē fābulae dēlectant nisi Plautī,** *no plays delight me except those of Plautus.*

4. Note the phrases **et is, et ea,** *etc.*, in the sense : *and that too* ; as,—
**vincula, et ea sempiterna,** *imprisonment, and that too permanently.*

## Īdem.

**248.** 1. **Īdem** in apposition with the subject or object often has the force of *also, likewise* ; as, —

**quod idem mihi contigit,** *which likewise happened to me* (lit. *which the same thing*) ;

**bonus vir, quem eundem sapientem appellāmus,** *a good man, whom we call also wise.*

For **īdem atque (ac),** *the same as,* see § 341. 1. *c.*

### Ipse.

**249.** 1. **Ipse**, literally *self*, acquires its special force from the context; as, —

eō ipsō diē, *on that very day*;
ad ipsam rīpam, *close to the bank*;
ipsō terrōre, *by mere fright*;
valvae sē ipsae aperuērunt, *the doors opened of their own accord*,
ipse aderat, *he was present in person.*

2. The reflexive pronouns are often emphasized by the addition of **ipse**, but **ipse** in such cases, instead of standing in apposition with the reflexive, more commonly agrees with the subject; as, —

sēcum ipsī loquuntur, *they talk with themselves*;
sē ipse continēre nōn potest, *he cannot contain himself.*

3. **Ipse** is also used as an Indirect Reflexive for the purpose of *marking a contrast* or *avoiding an ambiguity*; as, —

Persae pertimuērunt nē Alcibiadēs ab ipsīs dēscīsceret et cum suīs in grātiam redīret, *the Persians feared that Alcibiades would break with them and become reconciled with his countrymen.*
ea molestissimē ferre dēbent hominēs quae ipsōrum culpā contrācta sunt, *men ought to chafe most over those things which have been brought about by their own fault* (as opposed to the fault of others).

### RELATIVE PRONOUNS.

**250.** **Agreement.** 1. The Relative Pronoun agrees with its antecedent in Gender, Number, and Person, but its case is determined by its construction in the clause in which it stands; as, —

mulier quam vidēbāmus, *the woman whom we saw*;
bona quibus fruimur, *the blessings which we enjoy.*

2. Where the antecedent is compound, the same principles for number and gender prevail as in case of predicate adjectives under similar conditions (see § 235. *B.* 2). Thus : —

pater et fīlius, qui captī sunt, *the father and son who were captured*;
stultitia et timiditās quae fugienda sunt, *folly and cowardice which must be shunned*;
honōrēs et victōriae quae sunt fortuīta, *honors and victories, which are accidental.*

3. The Relative regularly agrees with a predicate noun (either Nominative or Accusative) instead of its antecedent ; as, —

**carcer, quae lautumiae vocantur,** *the prison, which is called Lautumiae ;*

**Belgae, quae est tertia pars,** *the Belgians, who are the third part.*

4. Sometimes the Relative takes its gender and number from the meaning of its antecedent ; as, —

**pars quī bēstiīs objectī sunt,** *a part (of the men) who were thrown to beasts.*

5. Occasionally the Relative is attracted into the case of its antecedent ; as, —

**nātus eō patre quō dīxī,** *born of the father that I said.*

**251. Antecedent.** 1. The antecedent of the Relative is sometimes omitted ; as, —

**quī nātūram sequitur sapiēns est,** *he who follows Nature is wise.*

2. The antecedent may be implied in a possessive pronoun (or rarely an adjective) ; as, —

**nostra quī remānsimus caedēs,** *the slaughter of us who remained ;*

**servīlī tumultū, quōs ūsus ac disciplīna sublevārunt,** *at the uprising of the slaves, whom experience and discipline assisted* (**servīlī = servōrum**).

3. Sometimes the antecedent is repeated with the Relative ; as, —

**erant itinera duo, quibus itineribus,** *there were two routes, by which (routes).*

4. **Incorporation of Antecedent in Relative Clause.** The antecedent is often incorporated in the relative clause. Thus : —

  *a)* When the relative clause stands first ; as, —

   **quam quisque nōvit artem, in hāc sē exerceat,** *let each one practice the branch which he knows.*

  *b)* When the antecedent is an appositive ; as, —

   **nōn longē ā Tolōsātium fīnibus absunt, quae cīvitās est in prōvinciā,** *they are not far from the borders of the Tolosates, a state which is in our province.*

  *c)* When the logical antecedent is a superlative ; as, —

   **Themistoclēs dē servīs suīs, quem habuit fidēlissimum, mīsit,** *Themistocles sent the most trusty slave he had.*

*d*) In expressions of the following type —

quā es prūdentiā ; quae tua est prūdentia, *such is your prudence* (lit. *of which prudence you are ; which is your prudence*).

5. The Relative is never omitted in Latin as it is in English.   Thus *the boy I saw* must be **puer quem vīdī**.

6. The Relative is used freely in Latin, particularly at the beginning of a sentence, where in English we employ a demonstrative; as, —

quō factum est, *by this it happened ;*
quae cum ita sint, *since this is so ;*
quibus rēbus cognitīs, *when these things became known.*

7. The Relative introducing a subordinate clause may belong grammatically to a clause which is subordinate to the one it introduces; as, —

numquam dignē satis laudārī philosophia poterit, cui quī pāreat, omne tempus aetātis sine molestiā possit dēgere, *philosophy can never be praised enough, since he who obeys her can pass every period of life without annoyance* (lit. *he who obeys which, etc.*).

Here **cui** introduces the subordinate clause **possit** and connects it with **philosophia**; but **cui** is governed by **pāreat**, which is subordinate to **possit**.

### INDEFINITE PRONOUNS.

**252.**  1.  **Quis**, *any one*, is the weakest of the Indefinites, and stands usually in combination with **sī, nisi, nē, num** ; as, —

sī quis putat, *if any one thinks.*

2. **Aliquis** (adj. **aliquī**) is more definite than **quis**, and corresponds usually to the English *some one, somebody, some* ; as, —

nunc aliquis dīcat mihi, *now let somebody tell me ;*
utinam modo agātur aliquid, *oh that something may be done.*

3. **Quīdam**, *a certain one*, is still more definite than **aliquis** ; as, —

homō quīdam, *a certain man (i.e. one whom I have in mind).*

  *a.* **Quīdam** (with or without **quasi**, *as if*) is sometimes used in the sense: *a sort of, kind of* ; as, —
  cognātiō quaedam, *a sort of relationship ;*
  mors est quasi quaedam migrātiō, *death is a kind of transfer, as it were.*

4. **Quisquam**, *any one, any one whoever* (more general than **quis**), and its corresponding adjective **ūllus**, *any*, occur mostly in negative and conditional sentences, in interrogative sentences implying a negative, and in clauses of comparison; as, —

**jūstitia numquam nocet cuiquam**, *justice never harms anybody;*
**sī quisquam, Catō sapiēns fuit**, *if anybody was ever wise, Cato was;*
**potestne quisquam sine perturbātiōne animī īrāscī**, *can anybody be angry without excitement?*
**sī ūllō modō poterit**, *if it can be done in any way;*
**taetrior hīc tyrannus fuit quam quisquam superiōrum**, *he was a viler tyrant than any of his predecessors.*

5. **Quisque**, *each one*, is used especially under the following circumstances: —

    *a)* In connection with **suus**. See § 244. 4. *a*.

    *b)* In connection with a Relative or Interrogative Pronoun; as, —

        **quod cuique obtigit, id teneat**, *what falls to each, that let him hold.*

    *c)* In connection with superlatives; as, —

        **optimus quisque**, *all the best* (lit. *each best one*).

    *d)* With ordinal numerals; as, —

        **quīntō quōque annō**, *every four years* (lit. *each fifth year*).

6. **Nēmō**, *no one*, in addition to its other uses, stands regularly with adjectives used substantively; as, —

        **nēmō mortālis**, *no mortal;*
        **nēmō Rōmānus**, *no Roman.*

## PRONOMINAL ADJECTIVES.

**253.** 1. **Alius**, *another*, and **alter**, *the other*, are often used correlatively; as, —

**aliud loquitur, aliud sentit**, *he says one thing, he thinks another;*
**aliī resistunt, aliī fugiunt**, *some resist, others flee;*
**alter exercitum perdidit, alter vēndidit**, *one ruined the army, the other sold it;*
**alterī sē in montem recēpērunt, alterī ad impedīmenta sē contulērunt**, *the one party retreated to the mountain, the others betook themselves to the baggage.*

2. Where the English says *one does one thing, another another*, the Latin uses a more condensed form of statement; as, —

> **alius aliud amat**, *one likes one thing, another another* ;
> **aliud aliīs placet**, *one thing pleases some, another others.*

> *a.* So sometimes with adverbs; as, —
> > **aliī aliō fugiunt**, *some flee in one direction, others in another.*

3. The Latin also expresses the notion '*each other*' by means of **alius** repeated; as, —

**Gallī alius alium cohortātī sunt**, *the Gauls encouraged each other.*

4. **Cēterī** means *the rest, all the others* ; as, —

> **cēterīs praestāre**, *to be superior to all the others.*

5. **Reliquī** means *the others* in the sense of *the rest, those remaining,* — hence is the regular word with numerals ; as, —

> > **reliquī sex**, *the six others.*

6. **Nescio quis** forms a compound indefinite pronoun with the force of *some one or other* ; as, —

> **causidicus nescio quis**, *some pettifogger or other* ;
> **mīsit nescio quem**, *he sent some one or other* ;
> **nescio quō pactō**, *somehow or other.*

---

# CHAPTER V. — *Syntax of Verbs.*

## AGREEMENT.

### With One Subject.

**254.** I. **Agreement in Number and Person.** A Finite Verb agrees with its subject in Number and Person ; as, —

> **vōs vidētis**, *you see* ;
> **pater fīliōs īnstituit**, *the father trains his sons.*

2. **Agreement in Gender.** In the compound forms of the verb the participle regularly agrees with its subject in gender ; as, —

> **sēditiō repressa est**, *the mutiny was checked.*

3. But when a predicate noun is of differ.nt gender or number from its subject, the verb usually agrees with its nearest substantive; as, —

**Tarquiniī māterna patria erat,** *Tarquinii was his native country on his mother's side;*

**nōn omnis error stultitia est dīcenda,** *not every error is to be called folly.*

> *a.* Less frequently the verb agrees with an appositive; as, —
>
> > **Coriolī, oppidum Volscōrum, captum est,** *Corioli, a town of the Volsci, was captured.*

4. **Construction according to Sense.** Sometimes the verb **agrees** with its subject according to sense instead of strict grammatical form. Thus: —

> *a)* In Number; as, —
>
> > **multitūdō hominum convēnerant,** *a crowd of men had gathered.*
>
> *b)* In Gender; as, —
>
> > **duo mīlia crucibus adfīxī sunt,** *two thousand (men) were crucified.*

### With Two or More Subjects.

**255.** I. **Agreement in Number.** With two or more subjects the verb is regularly plural; as, —

> **pater et fīlius mortuī sunt,** *the father and son died.*

2. But sometimes the verb agrees with the nearest subject; *viz.,* —

> *a)* When the verb precedes both subjects or stands between them; as, —
>
> > **mortuus est pater et fīlius;**
> > **pater mortuus est et fīlius.**
>
> *b)* When the subjects are connected by **aut; aut . . . aut; vel . . . vei; neque . . . neque;** as, —
>
> > **neque pater neque fīlius mortuus est,** *neither father nor son died.*

3. When the different subjects are felt together as constituting a whole, the singular is used; as, —

**temeritās ignōrātiōque vitiōsa est,** *rashness and ignorance are bad.*

> *a.* This is regularly the case in **senātus populusque Rōmānus.**

4. **Agreement in Person.** With compound subjects of different persons the verb always takes the *first* person rather than the *second*, and the *second* rather than the *third*; as, —

**sī tū et Tullia valētis, ego et Cicerō valēmus,** *if you and Tullia are well, Cicero and I are well.*

5. **Agreement in Gender.** With subjects of different genders the participle in the compound tenses follows the same principles as laid down for predicate adjectives. See § 235, *B*, 2.

## VOICES.

**256.** 1. The Passive Voice sometimes retains traces of its original middle or reflexive meaning; as, —

**ego nōn patiar eum dēfendī,** *I shall not allow him to defend himself.*

2. In imitation of Greek usage many perfect passive participles are used by the poets as indirect middles, *i.e.* the subject is viewed as acting not upon itself, but as doing something *in his own interest*; as, —

    **vēlātus tempora,** *having veiled his temples.*

    *a.* Occasionally finite forms of the verb are thus used; as. —
    **tunicā indūcitur artūs,** *he covers his limbs with a tunic.*

3. Intransitive Verbs may be used impersonally in the passive; as, —

    **curritur,** *people run* (lit. *it is run*);
    **ventum est,** *he (they, etc.) came* (lit. *it was come*).

## TENSES.

### TENSES OF THE INDICATIVE.

**257.** 1. The Latin tenses express two distinct notions : —

    *a)* The *period of time* to which the action belongs : Present, Past, or Future.
    *b)* The *kind of action :* Undefined, Going on, or Completed.

The Latin with its six tenses is able to express each of the three kinds of action for each of the three periods of time (making practically nine tenses). It does this by employing certain tenses in more than one way, as may be seen by the following table: —

PERIOD OF TIME.

| | | PRESENT. | PAST. | FUTURE. |
|---|---|---|---|---|
| KIND OF ACTION. | UNDEFINED. | Present: scrībō, *I write.* | Historical Perfect: scrīpsī, *I wrote.* | Future: scrībam, *I shall write.* |
| | GOING ON. | Present: scrībō, *I am writing.* | Imperfect: scrībēbam, *I was writing.* | Future: scrībam, *I shall be writing.* |
| | COMPLETED. | Present Perfect: scrīpsī, *I have written.* | Pluperfect: scrīpseram, *I had written.* | Future Perfect: scrīpserō, *I shall have written.* |

2. It will be seen that the Present may express Undefined action or action Going on; so also the Future. The Perfect likewise has a double use, according as it denotes action Completed in present time (Present Perfect) or Undefined action belonging to past time (Historical Perfect).

#### Principal and Historical Tenses.

**258.** Tenses which denote Present or Future time are called **Principal** (or Primary) Tenses; those which denote Past time are called **Historical** (or Secondary).

The Principal Tenses of the Indicative are: Present, Future, Present Perfect, Future Perfect.

The Historical Tenses are: Imperfect, Historical Perfect, Pluperfect.

#### Present Indicative.

**259.** Besides the two uses indicated in the table, the Present Indicative presents the following peculiarities: —

It is used to denote *a general truth,* *i.e.* something true not merely in the present but at all times ('Gnomic Present'); as, —

virtūs conciliat amīcitiās et cōnservat, *virtue establishes ties of friendship and maintains them* (*i.e.* always does so).

2. It is used of an attempted action ('Conative Present'); as, —

**dum vītant vitia, in contrāria currunt,** *while they try to avoid* (**vītant**) *vices, they rush into opposite ones.*

3. In lively narration the Present is often used of a past action ('Historical Present'); as, — *see Livy*

**Caesar imperat magnum numerum obsidum,** *Caesar demanded a large number of hostages* (lit. *demands*).

4. In combination with **jam, jam diū, jam prīdem,** and similar words, the Present is frequently used of an action originating in the past and continuing in the present; as, —

**jam prīdem cupiō tē vīsere,** *I have long been desiring to visit you* (*i.e.* I desire and have long desired).

### Imperfect Indicative.

**260.** 1. The Imperfect primarily denotes action *going on in past time;* as, —

**librum legēbam,** *I was reading a book.*

> *a.* This force makes the Imperfect especially adapted to serve as the tense of *description* (as opposed to mere *narration*).

2. From the notion of action *going on,* there easily develops the notion of *repeated* or *customary* action; as, —

**lēgātōs interrogābat,** *he kept asking the envoys;*
**C. Duīlium vidēbam puer,** *as a boy I often used to see Gaius Duilius.*

3. The Imperfect often denotes an attempted action ('Conative Imperfect') or an action as beginning ('Inceptive Imperfect'); as, —

**hostēs nostrōs intrā mūnītiōnēs prōgredī prohibēbant,** *the enemy tried to prevent* (**prohibēbant**) *our men from advancing within the fortifications* ('Conative');
**ad proelium sē expediēbant,** *they were beginning to get ready for battle* ('Inceptive').

4. The Imperfect, with **jam, jam diū, jam dūdum,** *etc.,* is sometimes used of an action which had been continuing some time; as, —

**domicilium Rōmae multōs jam annōs habēbat,** *he had had his residence at Rome for many years* (*i.e.* he had it at this time and had long had it).

### Future Indicative.

**261.** 1. The Latin is much more exact in the use of the Future than is the English. We say: '*If he comes, I shall be glad,*' where we really mean : '*If he shall come,*' etc. In such cases the Latin rarely admits the Present, but generally employs the Future.

2. Sometimes the Future has Imperative force; as, **dīcēs**, *say !*

### Perfect Indicative.

**262.** *A.* PRESENT PERFECT. Several Present Perfects denote the *state resulting from a completed act,* and so seem equivalent to the Present; as, —

    **nōvī, cognōvī,** *I know* (lit. *I have become acquainted with*);

    **cōnsuēvī,** *I am wont* (lit. *I have become accustomed*).

*B.* HISTORICAL PERFECT. The Historical Perfect is the tense of *narration* (as opposed to the Imperfect, the tense of *description*); as, —

**Rēgulus in senātum vēnit, mandāta exposuit, reddī captīvōs**
    **negāvit esse ūtile,** *Regulus came into the Senate, set forth his*
    *commission, said it was useless for captives to be returned.*

1. Occasionally the Historical Perfect is used of a general truth ('Gnomic Perfect').

### Pluperfect Indicative.

**263.** The Latin Pluperfect, like the English Past Perfect, denotes an act *completed in the past ;* as, —

**Caesar Rhēnum trānsīre dēcrēverat, sed nāvēs deerant,** *Caesar*
    *had decided to cross the Rhine, but had no boats.*

    *a.* In those verbs whose Perfect has Present force (§ 262, *A*),
    the Pluperfect has the force of an Imperfect; as, —
    **nōveram,** *I knew.*

### Future Perfect Indicative.

**264.** The Future Perfect denotes an action *completed in future time.* Thus : —

**scrībam epistulam, cum redieris,** *I will write the letter when you*
    *have returned* (lit. *when you shall have returned*).

    *a.* The Latin is much more exact in the use of the Future Per-
    fect than the English, which commonly employs the Present
    Perfect instead of the Future Perfect.

    *b.* In those verbs whose Perfect has Present force (§ 262, *A*)
    the Future Perfect has the force of a Future; as, —
    **nōverō,** *I shall know.*

### Epistolary Tenses.

**265.** In letters the writer often uses tenses which are not appropriate at the time of writing, but which will be so at the time when his
letter is received; he thus employs the Imperfect and the Perfect for
the Present, and the Pluperfect for the Present Perfect; as, —

nihil habēbam quod scrīberem, neque enim novī quidquam
audieram et ad tuās omnēs epistulās jam rescrīpseram,
*I have nothing to write, for I have heard no news and have
already answered all your letters.*

## TENSES OF THE SUBJUNCTIVE.

**266.** *A.* **In Independent Sentences.** See §§ 272–280.

*B.* **In Dependent Sentences.** In dependent sentences the
tenses of the subjunctive usually conform to the so-called

### Sequence of Tenses.

**267.** 1. In the Subjunctive the Present and Perfect are
Principal tenses, the Imperfect and Pluperfect, Historical.

2. By the Sequence of Tenses Principal tenses are followed by Principal, Historical by Historical. Thus : —

PRINCIPAL SEQUENCE, —

videō quid faciās, *I see what you are doing.*
vidēbō quid faciās, *I shall see what you are doing.*
vīderō quid faciās, *I shall have seen what you are doing.*
videō quid fēcerīs, *I see what you have done.*
vidēbō quid fēcerīs, *I shall see what you have done.*
vīderō quid fēcerīs, *I shall have seen what you have done.*

HISTORICAL SEQUENCE, —

vidēbam quid facerēs, *I saw what you were doing.*
vīdī quid facerēs, *I saw what you were doing.*
vīderam quid facerēs, *I had seen what you were doi.*
vidēbam quid fēcissēs, *I saw what you had done.*
vīdī quid fēcissēs, *I saw what you had done.*
vīderam quid fēcissēs, *I had seen what you had done.*

3. The Present and Imperfect Subjunctive denote incomplete
action, the Perfect and Pluperfect completed action, exactly as in the
Indicative.

### Peculiarities of Sequence.

**268.** 1. The Perfect Indicative is usually an historical tense (even when translated in English as a Present Perfect), and so is followed by the Imperfect and Pluperfect Subjunctive; as, —

dēmōnstrāvī quārē ad causam accēderem, *I have shown why I took the case* (lit. *I showed why, etc.*).

2. A dependent Perfect Infinitive is treated as an historical tense wherever, if resolved into an equivalent Indicative, it would be historical; as, —

videor ostendisse quālēs deī essent, *I seem to have shown of what nature the gods are* (ostendisse here corresponds to an Indicative, ostendī, *I showed*).

3. The Historical Present is sometimes regarded as a principal tense, sometimes as historical. Thus: —

Sulla suōs hortātur ut fortī animō sint, *Sulla exhorts his soldiers to be stout-hearted;*

Gallōs hortātur ut arma caperent, *he exhorted the Gauls to take arms.*

4. Conditional sentences of the 'contrary-to-fact' type are not affected by the principles for the Sequence of Tenses; as, —

honestum tāle est ut, vel sī ignōrārent id hominēs, suā tamen pulchritūdine laudābile esset, *virtue is such a thing that even if men were ignorant of it, it would still be worthy of praise for its own loveliness.*

5. In conditional sentences of the 'contrary-to-fact' type the Imperfect Subjunctive is usually treated as an Historical tense; as, —

sī sōlōs eōs dīcerēs miserōs, quibus moriendum esset, nēminem tū quidem eōrum quī vīverent exciperēs, *if you called only those wretched who must die, you would except no one of those who live.*

6. In clauses of Result and some others, the Perfect Subjunctive is sometimes used as an historical tense. Thus: —

rēx tantum mōtus est, ut Tissaphernem hostem jūdicārit, *the king was so much moved that he adjudged Tissaphernes an enemy.*

This construction is rare in Cicero, but frequent in Nepos and subsequent historians. The Perfect Subjunctive in this use represents a result simply *as a fact without reference to the continuance of the act,* and therefore corresponds to an Historical Perfect Indicative of direct statement. Thus, **jūdicārit** in the above example corresponds to a **jūdicāvit,** *he adjudged.* To denote a result as *something continuous,* all writers use the Imperfect Subjunctive after historical tenses.

7. Sometimes perspicuity demands that the ordinary principles of Sequence be abandoned altogether. Thus: —

> *a*) We may have the Present or Perfect Subjunctive after an historical tense; as, —

> > **Verrēs Siciliam ita perdidit ut ea restituī nōn possit,** *Verres so ruined Sicily that it cannot be restored* (Direct statement: **nōn potest restitui**);

> > **ārdēbat Hortēnsius dīcendī cupiditāte sīc, ut in nūllō flagrantius studium vīderim,** *Hortensius burned so with eagerness to speak that I have seen in no one a greater desire* (Direct statement: **in nūllō vīdī,** *I have seen in no one*).

NOTE. — This usage is different from that cited under 6. Here, by neglect of Sequence, the Perfect is used, though a principal tense; there the Perfect was used as an historical tense.

> *b*) We may have a principal tense followed by the Perfect Subjunctive used historically; as, —

> > **nesciō quid causae fuerit cūr nūllās ad mē litterās darēs,** *I do not know what reason there was why you did not send me a letter.*

> Here **fuerit** is historical, as is shown by the following Imperfect Subjunctive.

**Method of Expressing Future Time in the Subjunctive.**

**269.** The Future and Future Perfect, which are lacking to the Latin Subjunctive, are supplied in subordinate clauses as follows: —

> 1. *a*) The Future is supplied by the Present after principal tenses, by the Imperfect after historical tenses.

> *b*) The Future Perfect is supplied by the Perfect after principal tenses, by the Pluperfect after historical tenses.

> This is especially frequent when the context clearly shows, by the presence of a future tense in the main clause, that the reference is to future time. Thus: —

Gallī pollicentur sē factūrōs, quae Caesar imperet, *the Gauls promise they will do what Caesar shall order;*

Gallī pollicēbantur sē factūrōs, quae Caesar imperāret, *the Gauls promised they would do what Caesar should order;*

Gallī pollicentur sē factūrōs quae Caesar imperāverit, *the Gauls promise they will do what Caesar shall have ordered;*

Gallī pollicēbantur sē factūrōs quae Caesar imperāvisset, *the Gauls promised they would do what Caesar should have ordered.*

2. Even where the context does not contain a Future tense in the main clause, Future time is often expressed in the subordinate clauses by the Present and Imperfect Subjunctive. Thus: —

timeō nē veniat, *I am afraid he will come;*

Caesar exspectābat quid cōnsilī hostēs caperent, *Caesar was waiting to see what plan the enemy would adopt.*

3. Where greater definiteness is necessary, the periphrastic forms in -ūrus sim and -ūrus essem are employed, especially in clauses of Result, Indirect Questions, and after nōn dubitō quīn; as, —

nōn dubitō quīn pater ventūrus sit, *I do not doubt that my father will come;*

nōn dubitābam quīn pater ventūrus esset, *I did not doubt that my father would come.*

4. Where the verb has no Future Active Participle, or where it stands in the passive voice, its Future character may be indicated by the use of the particles mox, brevī, statim, *etc.*, in connection with the Present and Imperfect Subjunctive; as, —

nōn dubitō quīn tē mox hūjus reī paeniteat, *I do not doubt that you will soon repent of this thing;*

nōn dubitābam quīn haec rēs brevī cōnficerētur, *I did not doubt that this thing would soon be finished.*

## TENSES OF THE INFINITIVE.

**270.** 1. The tenses of the Infinitive denote time not absolutely, but *with reference to the verb on which they depend.* Thus: —

a) The Present Infinitive represents an act as *contemporaneous with* the time of the verb on which it depends; as, —

vidētur honōrēs adsequī, *he seems to be gaining honors;*

vidēbātur honōrēs adsequī, *he seemed to be gaining honors.*

*b*) The Perfect Infinitive represents an act as *prior to* the time of the verb on which it depends; as, —

**vidētur honōrēs adsecūtus esse,** *he seems to have gained honors;*

**vīsus est honōrēs adsecūtus esse,** *he seemed to have gained honors.*

*c*) The Future Infinitive represents an act as *subsequent to* that of the verb on which it depends; as, —

**vidētur honōrēs adsecūtūrus esse,** *he seems to be about to gain honors;*

**vīsus est honōrēs adsecūtūrus esse,** *he seemed to be about to gain honors.*

2. Where the English says '*ought to have done*,' '*might have done*,' *etc.*, the Latin uses **dēbuī, oportuit, potuī** (**dēbēbam, oportēbat, poteram**), with the Present Infinitive; as, —

**dēbuit dīcere,** *he ought to have said* (lit. *owed it to say*);
**oportuit venīre,** *he ought to have come;*
**potuit vidēre,** *he might have seen.*

*a.* **Oportuit, volō, nōlō** (and in poetry some other verbs), may take a Perfect Infinitive instead of the Present; as, —

**hōc jam prīdem factum esse oportuit,** *this ought long ago to have been done.*

3. PERIPHRASTIC FUTURE INFINITIVE. Verbs that have no Participial Stem, express the Future Infinitive Active and Passive by **fore ut** or **futūrum esse ut,** with the Subjunctive; as, —

**spērō fore ut tē paeniteat levitātis,** *I hope you will repent of your fickleness* (lit. *hope it will happen that you repent*);
**spērō futūrum esse ut hostēs arceantur,** *I hope that the enemy will be kept off.*

*a.* The Periphrastic Future Infinitive is often used, especially in the Passive, even in case of verbs which have the Participial Stem; as, —

**spērō fore ut hostēs vincantur,** *I hope the enemy will be conquered.*

4. Passives and Deponents sometimes form a Future Perfect Infinitive with **fore;** as, —

**spērō epistulam scrīptam fore,** *I hope the letter will have been written;*
**dīcō mē satis adeptum fore,** *I say that I shall have gained enough.*

## THE MOODS.

## MOODS IN INDEPENDENT SENTENCES.

### The Indicative in Independent Sentences.

**271.** The Indicative is used for the *statement of facts,* *the supposition of facts,* or *inquiry after facts.*

1. Note the following idiomatic uses : —

    *a)* With **possum** ; as, —

    **possum multa dīcere,** *I might say much ;*
    **poteram multa dīcere,** *I might have said much* (§ 270, 2).

    *b)* In such expressions as **longum est, aequum est, melius est, difficile est, ūtilius est,** and some others ; as, —

    **longum est ea dīcere,** *it would be tedious to tell that ;*
    **difficile est omnia persequī,** *it would be difficult to enumerate everything.*

### The Subjunctive in Independent Sentences.

**272.** The Subjunctive is used in Independent Sentences to express something —

1. **As willed — Volitive Subjunctive ;**
2. **As desired — Optative Subjunctive ;**
3. **Conceived of as possible — Potential Subjunctive.**

## VOLITIVE SUBJUNCTIVE.

**273.** The Volitive Subjunctive represents the action *as willed.* It always implies authority on the part of the speaker, and has the following varieties : —

### *A.* Hortatory Subjunctive.

**274.** The Hortatory Subjunctive expresses *an exhortation.* This use is confined to the first person plural of the Present. The negative is **nē.** Thus : —

    **eāmus,** *let us go ;*
    **amēmus patriam,** *let us love our country ;*
    **nē dēspērēmus,** *let us not despair.*

**275.** The Jussive Subjunctive expresses a *command.* The Jussive stands regularly in the Present Tense, and is used —

1. Most frequently in the third singular and the third plural; as, —
   dīcat, *let him tell;*
   dīcant, *let them tell;*
   quārē sēcēdant improbī, *wherefore let the wicked depart!*

2. Less frequently in the second person, often with indefinite force; as, —
   istō bonō ūtāre, *use that advantage;*
   modestē vīvās, *live temperately.*

**276.** The Subjunctive is used in the second and third persons singular and plural, with **nē**, to express *a prohibition.* Both Present and Perfect occur, and without appreciable difference of meaning; as, —

   nē repugnētis, *do not resist!*
   tū vērō istam nē relīquerīs, *don't leave her!*
   impiī nē plācāre audeant deōs, *let not the impious dare to appease the gods!*

*a.* Neither of these constructions is frequent in classical prose.

*b.* A commoner method of expressing a prohibition in the second person is by the use of **nōlī** (**nōlīte**) with a following infinitive, or by **cavē** or **cavē nē** with the Subjunctive; as, —
   nōlī hōc facere, *don't do this* (lit. *be unwilling to do*)!
   nōlīte mentīrī, *do not lie!*
   cavē ignōscās, cavē tē misereat, *do not forgive, do not pity!*
   cavē nē haec faciās, *do not do this* (lit. *take care lest you do*)!

**277.** The Deliberative Subjunctive is used *in questions and exclamations implying doubt, indignation, the impossibility of an act, obligation, or propriety.* The Present is used referring to present time, the Imperfect referring to past. The negative is **nōn.** Thus: —

> **quid faciam,** *what shall I do?*
> **ego redeam,** *I go back!*
> **huic cēdāmus! hūjus condiciōnēs audiāmus!** *are we to bow to him! are we to listen to his terms!*
> **quid facerem,** *what was I to do?*
> **hunc ego nōn dīligam,** *should I not cherish this man?*

> *a.* These Deliberative Questions are usually purely Rhetorical in character, and do not expect an answer.

### E. CONCESSIVE SUBJUNCTIVE.

**278.** The Subjunctive is used to indicate something *as granted or conceded for the sake of argument.* The Present is used for present time, the Perfect regularly for past. The negative is **nē** Thus: —

> **sit hōc vērum,** *I grant that this is true* (lit. *let this be true*);
> **nē sint in senectūte vīrēs,** *I grant there is not strength in old age;*
> **fuerit malus cīvis aliīs; tibi quandō esse coepit,** *I grant that he was a bad citizen to others; when did he begin to be so toward you?*

### OPTATIVE SUBJUNCTIVE.

**279.** The Optative Subjunctive occurs in expressions of *wishing.* The negative is regularly **nē.**

> 1. The Present Tense, often accompanied by **utinam,** is used where the wish is conceived of *as possible.*

> **dī istaec prohibeant,** *may the gods prevent that!*
> **falsus utinam vātēs sim,** *oh that I may be a false prophet!*
> **nē veniant,** *may they not come!*

> 2. The Imperfect expresses, in the form of a wish, the *regret that something is not so now;* the Pluperfect that something *was not so in the past.* The Imperfect and Pluperfect are regularly accompanied by **utinam;** as, —

> **utinam istud ex animō dīcerēs,** *would that you were saying that in earnest* (*i.e.* I regret that you are not saying it in earnest);
> **Pēlīdēs utinam vītāsset Apollinis arcūs,** *would that Achilles had escaped the bow of Apollo;*
> **utinam nē nātus essem,** *would that I had not been born.*

## POTENTIAL SUBJUNCTIVE.

**280.** The Potential Subjunctive expresses *a possibility*. The negative is **nōn**. The following uses are to be noted:—

1. **The 'May' Potential.** — The Potential Subjunctive may designate *a mere possibility* (English auxiliary *may*). Both Present and Perfect occur, and without appreciable difference of meaning. Thus : —

> dīcat aliquis, *some one may say* ;
> dīxerit aliquis, *some one may say*.

    *a.* This construction is by no means frequent, and is confined mainly to a few phrases like those given as examples.

2. **'Should'-'Would' Potential.** — The Potential Subjunctive may represent something as *depending upon a condition expressed or understood* (English auxiliary *should, would*). Both Present and Perfect occur, and without appreciable difference of meaning. Thus : —

> fortūnam citius reperiās quam retineās, *one would more quickly find*
>     *Fortune than keep it* (*i.e.* if one should make the trial) ;
> crēdiderim, *I should believe*.

    *a.* Here belongs the use of **velim, mālim, nōlim,** as softened forms of statement for **volō, mālō, nōlō.** Thus : —

> velim mihi ignōscās, *I wish you would forgive me* ;
> nōlim putēs mē jocārī, *I don't want you to think I'm joking*.

    *b.* When the condition is expressed, we get one of the regular types of Conditional Sentences (see § 303) ; as, —

> diēs dēficiat, sī cōner ēnumerāre causās, *time would fail if I should attempt to enumerate the reasons*.

3. **'Can'-'Could' Potential.** — In the Present and Imperfect the Potential occurs in the second person singular (with *indefinite* force ; § 356, 3) of a few verbs of *perceiving, seeing, thinking,* and the like ; as, —

> videās, cernās, *one can see, one can perceive* ;
> crēderēs, *one could believe* ;
> vidērēs, cernerēs, *one could see, perceive* ;
> putārēs, *one could imagine*.

4. The Imperfect and Pluperfect in the Apodosis of conditional sentences of the contrary-to-fact type (see § 304) are also Potential in character. By omission of the Protasis, such an Apodosis sometimes stands alone, particularly **vellem, nōllem, mālem** ; as, —

> vellem id quidem, *I should wish that* (*i.e.* were I bold enough).

## The Imperative.

**281.** The Imperative is used in *commands, admonitions,* and *entreaties* (negative **nē**); as, —

> ēgredere ex urbe, *depart from the city;*
> mihi ignōsce, *pardon me;*
> valē, *farewell.*

1. The Present is the tense of the Imperative most commonly used, but the Future is employed —

 *a*) Where there is a distinct reference to future time, especially in the apodosis of conditional sentences; as, —

> rem vōbīs prōpōnam; vōs eam penditōte, *I will lay the matter before you; do you (then) consider it;*
> sī bene disputābit, tribuitō litterīs Graecis, *if he shall speak well, attribute it to Greek literature.*

 *b*) In laws, treaties, wills, maxims, *etc.*; as, —

> cōnsulēs summum jūs habentō, *the consuls shall have supreme power;*
> hominem mortuom in urbe nē sepelītō, *no one shall bury a dead body in the city;*
> amīcitia rēgī Antiochō cum populō Rōmānō hīs lēgibus et condiciōnibus estō, *let there be friendship between Antiochus and the Roman people on the following terms and conditions;*
> quārtae estō partis Mārcus hērēs, *let Marcus be heir to a fourth (of the property);*
> ignōscitō saepe alterī, numquam tibi, *forgive your neighbor often, yourself never.*

2. Except with the Future Imperative the negative is not used in classical prose. Prohibitions are regularly expressed in other ways. See § 276, *b.*

3. Questions in the Indicative introduced by **quīn** (*why not?*) are often equivalent to an Imperative or to the Hortatory Subjunctive; as, —

quīn abīs, *go away!* (lit. *why don't you go away?*);

quīn vōcem continētis, *keep still!* (lit. *why don't you stop your voices?*);

quīn equōs cōnscendimus, *let us mount our horses* (lit. *why do we not mount our horses?*).

## MOODS IN DEPENDENT CLAUSES.

### Clauses of Purpose.

**282.** 1. Clauses of Purpose are introduced most commonly by ut (utī), quō (*that, in order that*), nē (*in order that not, lest*), and stand in the Subjunctive; as, —

edimus ut vīvāmus, *we eat that we may live;*

adjūtā mē quō hōc fīat facilius, *help me, in order that this may be done more easily;*

portās clausit, nē quam oppidānī injūriam acciperent, *he closed the gates, lest the townspeople should receive any injury.*

> *a.* Quō, as a rule, is employed only when the purpose clause contains a comparative or a comparative idea. Occasional exceptions occur; as, —
>
> > haec faciunt quō Chremētem absterreant, *they are doing this in order to frighten Chremes.*
>
> *b.* Ut nē is sometimes found instead of nē. Thus : —
>
> > ut nē quid neglegenter agāmus, *in order that we may not do anything carelessly.*
>
> *c.* Ut nōn (not nē) is used where the negation belongs to some single word, instead of to the purpose clause as a whole. Thus : —
>
> > ut nōn ējectus ad aliēnōs, sed invītātus ad tuōs videāre, *that you may seem not driven out among strangers, but invited to your own friends.*
>
> *d.* To say '*and that not*' or '*or that not,*' the Latin regularly uses nēve (neu); as, —
>
> > ut eārum rērum vīs minuerētur, neu pontī nocērent, *that the violence of these things might be lessened, and that they might not harm the bridge;*
>
> > profūgit, nē caperētur nēve interficerētur, *he fled, that he might not be captured or killed.*
>
> *e.* But neque (for nēve) is sometimes used in a second Purpose Clause when ut stands in the first, and, after the Augustan era, even when the first clause is introduced by nē.
>
> *f.* Purpose Clauses sometimes stand in apposition with a preceding noun or pronoun; as, —
>
> > hāc causā, ut pācem habērent, *on this account, that they might have peace.*

2. A Relative Pronoun (**quī**) or Adverb (**ubi, unde, quō**) is frequently used to introduce a Purpose Clause; as, —

**Helvētiī lēgātōs mittunt, quī dīcerent**, *the Helvetii sent envoys to
say* (lit. *who should say*) ;

**haec habuī, dē senectūte quae dīcerem,** *I had these things to say
about old age ;*

**nōn habēbant quō sē reciperent,** *they had no place to which to flee*
(lit. *whither they might flee*).

> *a.* **Quī** in such clauses is equivalent to **ut is, ut ego,** *etc. ;* **ubi** to **ut
> ibi; unde** to **ut inde; quŏ** to **ut eō.**

3. Relative Clauses of purpose follow **dignus, indignus,** and **idōneus**; as, —

**idōneus fuit nēmō quem imitārēre,** *there was no one suitable for
you to imitate* (*cf.* **nēmō fuit quem imitārēre,** *there was no
one for you to imitate*) ;

**dignus est quī aliquandō imperet,** *he is worthy to rule sometime.*

4. Purpose Clauses often depend upon something to be supplied
from the context instead of upon the principal verb of their own sentences; as, —

**ut haec omnia omittam, abiimus,** *to pass over all this, (I will say
that) we departed.*

### Clauses of Characteristic.

**283.** 1. A relative clause used *to express a quality or
characteristic of a general or indefinite antecedent* is called
a Clause of Characteristic, and usually stands in the
Subjunctive; as, —

**multa sunt, quae mentem acuant,** *there are many things which
sharpen the wits.*

Clauses of Characteristic are opposed to those relative clauses which
are used merely to state some fact about a definite antecedent, and
which therefore take the Indicative; as, —

**Catō, senex jūcundus, quī Sapiēns appellātus est,** *Cato, a delight-
ful old man, who was called ' The Wise.'*

The Clause of Characteristic implies ' *a person of the sort that does
something*'; the Indicative relative clause implies ' *a particular person
who does something.*'

2. Clauses of Characteristic are used especially after such expressions as, **est quī**; **sunt quī**; **nēmō est quī**; **nūllus est quī**; **ūnus est quī**; **sōlus est quī**; **quis est quī**; **is quī**; *etc.* Thus: —

**sunt quī dīcant,** *there are (some) who say;*

**nēmō est quī nesciat,** *there is nobody who is ignorant;*

**sapientia est ūna quae maestitiam pellat,** *philosophy is the only thing that drives away sorrow;*

**quae cīvitās est quae nōn ēvertī possit,** *what state is there that cannot be overthrown?*

**nōn is sum quī improbōs laudem,** *I am not the sort of man that praises the wicked.*

> *a.* Sometimes (very rarely in Cicero and Caesar) the clause of characteristic is used after comparatives; as, —
>
> > **nōn longius hostēs aberant quam quō tēlum adigī posset,** *the enemy were not too far off for a dart to reach them* (lit. *further off than [a point] to which a dart could be cast*).

3. The Clause of Characteristic often conveys an accessory notion of **cause** (*since*) or **opposition** (*although*). Thus: —

> *a)* Cause. The relative is then frequently accompanied by **ut, quīppe, utpote**; as, —
>
> > **ō fortūnāte adulēscēns, quī tuae virtūtis Homērum praecōnem invēnerīs,** *O fortunate man, since you have found a Homer as the herald of your valor;*
> >
> > **ut quī optimō jūre eam prōvinciam obtinuerit,** *since he held that province by excellent right.*
>
> *b)* Opposition: —
>
> > **egomet quī sērō Graecās litterās attigissem, tamen complūrēs diēs Athēnīs commorātus sum,** *I, although I had taken up Greek literature late in life, nevertheless tarried several days at Athens.*

4. Clauses of Characteristic may also be introduced by **quīn = quī (quae, quod) nōn**; as, —

**nēmō est quīn saepe audierit,** *there is no one who has not often heard;*

**nēmō fuit mīlitum quīn vulnerārētur,** *there was no one of the soldiers who was not wounded.*

5. Related to Clauses of Characteristic are also phrases of the type: **quod sciam,** *so far as I know;* **quem (quam, quod), audierim,** *so far as I have heard.*

### Clauses of Result.

**284.** 1. Clauses of Result are usually introduced by **ut** (*that, so that*), negative **ut nōn** (*so that not*), and take the Subjunctive. The main clause often contains **tantus, tālis, tot, is** ( = tālis), **tam, ita, sīc, adeō**, or some similar word. Thus : —

**quis tam dēmēns est ut suā voluntāte maereat,** *who is so senseless as to mourn of his own volition ?*

**Siciliam ita vāstāvit ut restituī in antīquum statum nōn possit,** *he so ravaged Sicily that it cannot be restored to its former condition ;*

**mōns altissimus impendēbat, ut facile perpaucī prohibēre possent,** *a very high mountain overhung, so that a very few could easily stop them ;*

**nōn is es ut tē pudor umquam ā turpitūdine āvocārit,** *you are not so constituted that shame ever called you back from baseness.*

2. A Result Clause is often introduced by a Relative Pronoun or Adverb, **quī** ( = **ut is**), **quō** ( = **ut eō**), *etc.* ; as, —

**nēmō est tam senex quī sē annum nōn putet posse vīvere,** *nobody is so old as not to think he can live a year ;*

**habētis eum cōnsulem quī pārēre vestrīs dēcrētīs nōn dubitet,** *you have a consul such as does not hesitate to obey your decrees.*

> *a.* These Relative Clauses of Result are closely related to the Clause of Characteristic, and sometimes it is difficult to distinguish the two constructions. It is best to class the relative clause as one of Characteristic, unless the result idea is clear and unmistakable.

3. Result clauses may also be introduced by **quīn = ut nōn** ; as, —

**nihil tam difficile est quīn quaerendō invēstīgārī possit,** *nothing is so difficult that it cannot be discovered by searching ;*

**nēmō est tam fortis quīn reī novitāte perturbētur,** *no one is so steadfast as not to be thrown into confusion by a strange occurrence.*

4. Note the use of **quam ut** (sometimes **quam** alone) to denote Result after comparatives ; as, —

**urbs erat mūnītior quam ut prīmō impetū capī posset,** *the city was too strongly fortified to be taken at the first attack* (lit. *more strongly fortified than* [*so*] *that it could be taken, etc.*).

### Causal Clauses.

**285.** Causal clauses are introduced chiefly by the following particles : —

      1. Quod, quia, quoniam.
      2. Cum.
      3. Quandō.

**286.** The use of moods is as follows : —

1. **Quod, quia, quoniam** take the Indicative when the reason is *that of the writer or speaker;* they take the Subjunctive when the reason is viewed *as that of another.* Thus : —

**Parthōs timeō quod diffīdō cōpiīs nostrīs,** *I fear the Parthians, because I distrust our troops.*

**Themistoclēs, quia nōn tūtus erat, Corcȳram dēmigrāvit,** *Themistocles, since he was not safe, moved to Corcyra.*

**neque mē vīxisse paenitet, quoniam bene vīxī,** *I do not regret having lived, since I have lived well.*

**Sōcratēs accūsātus est quod corrumperet juventūtem,** *Socrates was arraigned on the ground that he was corrupting the young.* (Here the reason is not that of the writer but of the accuser. Hence the Subjunctive.)

**Haeduī Caesarī grātiās ēgērunt quod sē perīculō līberāvisset,** *the Haedui thanked Caesar because he had delivered them from danger.* (The reason of the Haedui.)

**quoniam Miltiadēs dīcere nōn posset, verba prō eō fēcit Tīsagorās,** *since Miltiades could not speak, Tisagoras spoke for him.* (The reason of Tisagoras.)

**noctū ambulābat Themistoclēs, quod somnum capere nōn posset,** *Themistocles used to walk at night because (as he said) he couldn't sleep.*

    *a.* Verbs of *thinking* and *saying* often stand in the Subjunctive in causal clauses as though the act of thinking or saying, and not the contents of the thought or language, constituted the reason. Thus : —

        **Bellovacī suum numerum nōn complēvērunt quod sē suō nōmine cum Rōmānīs bellum gestūrōs dīcerent,** *the Bellovaci did not furnish their complement* *because they said they were going to wage war with the Romans on their own account.*

*b.* **Nōn quod, nōn quō** (by attraction for **nōn eō quod**), **nōn quia**, *not that, not because*; and **nōn quod nōn, nōn quō nōn, nōn quīn,** *not that . . . not; not because . . . not; not but that*, are usually employed merely to introduce a hypothetical reason, and hence take the Subjunctive; as, —

    **id fēcī, nōn quod vōs hanc dēfēnsiōnem dēsīderāre arbitrārer, sed ut omnēs intellegerent,** *this I did, not because I thought you needed this defense, but that all might perceive;*

    **Crassō commendātiōnem nōn sum pollicitus, nōn quīn eam valitūram apud tē arbitrārer, sed egēre mihi commendātiōne nōn vidēbātur,** *I did not promise a recommendation to Crassus, not that I did not think it would have weight with you, but because he did not seem to me to need recommendation.*

*c.* But clauses introduced by **nōn quod, nōn quia** take the Indicative *if they state a fact*, even though that fact is denied to be the reason for something; as. —

    **hōc ita sentiō, nōn quia sum ipse augur, sed quia sīc exīstimāre nōs est necesse,** *this I think, not because I am myself an augur (which I really am), but because it is necessary for us to think so.*

2. **Cum** causal regularly takes the Subjunctive; as, —

**quae cum ita sint,** *since this is so;*
**cum sīs mortālis, quae mortālia sunt, cūrā,** *since you are mortal, care for what is mortal.*

    *a.* Note the phrase **cum praesertim (praesertim cum),** *especially since;* as, —

    **Haeduōs accūsat, praesertim cum eōrum precibus adductus bellum suscēperit,** *he blamed the Haedui, especially since he had undertaken the war at their entreaties.*

3. **Quandō** (less frequent than the other causal particles) governs the Indicative; as, —

**id omittō, quandō vōbīs ita placet,** *I pass over that, since you so wish.*

### Temporal Clauses introduced by *Postquam, Ut, Ubi, Simul ac, etc.*

**287.** 1. **Postquam** (posteāquam), *after;* ut, ubi, *when;* cum prīmum, simul, simul ac (simul atque), *as soon as,* when used to refer *to a single past act* regularly take the Perfect Indicative; as, —

Epamīnōndās postquam audīvit vīcisse Boeōtiōs, 'Satis' inquit 'vīxī,' *Epaminondas, after he heard that the Boeotians had conquered, said, 'I have lived enough;'*

id ut audīvit, Corcȳram dēmigrāvit, *when he heard this, he moved to Corcyra;*

Caesar cum prīmum potuit, ad exercitum contendit, *Caesar, as soon as he could, hurried to the army;*

ubi dē Caesaris adventū certiōrēs factī sunt, lēgātōs ad eum mittunt, *when they were informed of Caesar's arrival, they sent envoys to him.*

    *a.* The Historical Present may take the place of the Perfect in this construction.

    2. To denote *the repeated occurrence* of an act, ut, ubi, simul atque, *as often as,* when following an historical tense, take the Pluperfect Indicative (compare §§ 288, 3; 302, 3); as, —

ut quisque Verris animum offenderat, in lautumiās statim coniciēbātur, *whenever anybody had offended Verres's feelings, he was forthwith put in the stone-quarry;*

hostēs, ubi aliquōs ēgredientēs cōnspexerant, adoriēbantur, *whenever the enemy had seen any men disembarking, they attacked them.*

    *a.* In Livy and succeeding historians the Imperfect and Pluperfect Subjunctive are used to denote this repeated occurrence of an act ('Indefinite Frequency'); as, —

        id ubi dīxisset hastam mittēbat, *whenever he had said that, he hurled a spear.*

    3. Occasionally the above conjunctions are followed by the Pluperfect Indicative of a single occurrence. This is regularly the case with **postquam** in expressions denoting a definite interval of time (days, months, years, *etc.*), such as **post tertium annum quam, trienniō postquam.** Thus: —

quīnque post diēbus quam Lūcā discesserat, ad Sardiniam vēnit, *five days after he had depárted from Luca he came to Sardinia;*

postquam occupātae Syrācūsae erant, profectus est Carthāginem, *after Syracuse had been seized, he set out for Carthage.*

4. The Imperfect Indicative also sometimes occurs, to denote *a continued state;* as, —

postquam Rōmam adventābant, senātus cōnsultus est, *after they were on the march toward Rome, the Senate was consulted;*

postquam strūctī utrimque stābant, *after they had been drawn up on both sides and were in position.*

5. Rarely postquam, posteāquam, following the analogy of cum, take the Subjunctive, but only in the historical tenses; as, —

posteāquam sūmptuōsa fierī fūnera coepissent, lēge sublāta sunt, *after funerals had begun to be elaborate, they were done away with by law.*

### Temporal Clauses introduced by *Cum.*

#### *A.* Cum REFERRING TO THE PAST.

**288.** 1. Cum, when referring to the past, takes, —

*A.* The Indicative (Imperfect, Historical Perfect, or Pluperfect) to denote *the point of time at which* something occurs.

*B.* The Subjunctive (Imperfect or Pluperfect) to denote *the situation or circumstances under which* something occurs.

Examples: —

INDICATIVE.

an tum erās cōnsul, cum in Palātiō mea domus ārdēbat, *or were you consul at the time when my house burned up on the Palatine?*

crēdō tum cum Sicilia flōrēbat opibus et cōpiīs magna artificia fuisse in eā īnsulā, *I believe that at the time when Sicily was powerful in riches and resources there were great crafts in that island;*

eō tempore pāruit cum pārēre necesse erat, *he obeyed at the time when it was necessary to obey;*

illō diē, cum est lāta lēx dē mē, *on that day when the law concerning me was passed.*

Subjunctive.

**Lysander cum vellet Lycūrgī lēgēs commūtāre, prohibitus est,** *when Lysander desired to change the laws of Lycurgus, he was prevented;*

**Pȳthagorās cum in geōmetriā quiddam novī invēnisset, Mūsīs bovem immolāsse dīcitur,** *when Pythagoras had discovered something new in geometry, he is said to have sacrificed an ox to the Muses.*

> *a.* Note that the Indicative is much less frequent in such clauses than the Subjunctive, and is regularly confined to those cases where the main clause has **tum, eō diē, eō annō, eō tempore** or some similar correlative of the **cum**. Sometimes it depends entirely upon the point of view of the writer whether he shall employ the Indicative or Subjunctive.

2. **Cum Inversum.** When the logical order of the clauses is inverted, we find **cum** with the Perfect Indicative or Historical Present, in the sense of *when, when suddenly.* The main clause in such cases often has **jam, vix, aegrē, nōndum**; as, —

**jam Gallī ex oppidō fugere apparābant, cum mātrēs familiae repente prōcurrērunt,** *the Gauls were already preparing to flee, when suddenly the matrons rushed forth* (logically, *the matrons rushed forth as the Gauls were preparing to flee*) ;

**Trēvirī Labiēnum adorīrī parābant, cum duās legiōnēs vēnisse cognōscunt,** *the Treviri were preparing to attack, when (suddenly) they learned that two legions had arrived.*

3. To denote a *recurring action* in the past, **cum** is followed by the Indicative, particularly of the Pluperfect (compare §§ 287, 2 ; 302, 3) ; as, —

**cum ad aliquod oppidum vēnerat, eādem lectīcā ad cubiculum dēferēbātur,** *whenever he had arrived at some town, he was (always) carried in the same litter to his room;*

**cum equitātus noster sē in agrōs ējēcerat, essedāriōs ex silvīs ēmittēbat,** *whenever our cavalry had advanced into the fields, he would send his charioteers out from the woods.*

> *a.* Sometimes the Imperfect or Pluperfect Subjunctive is thus used; as, —
> **saepe cum aliquem vidēret minus bene vestītum, suum amiculum dedit,** *often, whenever he saw some one more poorly clothed, he gave him his own mantle ;*
> **cum prōcucurrissent, Numidae effugiēbant,** *as often as they had advanced, the Numidians ran away.*
> This construction is frequent in Livy and subsequent historians.

**289.** When **cum** refers to the Present or Future it regularly takes the Indicative; as, —

tum tua rēs agitur, pariēs cum proximus ārdet, *your own interests are at stake when your neighbor's house is burning;*
cum vidēbis, tum sciēs, *when you see, then you will know.*

> *a.* The Indicative of the Present or Future may denote also a *recurring action;* as, —
>
>> stabilitās amīcitiae cōnfīrmārī potest, cum hominēs cupīdinibus imperābunt, *firm friendship can be established whenever men shall control their desires.*

*C.* OTHER USES OF **Cum**.

**290.** 1. **Cum Explicative.** Cum, with the Indicative, is sometimes used to indicate the identity of one act with another; as, —

cum tacent clāmant, *their silence is a shout* (lit. *when they are silent, they shout*).

2. **Cum . . . tum.** When cum . . . tum mean *both . . . and,* the cum-clause is in the Indicative; but when cum has the force of *while, though,* it may take the Subjunctive; as, —

cum tē semper dīlēxerim, tum tuīs factīs incēnsus sum, *while I have always loved you, at the same time I am stirred by your conduct.*

**Clauses introduced by *Antequam* and *Priusquam*.**

*A.* WITH THE INDICATIVE.

**291.** **Antequam** and **priusquam** (often written **ante . . . quam, prius . . . quam**) take the Indicative to denote *an actual fact.*

1. Sometimes the Present or Future Perfect; as, —
prius respondēs quam rogō, *you answer before I ask;*
nihil contrā disputābō priusquam dīxerit, *I will say nothing in opposition, before he speaks.*

2. Sometimes the Perfect, especially after negative clauses; as, —
nōn prius jugulandī fīnis fuit, quam Sulla omnēs suōs dīvitiīs explēvit, *there was no end of murder until Sulla satisfied all his henchmen with wealth.*

**292.** **Antequam** and **priusquam** take the Subjunctive to denote an act as *anticipated*.

1. Thus the Subjunctive may denote —

   *a*) An act in preparation for which the main act takes place; as, —

   **priusquam dīmicārent, foedus īctum est,** *i.e. in anticipation of the fight, a treaty was struck.*

   By an extension of this usage, the Subjunctive is sometimes used of *general truths*, where the anticipatory notion has faded out; as, —

   **tempestās minātur antequam surgat,** *the tempest threatens before it rises.*

   *b*) An act anticipated and forestalled; as, —

   **priusquam tēlum adicī posset, omnis aciēs terga vertit,** *before a spear could be hurled, the whole army fled.*

   *c*) An act anticipated and deprecated; as, —

   **animum omittunt priusquam locō dēmigrent,** *they die rather than quit their post.*

2. After historical tenses the Imperfect Subjunctive is used, especially by some writers, where the notion of anticipation has practically vanished; as, —

   **sōl antequam sē abderet fugientem vīdit Antōnium,** *the sun before it set saw Antony fleeing.*

### Clauses introduced by *Dum, Dōnec, Quoad*

**293.** I. **Dum,** *while,* regularly takes the Indicative of the Historical Present; as, —

**Alexander, dum inter prīmōrēs pugnat, sagittā ictus est,** *Alexander, while he was fighting in the van, was struck by an arrow;*

**dum haec geruntur, in fīnēs Venellōrum pervēnit,** *while these things were being done, he arrived in the territory of the Venelli.*

II. **Dum, dōnec,** and **quoad,** *as long as,* take the Indicative; as, —

**dum anima est, spēs est,** *as long as there is life, there is hope;*

**Lacedaemoniōrum gēns fortis fuit, dum Lycūrgī lēgēs vigēbant,** *the race of the Lacedaemonians was powerful, as long as the laws of Lycurgus were in force;*

**Catō, quoad vīxit, virtūtum laude crēvit,** *Cato, as long as he lived, increased in the fame of his virtues.*

III. **Dum, dōnec,** and **quoad,** *until,* take : —

1. The Indicative, to denote *an actual event;* as, —

**dōnec rediit, fuit silentium,** *there was silence till he came;*

**ferrum in corpore retinuit, quoad renūntiātum est Boeōtiōs vīcisse,** *he kept the iron in his body until word was brought that the Boeotians had conquered.*

> *a.* In Livy and subsequent historians **dum** and **dōnec** in this sense often take the Subjunctive instead of the Indicative; as, —
>
> > **trepidātiōnis aliquantum ēdēbant dōnec timor quiētem fēcisset,** *they showed some trepidation, until fear produced quiet.*

2. The Subjunctive, to denote *anticipation* or *expectancy;* as, —

**exspectāvit Caesar dum nāvēs convenīrent,** *Caesar waited for the ships to assemble;*

**dum litterae veniant, morābor,** *I shall wait for the letter to come.*

### Substantive Clauses.

**294.** A Substantive Clause is one which as a whole serves as the Subject or Object of a verb, or stands in some other case relation.

**A. Substantive Clauses developed from the Volitive.**

**295.** Substantive Clauses Developed from the Volitive are used with the following classes of verbs : —

1. With verbs signifying *to admonish, request, command, urge, persuade, induce,*[1] *etc.* (conjunctions **ut, nē,** or **ut nē**) ; as, —

**postulō ut fīat,** *I demand that it be done* (dependent form of the Jussive **fīat,** *let it be done!*) ;

**ōrat, nē abeās,** *he begs that you will not go away;*

**mīlitēs cohortātus est ut hostium impetum sustinērent,** *he exhorted his soldiers to withstand the attack of the enemy :*

**Helvētiīs persuāsit ut exīrent,** *he persuaded the Helvetii to march forth.*

> *a.* **Jubeō,** *command, order,* regularly takes the Infinitive.

---

[1] Especially: **moneō, admoneō; rogō, ōrō, petō, postulō, precor, flāgitō; mandō, imperō, praecipiō·suāde ɔ, hortor, cohortor : persuādeō, impellō**

2. With verbs signifying *to grant, concede, permit, allow,*[1] *etc.* (conjunction **ut**) ; as, —

**huic concēdō ut ea praetereat,** *I allow him to pass that by* (dependent form of the Jussive **ea praetereat,** *let him pass that by !*) ;

**cōnsulī permissum est ut duās legiōnēs scrīberet,** *the consul was permitted to enroll two legions.*

3. With verbs of *hindering, preventing,*[2] *etc.* (conjunctions **nē**, **quōminus, quīn**) ; as, —

**nē lūstrum perficeret, mors prohibuit,** *death prevented him from finishing the lustrum* (dependent form after past tense of **nē lūstrum perficiat,** *let him not finish, etc.*) ;

**prohibuit quōminus in ūnum coīrent,** *he prevented them from coming together ;*

**nec quīn ērumperet, prohibērī poterat,** *nor could he be prevented from rushing forth.*

> *a.* **Quīn** is used only when the verb of *hindering* is accompanied by a negative, or stands in a question implying a negative; it is not *necessarily* used even then.

4. With verbs of *deciding, resolving,*[3] *etc.* (conjunctions **ut, nē**, or **ut nē**) ; as, —

**cōnstitueram ut prīdiē Īdūs Aquīnī manērem,** *I had decided to remain at Aquinum on the* 12*th ;*

**dēcrēvit senātus ut Opīmius vidēret,** *the Senate decreed that Opimius should see to it ;*

**convēnit ut ūnīs castrīs miscērentur,** *it was agreed that they should be united in one camp.*

5. With verbs of *striving,*[4] *etc.* (conjunctions **ut, nē**, or **ut nē**) ; as, —

**fac ut eum exōrēs,** *see to it that you prevail upon him !*
**cūrā ut vir sīs,** *see to it that you are a man !*
**labōrābat ut reliquās cīvitātēs adjungeret,** *he was striving to join the remaining states to him.*

> *a.* **Cōnor,** *try,* always takes the Infinitive.

NOTE. — Verbs of all the above classes also admit the Infinitive, especially in poetry.

---

[1] Especially : **permittō, concēdō, nōn patior.**
[2] Especially : **prohibeō, impediō, dēterreō.**
[3] Especially : **cōnstituō, dēcernō, cēnseō, placuit, convenit, pacīscor.**
[4] Especially : **labōrō, dō operam, id agō, contendō. impetrō.**

6. With a few other expressions, such as **necesse est, reliquum est, sequitur, licet, oportet**; as, —

> **sequitur ut doceam,** *it remains for me to show;*
> **licet redeās,** *you may return;*
> **oportet loquāmur,** *we must speak.*

On the absence of **ut** with **licet** and **oportet**, see paragraph 8.

7. Here also belong phrases of the type: **nūlla causa est cūr, quīn; nōn est cūr,** *etc.*; **nihil est cūr,** *etc.*; as, —

**nūlla causa est cūr timeam,** *there is no reason why I should fear* (originally Deliberative: *why should I fear? There's no reason*);
**nihil est quīn dīcam,** *there is no reason why I should not say.*

8. Many of the above classes of verbs at times take the simple Subjunctive without **ut**. In such cases we must not recognize any omission of **ut**, but simply an earlier form of expression which existed before the **ut**-clause arose. This is regularly the case with **necesse est, licet,** and **oportet**; see 6. Other examples are: —

> **eōs moneō dēsinant,** *I warn them to stop;*
> **huic imperat adeat cīvitātēs,** *he orders him to visit the states.*

### B. Substantive Clauses developed from the Optative.

**296.** Substantive Clauses Developed from the Optative occur: —

1. With verbs of *wishing, desiring*, especially **cupiō, optō, volō, mālō** (conjunctions **ut, nē, ut nē**); as, —

**optō ut in hōc jūdiciō nēmō improbus reperiātur,** *I hope that in this court no bad man may be found* (here **ut reperiātur** represents a simple optative of direct statement, *viz.* **reperiātur,** *may no bad man be found!*);
**cupiō nē veniat,** *I desire that he may not come.*

> *a.* The simple Subjunctive (without **ut**) sometimes occurs with verbs of this class. (See § 295, 8.) Examples are: **velim scrībās,** *I wish you would write;* **vellem scrīpsisset,** *I wish he had written.*

2. With expressions of *fearing* (**timeō, metuō, vereor,** etc.). Here **nē** means *that, lest*, and **ut** means *that not*; as, —

**timeō nē veniat,** *I fear that he will come* (originally: *may he not come! I'm afràid [he will]*);

**timeō ut veniat,** *I fear that he will not come* (originally: *may he come! I'm afraid [he won't]*).

*a.* **Nē nōn** sometimes occurs instead of **ut**, especially where the verb of *fearing* has a negative, or where the writer desires to emphasize some particular word in the dependent clause ; as, —

**nōn vereor nē hōc nōn fīat**, *I am not afraid that this will not happen ;*

**vereor nē exercitum fīrmum habēre nōn possit,** *I fear that he is unable* (**nōn possit**) *to have a strong army.*

### *C.* Substantive Clauses of Result.

**297.** Substantive Clauses of Result (introduced by **ut, ut nōn**) are a development of pure Result clauses, and occur with the following classes of words : —

1. As object clauses after verbs of *doing, accomplishing* (especially **faciō, efficiō, cōnficiō**). Thus : —

**gravitās morbī facit ut medicīnā egeāmus,** *the severity of disease makes us need medicine.*

2. As the subject of several impersonal verbs, particularly **fit, efficitur, accidit, ēvenit, contingit, accēdit, fierī potest, fore, sequitur, relinquitur.** Thus : —

**ex quō efficitur, ut voluptās nōn sit summum bonum,** *from which it follows that pleasure is not the greatest good ;*

**ita fit, ut nēmō esse possit beātus,** *thus it happens that no one can be happy ;*

**accēdēbat ut nāvēs deessent,** *another thing was the lack of ships* (lit. *it was added that ships were lacking*).

3. As predicate or appositive after expressions like **jūs est, mōs est, cōnsuētūdō est;** also after neuter pronouns, **hōc, illud,** *etc.* Thus : —

**est mōs hominum ut nōlint eundem plūribus rēbus excellere,** *it is the way of men not to wish the same person to excel in many things.*

### *D.* Substantive Clauses introduced by *Quīn.*

**298.** Substantive Clauses introduced by **quīn** (used sometimes as subject, sometimes as object) occur after negative and interrogative expressions of *doubt, omission,* and the like, particularly after **nōn dubitō,** *I do not doubt ;* **quis**

dubitat, *who doubts?;* nōn (haud) dubium est, *there is no doubt.* The mood is the Subjunctive. Examples: —

quis dubitat quīn in virtūte dīvitiae sint, *who doubts that in virtue there are riches?*

nōn dubium erat quīn ventūrus esset, *there was no doubt that he was about to come.*

> *a.* In Nepos, Livy, and post-Augustan writers an Infinitive sometimes takes the place of the quīn-clause after nōn dubitō; as, —
>
> nōn dubitāmus inventōs esse, *we do not doubt that men were found.*
>
> *b.* Nōn dubitō, *I do not hesitate,* is regularly followed by the Infinitive, though sometimes by a quīn-clause.

### E. Substantive Clauses Introduced by *Quod*.

**299.** 1. Quod, *the fact that, that,* introduces Substantive Clauses in the Indicative. This construction occurs especially —

> *a)* In apposition with a preceding demonstrative, as hōc, id, illud, illa, ex eō, inde, *etc.* Thus: —
>
> illud est admīrātiōne dignum, quod captīvōs retinendōs cēnsuit, *this is especially worthy of admiration, that he thought the prisoners ought to be kept;*
>
> hōc ūnō praestāmus vel maximē ferīs, quod colloquimur inter nōs, *in this one respect we are especially superior to the beasts, that we talk with each other.*
>
> *b)* After bene fit, bene accidit, male fit, bene facere, mīror, *etc.*; as, —
>
> bene mihi ēvenit, quod mittor ad mortem, *it is well for me that I am sent to death;*
>
> bene fēcistī quod mānsistī, *you did well in remaining.*

2. Quod at the beginning of the sentence sometimes has the force of *as regards the fact that.* Thus: —

quod multitūdinem Germānōrum in Galliam trādūcō, id meī mūniendī causā faciō, *as regards the fact that I am transporting a multitude of Germans into Gaul, I am doing it for the sake of strengthening myself;*

quod mē Agamemnona aemulārī putās, falleris, *as regards your thinking that I emulate Agamemnon, you are mistaken.*

### F. Indirect Questions.

**300.** 1. Indirect Questions are Substantive Clauses used after verbs of *asking, inquiring, telling,* and the like. They take their verb in the Subjunctive.[1] Like Direct Questions (see § 162) they may be introduced —

    *a*) By Interrogative Pronouns or Adverbs; as, —

        **dīc mihi ubi fuerīs, quid fēcerīs,** *tell me where you were, what you did;*

        **oculīs jūdicārī nōn potest in utram partem fluat Arar,** *it cannot be determined by the eye in which direction the Arar flows;*

        **bis bīna quot essent, nesciēbat,** *he did not know how many two times two were.*

NOTE. — Care should be taken to distinguish Indirect Questions from Relative Clauses. The difference between the two appears clearly in the following : —

**effugere nēmō id potest quod futūrum est,** *no one can escape what is destined to come to pass;* but

**saepe autem ne ūtile quidem est scīre quid futūrum sit,** *but often it is not even useful to know what is coming to pass.*

    *b*) By **num** or **-ne,** without distinction of meaning; as, —

        **Epamīnōndās quaesīvit num salvus esset clipeus,** or **salvusne esset clipeus,** *Epaminondas asked whether his shield was safe;*

        **disputātur num interīre virtūs in homine possit,** *the question is raised whether virtue can die in a man;*

        **ex Sōcrate quaesītum est nōnne Archelāum beātum putāret,** *the question was asked of Socrates whether he did not think Archelaus happy.*

NOTE. — **Nōnne** in Indirect Questions occurs only after **quaerō,** as in the last example above.

    2. Often the Indirect Question represents a Deliberative Subjunctive of the direct discourse; as, —

**nesciō quid faciam,** *I do not know what to do.* (Direct : **quid faciam,** *what shall I do!*)

---

[1] Exclamations, also, upon becoming indirect, take the Subjunctive, as **cōnsiderā quam variae sint hominum cupīdinēs,** *consider how varied are the desires of men.* (Direct: **quam variae sunt hominum cupīdinēs!**)

3. After verbs of *expectation* and *endeavor* (**exspectō, cōnor, experior, temptō**) we sometimes find an Indirect Question introduced by **sī**; as, —

**cōnantur sī perrumpere possint,** *they try whether they can break through.*

> *a.* Sometimes the governing verb is omitted; as, —
>
> > **pergit ad proximam spēluncam sī forte eō vēstīgia ferrent,** *he proceeded to the nearest cave (to see) if the tracks led thither.*

4. **Indirect Double Questions** are introduced in the main by the same particles as direct double questions (§ 162, 4); *viz.*: —

utrum . . . an;

-ne . . . . . an;

——   . . . . an;

——   . . . . ne.

Examples: —

**quaerō utrum vērum an falsum sit,**
**quaerō vērumne an falsum sit,**   } *I ask whether it is true or false?*
**quaerō vērum an falsum sit,**
**quaerō vērum falsumne sit,**

> *a.* '*Or not*' in the second member of the double question is ordinarily expressed by **necne**, less frequently by **an nōn**; as, —
> **dī utrum sint necne, quaeritur,** *it is asked whether there are gods or not.*

5. **Haud sciō an, nesciō an,** by omission of the first member of the double question, occur with the Subjunctive in the sense : *I am inclined to think, probably, perhaps*; as, —

**haud sciō an ita sit,** *I am inclined to think this is so.*

6. In early Latin and in poetry the Indicative is sometimes used in Indirect Questions.

### CONDITIONAL SENTENCES.

**301.** Conditional Sentences are compound sentences (§ 164) consisting of two parts, the Protasis (or *condition*), usually introduced by **sī, nisi,** or **sīn,** and the Apodosis (or *conclusion*). There are the following types of Conditional Sentences : —

**First Type. — Nothing Implied as to the Reality of the Supposed Case.**

**302.** 1. Here we regularly have the Indicative in both Protasis and Apodosis. Any tense may be used; as, —

sī hōc crēdis, errās, *if you believe this, you are mistaken* ;
nātūram sī sequēmur, numquam aberrābimus, *if we follow Nature, we shall never go astray* ;
sī hōc dīxistī, errāstī, *if you said this, you were in error.*

2. Sometimes the Protasis takes the Indefinite Second Person Singular (§ 356, 3) of the Present or Perfect Subjunctive, with the force of the Indicative ; as, —

memoria minuitur, nisi eam exerceās, *memory is impaired unless you exercise it.*

3. Here belong also those conditional sentences in which the Protasis denotes a repeated action (compare §§ 287, 2 ; 288, 3) ; as, —

sī quis equitum dēciderat, peditēs circumsistēbant, *if any one of the horsemen fell, the foot-soldiers gathered about him.*

    *a.* Instead of the Indicative, Livy and subsequent writers employ the Subjunctive of the Historical tenses in the Protasis to denote repeated action ; as, —

        sī dīcendō quis diem eximeret, *if (ever) anybody consumed a day in pleading ;* sī quandō adsidēret, *if ever he sat by.*

4. Where the sense demands it, the Apodosis in conditional sentences of the First Type may be an Imperative or one of the Independent Subjunctives (Hortatory, Deliberative, *etc.*) ; as, —

sī hōc crēditis, tacēte, *if you believe this, be silent* ;
sī hōc crēdimus, taceāmus, *if we believe this, let us keep silent.*

**Second Type. — 'Should'-'Would' Conditions.**

**303.** Here we regularly have the Subjunctive (of the Present or Perfect tense) in both Protasis and Apodosis ; as, —

sī hōc dīcās, errēs,    } *if you should say this, you would be mis-*
sī hōc dīxerīs, errāverīs, }   *taken.*
sī velim Hannibalis proelia omnia dēscrībere, diēs mē dēficiat, *if I should wish to describe all the battles of Hannibal, time would fail me* ;

**mentiar, sī negem,** *I should lie, if I should deny it* ;

**haec sī tēcum patria loquātur, nōnne impetrāre dēbeat,** *if your country should plead thus with you, would she not deserve to obtain her request ?*

a. The Subjunctive in the Apodosis of conditional sentences of this type is of the Potential variety.

b. Sometimes we find the Indicative in the Apodosis of sentences of the Second Type, where the writer wishes to assert the accomplishment of a result more positively ; as, —

> **aliter sī faciat, nūllam habet auctōritātem,** *if he should do otherwise, he has no authority.*

**Third Type. — Supposed Case Represented as Contrary to Fact.**

**304.** 1. Here we regularly have the Subjunctive in both Protasis and Apodosis, the Imperfect referring *to present time*, and the Pluperfect referring *to past ;* as, —

**sī amīcī meī adessent, opis nōn indigērem,** *if my friends were here, I should not lack assistance ;*

**sī hōc dīxissēs, errāssēs,** *if you had said this, you would have erred ;*

**sapientia nōn expeterētur, sī nihil efficeret,** *philosophy would not be desired, if it accomplished nothing ;*

**cōnsilium, ratiō, sententia nisi essent in senibus, nōn summum cōnsilium majōrēs nostrī appellāssent senātum,** *unless deliberation, reason, and wisdom existed in old men, our ancestors would not have called their highest deliberative body a senate.*

2. Sometimes the Imperfect Subjunctive is found referring to the past, especially to denote *a continued act, or a state of things still existing ;* as, —

**Laelius, Fūrius, Catō sī nihil litterīs adjuvārentur, numquam sē ad eārum studium contulissent,** *Laelius, Furius, and Cato would never have devoted themselves to the study of letters, unless they had been (constantly) helped by them ;*

**num igitur sī ad centēsimum annum vīxisset, senectūtis eum suae paenitēret,** *if he had lived to his hundredth year, would he have regretted (and now be regretting) his old age ?*

3. The Apodosis in conditional sentences of this type sometimes stands in the Indicative (Imperfect, Perfect, or Pluperfect), *viz.* —

    *a*) Frequently in expressions of *ability, obligation,* or *necessity*; as, —

        **nisi fēlīcitās in sōcordiam vertisset, exuere jugum potuērunt,** *unless their prosperity had turned to folly, they could have thrown off the yoke;*

NOTE. — In sentences of this type, however, it is not the *possibility* that is represented as-contrary-to-fact, but something to be supplied in thought from the context. Thus in the foregoing sentence the logical apodosis is **et exuissent** understood (*and they would have shaken it off*). When the *possibility* itself is conditioned, the Subjunctive is used.

        **eum patris locō colere dēbēbās, sī ūlla in tē pietās esset,** *you ought to revere him as a father, if you had any sense of devotion.*

    *b*) With both the Periphrastic Conjugations; as, —

        **sī Sēstius occīsus esset, fuistisne ad arma itūrī,** *if Sestius had been slain, would you have proceeded to arms?*

        **sī ūnum diem morātī essētis, moriendum omnibus fuit,** *if you had delayed one day, you would all have had to die.*

### Protasis expressed without *Sī.*

**305.** 1. The Protasis is not always expressed by a clause with **sī,** but may be implied in a word, a phrase, or merely by the context; as, —

**aliōquī haec nōn scrīberentur,** *otherwise* (*i.e.* if matters were otherwise) *these things would not be written;*

**nōn potestis, voluptāte omnia dīrigentēs, retinēre virtūtem,** *you cannot retain virtue, if you direct everything with reference to pleasure.*

    2. Sometimes an Imperative, or a Jussive Subjunctive, serves as Protasis. Thus: —

**crās petitō, dabitur,** *if you ask to-morrow, it shall be given you* (lit. *ask to-morrow, etc.*) ;

**haec reputent, vidēbunt,** *if they consider this, they will see* (lit. *let them consider, etc.*) ;

**rogēs Zēnōnem, respondeat,** *if you should ask Zeno, he would answer.*

## Use of *Nisi*, *Sī Nōn*, *Sīn*.

**306.** 1. **Nisi**, *unless*, negatives the entire protasis; **sī nōn** negatives a single word; as, —

**ferreus essem, nisi tē amārem,** *I should be hard-hearted unless I
loved you;* but —

**ferreus essem, sī tē nōn amārem,** *I should be hard-hearted if I did
NOT love you.*

In the first example, it is the notion of *loving you* that is negatived,
in the second, the notion of *loving*.

   2. **Sī nōn (sī minus)** is regularly employed : —

   *a)* When an apodosis with **at, tamen, certē** follows; as, —

   **dolōrem sī nōn potuerō frangere, tamen occultābō,** *if
   I cannot crush my sorrow, yet I will hide it.*

   *b)* When an affirmative protasis is repeated in negative form;
   as, —

   **sī fēceris, magnam habēbō grātiam; sī nōn fēceris,
   ignōscam,** *if you do it, I shall be deeply grateful; if you
   do not do it, I shall pardon you.*

   *a.* But if the verb is omitted in the repetition, only **sī minus** or **sīn
   minus** is admissible; as, —

   **hōc sī assecūtus sum, gaudeō; sī minus, mē cōnsōlor,** *if I
   have attained this, I am glad; if not, I console myself.*

3. **Sīn.** Where one protasis is followed by another opposed in
meaning, but affirmative in form, the second is introduced by **sīn**; as, —

**hunc mihi timōrem ēripe; sī vērus est, nē opprimar, sīn falsus,
ut timēre dēsinam,** *relieve me of this fear; if it is well
founded, that I may not be destroyed; but if it is groundless,
that I may cease to fear.*

   4. **Nisi** has a fondness for combining with negatives (**nōn, nēmō,
nihil**) ; as, —

**nihil cōgitāvit nisi caedem,** *he had no thought but murder.*

   *a.* Nōn and nisi are always separated in the best Latinity.

   5. **Nisi forte, nisi vērō, nisi sī,** *unless perchance, unless indeed*
(often with ironical force), take the Indicative ; as, —

**nisi vērō, quia perfecta rēs nōn est, nōn vidētur pūnienda,**
*unless indeed, because an act is not consummated, it does not
seem to merit punishment.*

### Conditional Clauses of Comparison.

**307.** 1. Conditional Clauses of Comparison are introduced by the particles, **ac sī, ut sī, quasi, quam sī, tamquam
sī, velut sī,** or simply by **velut** or **tamquam.** They stand in
the Subjunctive mood and regularly involve an ellipsis (see
§ 374, 1), as indicated in the following examples : —

**tantus patrēs metus cēpit, velut sī jam ad portās hostis esset,** *as
great fear seized the senators as (would have seized them) if the
enemy were already at the gates ;*

**sed quid ego hīs testibus ūtor quasi rēs dubia aut obscūra sit,**
*but why do I use these witnesses, as (I should do) if the matter
were doubtful or obscure ;*

**serviam tibi tam quasi ēmerīs mē argentō,** *I will serve you as
though you had bought me for money.*

2. Note that in sentences of this kind the Latin observes the regular principles for the Sequence of Tenses. Thus after principal tenses
the Latin uses the Present and Perfect (as in the second and third examples), where the English uses the Past and Past Perfect.

### Concessive Clauses.

**308.** The term 'Concessive' is best restricted to those
clauses developed from the Jussive Subjunctive which
have the force of *granted that, etc.;* (see § 278) as, —

**sit fūr, sit sacrilegus, at est bonus imperātor,** *granted that he is a
thief and a robber, yet he is a good commander ;*

**haec sint falsa,** *granted that this is false ;*

**nē sit summum malum dolor, malum certē est,** *granted that pain
is not the greatest evil, yet it is certainly an evil.*

### Adversative Clauses with *Quamvīs, Quamquam, etc.*

**309.** Clauses introduced by **quamvīs, quamquam, etsī,
tametsī, cum,** *although,* while often classed as 'Concessive,' are yet essentially different from genuine Concessive
clauses. As a rule, they do not *grant* or *concede* anything, but rather state that something is true *in spite of*

*something else.* They accordingly emphasize the adversative idea, and are properly Subordinate Adversative Clauses. The different particles used to introduce these clauses have different meanings and take different constructions, as follows:—

1. **Quamvīs,** *however much, although,* does not introduce a statement of fact, but represents an act merely as conceived. It is followed by the Subjunctive, usually of the present tense; as,—

**hominēs quamvīs in turbidīs rēbus sint, tamen interdum animīs relaxantur,** *in however stirring events men may engage, yet at times they relax their energies;*

**nōn est potestās opitulandī reī pūblicae quamvīs ea premātur perīculīs,** *there is no opportunity to succor the state, though it be beset by dangers.*

2. **Quamquam, etsī, tametsī,** *although,* introduce a statement of fact, and are followed by the Indicative (of any tense); as,—

**quamquam omnis virtūs nōs allicit, tamen jūstitia id maximē efficit,** *although all virtue attracts us, yet justice does so especially;*

**Caesar, etsī nōndum cōnsilium hostium cognōverat, tamen id quod accidit suspicābātur,** *Caesar, though he did not yet know the plans of the enemy, yet was suspecting what actually occurred.*

    *a.* **Etsī,** *although,* must be distinguished from **etsī,** *even if.* The latter is a conditional particle and takes any of the constructions admissible for **sī.** (See §§ 302–304.)

3. **Cum,** *although,* is followed by the Subjunctive; as,—

**Atticus honōrēs nōn petiit, cum eī patērent,** *Atticus did not seek honors, though they were open to him.*

4. **Licet** sometimes loses its verbal force (see § 295, 6) and sinks to the level of a conjunction with the force of *although.* It takes the Subjunctive, Present or Perfect; as,—

**licet omnēs terrōrēs impendeant, succurram,** *though all terrors hang over me, (yet) I will lend aid.*

5. **Quamquam,** with the force *and yet,* is often used to introduce principal clauses; as,—

**quamquam quid loquor,** *and yet why do I speak?*

6. In post-Augustan writers **quamquam** is freely construed with the Subjunctive, while **quamvīs** is often used to introduce statements of fact, and takes either the Indicative or the Subjunctive. Thus: —

**quamquam movērētur hīs vōcibus,** *although he was moved by these words;*
**quamvīs multī opīnārentur,** *though many thought;*
**quamvīs īnfēstō animō pervēnerās,** *though you had come with hostile intent.*

### Clauses with *Dum, Modo, Dummodo,* denoting a Wish or a Proviso.

**310.** These particles are followed by the Subjunctive (negative **nē**) and have two distinct uses: —

I. They are used to introduce clauses *embodying a wish* entertained by the subject of the leading verb; as, —

**multī honesta neglegunt dummodo potentiam cōnsequantur,** *many neglect honor in their desire to obtain power (if only they may attain);*
**omnia postposuī, dum praeceptīs patris pārērem,** *I made everything else secondary, in my desire to obey the injunctions of my father;*
**nīl obstat tibi, dum nē sit dītior alter,** *nothing hinders you in your desire that your neighbor may not be richer than you.*

II. They are used to express a *proviso* ('*provided that*'); as, —

**ōderint, dum metuant,** *let them hate, provided they fear;*
**manent ingenia senibus, modo permaneat studium et industria,** *old men retain their faculties, provided only they retain their interest and vigor;*
**nūbant, dum nē dōs fīat comes,** *let them marry, provided no dowry goes with it.*

### Relative Clauses.

**311.** Relative Clauses are introduced by Relative Pronouns, Adjectives, or Adverbs.

**312.** 1. Relative clauses usually stand in the Indicative Mood, especially clauses introduced by those General Relatives which are doubled or have the suffix **-cumque**; as, —

quidquid id est, timeō Danaōs et dōna ferentēs, *whatever it is, I
fear the Greeks even when they offer gifts;*
quidquid oritur, quālecumque est, causam ā nātūrā habet, *whatever comes into being, of whatever sort it is, has its primal cause
in Nature.*

2. Any simple Relative may introduce a conditional sentence of
any of the three types mentioned in §§ 302–304; as, —

quī hōc dīcit, errat, *he who says this is mistaken* (First Type);
quī hōc dīcat, erret, *he would be mistaken who should say this*
(Second Type);
quī hōc dīxisset, errāsset, *the man who had said this would have
been mistaken.*

### INDIRECT DISCOURSE (*ŌRĀTIŌ OBLĪQUA*).

**313.** When the language or thought of any person is
reproduced without change, that is called Direct Discourse
(*Ōrātiō Rēcta*); as, *Caesar said, ' The die is cast.'* When,
on the other hand, one's language or thought is made to
depend upon a verb of *saying, thinking, etc.*, that is called
Indirect Discourse (*Ōrātiō Oblīqua*); as, *Caesar said that
the die was cast; Caesar thought that his troops were
victorious.*

   *a.* For the verbs most frequently employed to introduce Indirect
   Discourse, see § 331.

### MOODS IN INDIRECT DISCOURSE.

#### Declarative Sentences.

**314.** 1. Declarative Sentences upon becoming Indirect
change their main clause to the Infinitive with Subject
Accusative, while all subordinate clauses take the Subjunctive; as, —

Rēgulus dīxit quam diū jūre jūrandō hostium tenērētur nōn esse
sē senātōrem, *Regulus said that as long as he was held by his
pledge to the enemy he was not a senator.* (Direct: **quam diū
teneor nōn sum senātor.**)

2. The verb of *saying, thinking, etc.,* is sometimes to be inferred from the context; as, —

tum Rōmulus lēgātōs circā vīcīnās gentēs mīsit quī societātem cōnūbiumque peterent: urbēs quoque, ut cētera, ex īnfimō nāscī, *then Romulus sent envoys around among the neighboring tribes, to ask for alliance and the right of inter-marriage, (saying that) cities, like everything else, start from a modest beginning.*

3. Subordinate clauses which contain an explanatory statement of the writer and so are not properly a part of the Indirect Discourse, or which emphasize the fact stated, take the Indicative; as, —

nūntiātum est Ariovistum ad occupandum Vesontiōnem, quod est oppidum maximum Sēquanōrum contendere, *it was reported that Ariovistus was hastening to seize Vesontio, which is the largest town of the Sequani.*

4. Sometimes a subordinate clause is such only in its external form, and in sense is principal. It then takes the Infinitive with Subject Accusative. This occurs especially in case of relative clauses, where quī is equivalent to et hīc, nam hīc, *etc.*; as, —

dīxit urbem Athēniēnsium prōpugnāculum oppositum esse bar-barīs, apud quam jam bis classēs rēgiās fēcisse naufra-gium, *he said the city of the Athenians had been set against the barbarians like a bulwark, near which ( = and near it) the fleets of the King had twice met disaster.*

5. The Subject Accusative of the Infinitive is sometimes omitted when it refers to the same person as the subject of the leading verb, or can easily be supplied from the context; as, —

cum id nescīre Māgō dīceret, *when Mago said he did not know this* (for sē nescīre).

### Interrogative Sentences.

**315.** 1. Real questions of the Direct Discourse, upon becoming indirect, are regularly put in the Subjunctive; as, —

Ariovistus Caesarī respondit: sē prius in Galliam vēnisse quam populum Rōmānum. Quid sibi vellet? Cūr in suās pos-sessiōnēs venīret, *Ariovistus replied to Caesar that he*

*had come into Gaul before the Roman people. What did he
(Caesar) mean? Why did he come into his domain?* (Direct:
**quid tibi vīs? cūr in meās possessiōnēs venīs?**)

2. Rhetorical questions, on the other hand, being asked
merely for effect, and being equivalent in force to emphatic
statements, regularly stand in the Infinitive in Indirect Discourse. Thus: —

**quid est levius** (lit. *what is more trivial*, = nothing is more trivial)
of the Direct Discourse becomes **quid esse levius** in the Indirect.

3. Deliberative Subjunctives of the Direct Discourse remain unchanged in mood in the Indirect: as, —

**quid faceret,** *what was he to do?* (Direct: **quid faciat?**)

### Imperative Sentences.

**316.** All Imperatives or Jussive Subjunctives of the
Direct Discourse appear as Subjunctives in the Indirect; as, —

**mīlitēs certiōrēs fēcit paulisper intermitterent proelium,** *he
told the soldiers to stop the battle for a little.* (Direct:
**intermittite.**)

*a.* The negative in such sentences is **nē**; as, —

**nē suae virtūtī tribueret,** *let him not attribute it to his own
valor!*

### TENSES IN INDIRECT DISCOURSE.

#### A. Tenses of the Infinitive.

**317.** These are used in accordance with the regular
principles for the use of the Infinitive as given in § 270.

*a.* The Perfect Infinitive may represent any past tense of the
Indicative of Direct Discourse. Thus: —

**sciō tē haec ēgisse** may mean —

| | |
|---|---|
| *I know you were doing this.* | (Direct: **haec agēbās.**) |
| *I know you did this.* | (Direct: **haec ēgistī.**) |
| *I know you had done this.* | (Direct: **haec ēgerās.**) |

### B. Tenses of the Subjunctive.

**318.** These follow the regular principle for the Sequence of Tenses, being Principal if the verb of *saying* is Principal; Historical if it is Historical. Yet for the sake of vividness, we often find the Present Subjunctive used after an historical tense (*Repraesentātiō*); as, —

**Caesar respondit, sī obsidēs dentur, sēsē pācem esse factūrum.** *Caesar replied that, if hostages be given, he would make peace.*

    *a.* For the sequence after the Perfect Infinitive, see § 268, 2.

## CONDITIONAL SENTENCES IN INDIRECT DISCOURSE.

### Conditional Sentences of the First Type.

**319.** *A.* THE APODOSIS. Any tense of the Indicative is changed to the corresponding tense of the Infinitive (§§ 270; 317, *a*).

*B.* THE PROTASIS. The protasis takes those tenses of the Subjunctive which are required by the Sequence of Tenses.

Examples : —

| DIRECT. | INDIRECT. |
|---|---|
| sī hōc crēdis, errās, | dīcō, sī hōc crēdās, tē errāre ;<br>dīxī, sī hōc crēderēs, tē errāre. |
| sī hōc crēdēs, errābis, | dīcō, sī hōc crēdās, tē errātūrum essé ;<br>dīxī, sī hōc crēderēs, tē errātūrum esse. |
| sī hōc crēdideris, errābis, | dīcō, sī hōc crēdiderīs, tē errātūrum esse ;<br>dīxī, sī hōc crēdidissēs, tē errātūrum esse. |
| sī hōc crēdēbās, errāvistī, | dīcō, sī hōc crēderēs, tē errāvisse ;<br>dīxī, sī hōc crēderēs, tē errāvisse. |

    *a.* Note that a Future Perfect Indicative of the Direct Discourse regularly appears in the Indirect as a Perfect Subjunctive after a principal tense, and as a Pluperfect Subjunctive after an historical tense.

### Conditional Sentences of the Second Type.

**320.** *A.* THE APODOSIS. The Present Subjunctive of the Direct Discourse regularly becomes the Future Infinitive of the Indirect.

*B.* THE PROTASIS. The Protasis takes those tenses of the Subjunctive demanded by the sequence of tenses.

Examples: —

sī hōc **crēdās, errēs,**  { dīcō, sī hōc **crēdās,** tē **errātūrum esse** ;
  dīxī, sī hōc **crēderēs,** tē **errātūrum esse.**

### Conditional Sentences of the Third Type.

**321.** *A.* THE APODOSIS.

1. The Imperfect Subjunctive of the Direct Discourse becomes the Future Infinitive.

   *a.* But this construction is rare, being represented in the classical Latinity by a single example (Caesar, V. 29. 2). Some scholars question the correctness of this passage.

2. The Pluperfect Subjunctive of the Direct Discourse becomes : —

   *a*) In the Active Voice the Infinitive in **-ūrus fuisse.**
   *b*) In the Passive Voice it takes the form **futūrum fuisse ut** with the Imperfect Subjunctive.

*B.* THE PROTASIS. The protasis in Conditional Sentences of this type always remains unchanged.

Examples: —

sī hōc **crēderēs, errārēs,**      dīcō (dīxī), sī hōc **crēderēs,** tē **errātūrum esse** ;

sī hōc **crēdidissēs, errāvissēs,**   dīcō (dīxī), sī hōc **crēdidissēs,** tē **errātūrum fuisse** ;

sī hōc **dīxissēs, pūnītus essēs.**   dīcō (dīxī), sī hōc **dīxissēs, futūrum fuisse ut pūnīrēris.**

**322.** When an apodosis of a conditional sentence of the Third Type referring to the past is at the same time a Result clause, or a

**quīn**-clause (after **nōn dubitō**, *etc.*), it stands in the Perfect Subjunctive in the form -**ūrus fuerim**; as, —

**ita territi sunt, ut arma trāditūrī fuerint,**[1] nisi Caesar subitō advēnisset, *they were so frightened that they would have given up their arms, had not Caesar suddenly arrived;*
**nōn dubitō quīn, sī hōc dīxissēs, errātūrus fuerīs,**[1] *I do not doubt that, if you had said this, you would have made a mistake.*

　　*a.* This peculiarity is confined to the Active Voice. In the Passive, such sentences, when they become dependent, remain unchanged; as, —

　　　　**nōn dubitō quīn, sī hōc dīxissēs, vituperātus essēs,** *I do not doubt that, if you had said this, you would have been blamed.*

　　*b.* When an Indirect Question becomes an apodosis in a conditional sentence of the Third Type, -**ūrus fuerim** (rarely -**ūrus fuissem**) is used; as, —

　　　　**quaerō, num, sī hōc dīxissēs, errātūrus fuerīs (ol fuissēs).**

　　*c.* **Potuī,** when it becomes a dependent apodosis in sentences of this Type, usually changes to the Perfect Subjunctive; as, —

　　　　**concursū tōtīus cīvitātis dēfēnsī sunt, ut frīgidissimōs quoque ōrātōrēs populī studia excitāre potuerint,** *they were defended before a gathering of all the citizens, so that the interest of the people would have been enough to excite even the most apathetic orators.*

## IMPLIED INDIRECT DISCOURSE.

**323.** The Subjunctive is often used in subordinate clauses whose indirect character is *merely implied by the context*; as, —

**dēmōnstrābantur mihi praetereā, quae Sōcratēs dē immortālitāte animōrum disseruisset,** *there were explained to me besides, the arguments which Socrates had set forth concerning the immortality of the soul* (*i.e.* the arguments which, it was said, Socrates had set forth);
**Paetus omnēs librōs quōs pater suus relīquisset mihi dōnāvit,** *Paetus gave me all the books which (as he said) his father had left.*

---

[1] **Trāditūrī fuerint** and **errātūrus fuerīs** are to be regarded as representing **trāditūrī fuērunt** and **errātūrus fuistī** of Direct Discourse. (See § 304. 3. *b.*)

## SUBJUNCTIVE BY ATTRACTION.

**324.** 1. Subordinate clauses dependent upon the Sub‧ junctive are frequently attracted into the same mood, especially when they do not express a fact, but constitute *an essential part of one complex idea;* as, —

nēmō avārus adhūc inventus est, cui, quod habēret, esset satis, *no miser has yet been found who was satisfied with what he had;*

cum dīversās causās afferrent, dum fōrmam suī quisque et animī et ingeniī redderent, *as they brought forward different arguments, while each mirrored his own individual type of mind and natural bent;*

quod ego fatear, pudeat? *should I be ashamed of a thing which I admit?*

2. Similarly a subordinate clause dependent upon an Infinitive is put in the Subjunctive when the two form one closely united whole; as,—

mōs est Athēnīs quotannīs in cōntiōne laudārī eōs quī sint in proeliīs interfectī, *it is the custom at Athens every year for those to be publicly eulogized who have been killed in battle.* (Here the notion of 'praising those who fell in battle' forms an inseparable whole.)

## NOUN AND ADJECTIVE FORMS OF THE VERB.

**325.** These are the Infinitive, Participle, Gerund, and Supine. All of these partake of the nature of the Verb, on the one hand, and of the Noun or Adjective, on the other. Thus: —

As Verbs, —

    *a*) They may be limited by adverbs;
    *b*) They admit an object;
    *c*) They have the properties of voice and tense.

As Nouns or Adjectives, —

    *a*) They are declined;
    *b*) They take Noun or Adjective constructions.

## THE INFINITIVE.

### Infinitive without Subject Accusative.

**326.** This is used chiefly as Subject or Object but also as Predicate or Appositive.

NOTE. — The Infinitive was originally a Dative, and traces of this are still to be seen in the poetical use of the Infinitive to express *purpose ;* as, **nec dulcēs occurrent ōscula nātī praeripere**, *and no sweet children will run to snatch kisses.*

### *A. As Subject.*

**327.** 1. The Infinitive without Subject Accusative is used as the Subject of **esse** and various impersonal verbs, particularly **opus est, necesse est, oportet, juvat, dēlectat, placet, libet, licet, praestat, decet, pudet, interest,** *etc. ;* as, —

**dulce et decōrum est prō patriā morī,** *it is sweet and noble to die for one's country ;*

**virōrum est fortium toleranter dolōrem patī,** *it is the part of brave men to endure pain with patience ;*

**senātuī placuit lēgātōs mittere,** *the Senate decided* (lit. *it pleased the Senate) to send envoys.*

2. Even though the Infinitive itself appears without Subject, it may take a Predicate Noun or Adjective in the Accusative ; as, —

**aliud est īrācundum esse, aliud īrātum,** *it is one thing to be irascible, another to be angry ;*

**impūne quaelibet facere, id est rēgem esse,** *to do whatever you please with impunity, that is to be a king.*

a. But when **licet** is followed by a Dative of the person, a Predicate Noun or Adjective with **esse** is attracted into the same case; as, **licuit esse ōtiōsō Themistoclī,** lit. *it was permitted to Themistocles to be at leisure.* So sometimes with other Impersonals.

### *B. As Object.*

**328.** 1. The Infinitive without Subject Accusative is used as the Object of many verbs, to denote another action of the same subject, particularly after —

**volō, cupiō, mālō, nōlō ;**     **cōgitō, meditor,** *purpose, intend;*
    **dēbeō,** *ought ;*     **neglegō,** *neglect ;*
  **statuō, cōnstituō,** *decide ;*     **vereor, timeō,** *fear ;*

audeō, *dare*;                     mātūrō, festīnō, properō, con-
studeō, contendō, *strive*;          tendō, *hasten*;
parō, *prepare* (so parātus);      assuēscō, cōnsuēscō, *accustom*
incipiō, coepī, īnstituō, *begin*;     *myself* (so assuētus, īnsuētus,
pergō, *continue*;                   assuēfactus);
dēsinō, dēsistō, *cease*;          discō, *learn*;
possum, *can*;                     sciō, *know how*;
cōnor, *try*;                      soleō, *am wont*; as, —

tū hōs intuērī audēs, *do you dare to look on these men ?*

Dēmosthenēs ad flūctūs maris dēclāmāre solēbat, *Demosthenes used to declaim by the waves of the sea.*

2. A Predicate Noun or Adjective with these Infinitives is attracted into the Nominative; as,—

beātus esse sine virtūte nēmō potest, *no one can be happy without virtue;*

Catō esse quam vidērī bonus mālēbat, *Cato preferred to be good rather than to seem so.*

### Infinitive with Subject Accusative.

**329.** This is used chiefly as Subject or Object but also as Predicate or Appositive.

#### A. As Subject.

**330.** The Infinitive with Subject Accusative (like the simple Infinitive) is used as Subject with esse and Impersonal verbs, particularly with aequum est, ūtile est, turpe est, fāma est, spēs est, fās est, nefās est, opus est, necesse est, oportet, cōnstat, praestat, licet, *etc.*; as, —

nihil in bellō oportet contemnī, *nothing ought to be despised in war;*

apertum est sibi quemque nātūrā esse cārum, *it is manifest that by nature everybody is dear to himself.*

#### B. As Object.

**331.** The Infinitive with Subject Accusative is used as Object after the following classes of verbs:

I. Most frequently after verbs of *saying, thinking, knowing, perceiving,* and the like (*Verba Sentiendī et Dēclārandī*). This is the regular construction of Principal Clauses of Indirect Discourse. Verbs that take this construction are, among others, the following: **sentiō, audiō, videō, cognōscō; putō, jūdicō, spērō, cōnfīdō; sciō, meminī; dīcō, affīrmō, negō** (*say that . . . not*), **trādō, nārrō, fateor, respondeō, scrībō, prōmittō, glōrior.** Also the phrases **certiōrem faciō** (*inform*), **memoriā teneō** (*remember*), *etc.*

Examples: —

**Epicūrēī putant cum corporibus simul animōs interīre,** *the Epicureans think that the soul perishes with the body;*

**Thalēs dīxit aquam esse initium rērum,** *Thales said that water was the first principle of the universe;*

**Dēmocritus negat quicquid esse sempiternum,** *Democritus says nothing is everlasting;*

**spērō eum ventūrum esse,** *I hope that he will come.*

II. With **jubeō,** *order,* and **vetō,** *forbid*; as, —

**Caesar mīlitēs pontem facere jussit,** *Caesar ordered the soldiers to make a bridge.*

> *a.* When the name of the person who is ordered or forbidden to do something is omitted, the Infinitive with **jubeō** and **vetō** is put in the Passive; as, **Caesar pontem fierī jussit.**

III. With **patior** and **sinō,** *permit, allow*; as, —

**nūllō sē implicārī negōtiō passus est,** *he did not permit himself to be involved in any difficulty.*

IV. With **volō, nōlō, mālō, cupiō,** when the Subject of the Infinitive is different from that of the governing verb; as, —

**nec mihi hunc errōrem extorquērī volō,** *nor do I wish this error to be wrested from me;*

**eās rēs jactārī nōlēbat,** *he was unwilling that these matters should be discussed;*

**tē tuā fruī virtūte cupimus,** *we desire that you enjoy your worth.*

> *a.* When the Subject of both verbs is the same, the simple Infinitive is regularly used in accordance with § 328. 1. But exceptions occur, especially in case of **esse** and Passive Infinitives; as, —
>
> **cupiō mē esse clēmentem,** *I desire to be lenient;*
> **Tīmoleōn māluit sē dīligī quam metuī,** *Timoleon preferred to be loved rather than feared.*
>
> *b.* **Volō** also admits the Subjunctive, with or without **ut**; **nōlō** the Subjunctive alone. (See § 296. 1. *a.*)

V. With Verbs of *emotion* (*joy, sorrow, regret, etc.*), especially **gaudeō, laetor, doleō; aegrē ferō, molestē ferō, graviter ferō,** *am annoyed, distressed;* **mīror, queror, indignor;** as,—

**gaudeō tē salvum advenīre,** *I rejoice that you arrive safely;*
**nōn molestē ferunt sē libīdinum vinculīs laxātōs ēsse,** *they are not troubled at being released from the bonds of passion;*
**mīror tē ad mē nihil scrībere,** *I wonder that you write me nothing.*

    *a.* Instead of an Infinitive these verbs also sometimes admit a **quod**-clause as Object. (See § 299.) Thus:—

        **mīror quod nōn loqueris,** *I wonder that you do not speak.*

VI. Some verbs which take two Accusatives, one of the Person and the other of the Thing (§ 178, 1), may substitute an Infinitive for the second Accusative; as,—

**cōgō tē hōc facere,** *I compel you to do this* (*cf.* **tē hōc cōgō**);
**docuī tē contentum esse,** *I taught you to be content* (*cf.* **tē modestiam docuī,** *I taught you temperance*).

### Passive Construction of the Foregoing Verbs.

**332**. Those verbs which in the Active are followed by the Infinitive with Subject Accusative, usually admit the personal construction of the Passive. This is true of the following and of some others:—

    *a*) **jubeor, vetor, sinor;** as,—

        **mīlitēs pontem facere jussī sunt,** *the soldiers were ordered to build a bridge;*
        **pōns fierī jussus est,** *a bridge was ordered built;*
        **mīlitēs castrīs exīre vetitī sunt,** *the troops were forbidden to go out of the camp;*
        **Sēstius Clōdium accūsāre nōn est situs,** *Sestius was not allowed to accuse Clodius.*

    *b*) **videor,** *I am seen, I seem;* as,—

        **vidētur comperisse,** *he seems to have discovered.*

    *c*) **dīcor, putor, exīstimor, jūdicor** (in all persons); as,—

        **dīcitur in Italiam vēnisse,** *he is said to have come into Italy;*
        **Rōmulus prīmus rēx Rōmānōrum fuisse putātur,** *Romulus is thought to have been the first king of the Romans.*

*d*) **fertur, feruntur, trāditur, trāduntur** (only in the third person); as, —

> **fertur Homērus caecus fuisse,** *Homer is said to have been blind;*
> **carmina Archilochī contumēliīs referta esse trāduntur,** *Archilochus's poems are reported to have been full of abuse.*

NOTE. — In compound tenses and periphrastic forms, the last two classes of verbs, *c*), *d*), more commonly take the impersonal construction; as, —

**trāditum est Homērum caecum fuisse,** *the story goes that Homer was blind.*

### Infinitive with Adjectives.

**333.** The Infinitive with Adjectives (except **parātus, assuētus,** *etc.*; see § 328, 1) occurs only in poetry and post-Augustan prose writers; as, —

> **contentus dēmōnstrāsse,** *contented to have proved;*
> **audāx omnia perpetī,** *bold for enduring everything.*

### Infinitive in Exclamations.

**334.** The Infinitive is used in Exclamations implying *scorn, indignation,* or *regret.* An intensive **-ne** is often attached to some word in the clause. Examples : —

**huncine sōlem tam nigrum surrēxe mihi,** *to think that to-day's sun rose with such evil omen for me!*
**sedēre tōtōs diēs in vīllā,** *to stay whole days at the villa.*

### Historical Infinitive.

**335.** The Infinitive is often used in historical narrative instead of the Imperfect Indicative. The Subject stands in the Nominative; as, —

**interim cottīdiē Caesar Haeduōs frūmentum flāgitāre,** *meanwhile Caesar was daily demanding grain of the Haedui.*

## PARTICIPLES.

### Tenses of the Participle.

**336.** I. The tenses of the Participle, like those of the Infinitive (see § 270), express time not absolutely, but with reference to the verb upon which the Participle depends.

2. The Present Participle denotes action *contemporary with* that of the verb. Thus: —

**audiō tē loquentem** = *you* ARE *speaking and I hear you*;
**audiēbam tē loquentem** = *you* WERE *speaking and I heard you*;
**áudiam tē loquentem** = *you* WILL BE *speaking and I shall hear you.*

    *a.* The Present Participle is sometimes employed with Conative force; as, —

        **assurgentem rēgem resupīnat,** *as the king was trying to rise, he threw him down.*

3. The Perfect Passive Participle denotes action *prior to* that of the verb. Thus: —

    **locūtus taceō** = *I* HAVE *spoken and am silent;*
    **locūtus tacuī** = *I* HAD *spoken and then was silent;*
    **locūtus tacēbō** = *I* SHALL *speak and then shall be silent.*

4. The **absolute** time of the action of a participle, therefore, is determined entirely by the finite verb with which it is connected.

5. Certain Perfect Passive Participles of Deponent and Semi-Deponent Verbs are used as Presents; *viz.* **arbitrātus, ausus, ratus, gāvīsus, solitus, ūsus, cōnfīsus, diffīsus, secūtus, veritus.**

#### Use of Participles.

**337.** As an Adjective the Participle may be used either as an attributive or predicate modifier of a Substantive.

1. Attributive Use. This presents no special peculiarities. Examples are: —

**glōria est cōnsentiēns laus bonōrum,** *glory is the unanimous praise of the good;*
**Conōn mūrōs ā Lysandrō dīrutōs reficit,** *Conon restored the walls destroyed by Lysander.*

2. Predicate Use. Here the Participle is often equivalent to a subordinate clause. Thus the Participle may denote: —

    *a)* Time; as, —

        **omne malum nāscēns facile opprimitur,** *every evil is easily crushed at birth.*

    *b)* A Condition; as, —

        **mente ūtī nōn possumus cibō et pōtiōne complētī,** *if gorged with food and drink, we cannot use our intellects.*

*c*) Manner; as, —

**Solōn senēscere sē dīcēbat multa in diēs addiscentem,** *Solon said he grew old learning many new things daily.*

*d*) Means; as, —

**sōl oriēns diem cōnficit,** *the sun, by its rising, makes the day.*

*e*) Opposition (*'though'*); as, —

**mendācī hominī nē vērum quidem dīcentī crēdimus,** *we do not believe a liar, though he speaks the truth.*

*f*) Cause; as, —

**perfidiam veritus ad suōs recessit,** *since he feared treachery, he returned to his own troops.*

3. **Videō** and **audiō**, besides the Infinitive, take the Present Participle in the Predicate use; as, —

**videō tē fugientem,** *I see you fleeing.*

*a.* So frequently **faciō, fingō, indūcō,** *etc.;* as, —

**eīs Catōnem respondentem facimus,** *we represent Cato replying to them;*

**Homērus Laërtem colentem agrum facit,** *Homer represents Laërtes tilling the field.*

4. The Future Active Participle (except **futūrus**) is regularly confined to its use in the Periphrastic Conjugation, but in poets and later writers it is used independently, especially to denote *purpose;* as, —

**vēnērunt castra oppugnātūrī,** *they came to assault the camp.*

5. The Perfect Passive Participle is often equivalent to a coördinate clause; as, —

**urbem captam dīruit,** *he captured and destroyed the city* (lit. *he destroyed the city captured*).

6. The Perfect Passive Participle in combination with a noun is sometimes equivalent to an abstract noun with a dependent Genitive; as, —

**post urbem conditam,** *after the founding of the city;*

**Quīnctius dēfēnsus,** *the defense of Quinctius;*

**quibus animus occupātus,** *the preoccupation of the mind with which.*

7. **Habeō** sometimes takes a Perfect Passive Participle in the Predicate construction with a force not far removed from that of the Perfect or Pluperfect Indicative; as, —

**equitātus quem coāctum habēbat,** *the cavalry which he had collected.*

8. The Gerundive denotes *obligation, necessity, etc.* Like other Participles it may be used either as Attributive or Predicate.

*a*) Less frequently as Attributive. Thus : —

**liber legendus,** *a book worth reading;*
**lēgēs observandae,** *laws deserving of observance.*

*b*) More frequently as Predicate.

1) In the Passive Periphrastic Conjugation (**amandus est,** *etc.*). In this use Intransitive Verbs can be used only impersonally, but admit their ordinary case-construction (Gen., Dat., Abl.) ; as, —

**veniendum est,** *it is necessary to come;*
**oblīvīscendum est offēnsārum,** *one must forget injuries;*
**numquam prōditōrī crēdendum est,** *you must never trust a traitor;*
**suō cuique ūtendum est jūdiciō,** *every man must use his own judgment.*

2) After **cūrō,** *provide for;* **dō, trādō,** *give over;* **relinquō,** *leave;* **concēdō,** *hand over;* and some other verbs, instead of an object clause, or to denote purpose ; as, —

**Caesar pontem in Ararī faciendum cūrāvit,** *Caesar provided for the construction of a bridge over the Arar;*
**imperātor urbem mīlitibus dīripiendam concessit,** *the general handed over the city to the soldiers to plunder.*

9. For the Gerundive as the equivalent of the Gerund, see § 339, 1.

### THE GERUND.

**338.** As a verbal noun the Gerund admits noun constructions as follows : —

1. **Genitive.** The Genitive of the Gerund is used —
    *a*) With Nouns, as objective or Appositional Genitive (see §§ 200, 202) ; as, —
      **cupiditās dominandī,** *desire of ruling;*
      **ars scrībendī,** *the art of writing.*
    *b*) With Adjectives ; as, —
      **cupidus audiendī,** *desirous of hearing.*
    *c*) With **causā, grātiā** ; as, —
      **discendī causā,** *for the sake of learning.*

2. **Dative.**   The Dative of the Gerund is used —

*a*) With Adjectives ; as, —

**aqua ūtilis est bibendō,** *water is useful for drinking.*

*b*) With Verbs (rarely) ; as, —

**adfuī scrībendō,** *I was present at the writing.*

3. **Accusative.**   The Accusative of the Gerund is used only with Prepositions, chiefly **ad** and **in** to denote purpose ; as, —

**homō ad agendum nātus est,** *man is born for action.*

4. **Ablative.**   The Ablative of the Gerund is used —

*a*) Without a Preposition, as an Ablative of Means, Cause, *etc.* (see §§ 218, 219) ; as, —

**mēns discendō alitur et cōgitandō,** *the mind is nourished by learning and reflection.*

**Themistoclēs maritimōs praedōnēs cōnsectandō mare tūtum reddidit,** *Themistocles made the sea safe by following up the pirates.*

*b*) After the prepositions **ā, dē, ex, in** ; as, —

**summa voluptās ex discendō capitur,** *the keenest pleasure is derived from learning;*

**multa dē bene beātēque vīvendō ā Platōne disputāta sunt,** *there was much discussion by Plato on the subject of living well and happily.*

5. As a rule, only the Genitive of the Gerund and the Ablative (without a preposition) admit a Direct Object.

### Gerundive Construction instead of the Gerund.

**339.**   1. Instead of the Genitive or Ablative of the Gerund with a Direct Object, another construction *may be, and very often is, used.* This consists in putting the Direct Object in the case of the Gerund (Gen. or Abl.) and using the Gerundive in agreement with it.   This is called the Gerundive Construction.   Thus : —

| GERUND CONSTRUCTION. | GERUNDIVE CONSTRUCTION. |
|---|---|
| **cupidus urbem videndī,** *desirous of seeing the city.* | **cupidus urbis videndae;** |
| **dēlector ōrātōrēs legendō,** *I am charmed with reading the orators.* | **dēlector ōrātōribus legendīs.** |

2. The Gerundive Construction *must be used* to avoid a Direct Object with the Dative of the Gerund, or with a case dependent upon a Preposition ; as, —

**locus castrīs mūniendīs aptus,** *a place adapted to fortifying a camp;*
**ad pācem petendam vēnērunt,** *they came to ask peace;*
**multum temporis cōnsūmō in legendīs poētīs,** *I spend much time in reading the poets.*

3. In order to avoid ambiguity (see § 236, 2), the Gerundive Construction must not be employed in case of Neuter Adjectives used substantively. Thus regularly —

**philosophī cupidī sunt vērum invēstīgandī,** *philosophers are eager for discovering truth* (rarely **vērī invēstīgandī**) ;
**studium plūra cognōscendī,** *a desire of knowing more* (not **plūrium cognōscendōrum**).

4. From the nature of the case only Transitive Verbs can be used in the Gerundive construction ; but **ūtor, fruor, fungor, potior** (originally transitive) regularly admit it ; as, —

**hostēs in spem potiundōrum castrōrum vēnerant,** *the enemy had conceived the hope of gaining possession of the camp.*

5. The Genitives **meī, tuī, suī, nostrī, vestrī,** when used in the Gerundive Construction, are regularly employed without reference to Gender or Number, since they were originally Neuter Singular Adjectives used substantively. Thus : —

**mulier suī servandī causā aufūgit,** *the woman fled for the sake of saving herself;*
**lēgātī in castra vēnērunt suī pūrgandī causā,** *the envoys came into camp for the purpose of clearing themselves.*
So **nostrī servandī causā,** *for the sake of saving ourselves.*

6. Occasionally the Genitive of the Gerundive Construction is used to denote *purpose ;* as, —

**quae ille cēpit lēgum ac lībertātis subvertundae,** *which he undertook for the purpose of overthrowing the laws and liberty.*

7. The Dative of the Gerundive Construction occurs in some expressions which have the character of formulas ; as, —

**decemvirī lēgibus scrībundīs,** *decemvirs for codifying the laws ;*
**quīndecimvirī sacrīs faciundīs,** *quindecimvirs for performing the sacrifices.*

## THE SUPINE.

**340.** 1. The Supine in -**um** is used after Verbs of motion to express *purpose*; as, —

**lēgātī ad Caesarem grātulātum convēnērunt,** *envoys came to Caesar to congratulate him.*

> *a.* The Supine in -**um** may take an Object; as, —
>> **pācem petītum ōrātōrēs Rōmam mittunt,** *they send envoys to Rome to ask for peace.*
>
> *b.* Note the phrase: —
>> **dō (collocō) fīliam nūptum,** *I give my daughter in marriage.*

2. The Supine in -**ū** is used as an Ablative of Specification with **facilis, difficilis, incrēdibilis, jūcundus, optimus,** *etc.*; also with **fās est, nefās est, opus est;** as, —

> **haec rēs est facilis cognitū,** *this thing is easy to learn;*
> **hōc est optimum factū,** *this is best to do.*

> *a.* Only a few Supines in -**ū** are in common use, chiefly **audītū cognitū, dictū, factū, vīsū.**
> *b.* The Supine in -**ū** never takes an Object.

———•◦•———

## Chapter VI. — *Particles.*

### COÖRDINATE CONJUNCTIONS.

**341. Copulative Conjunctions.** These *join* one word phrase, or clause to another.

1. *a*) **et** simply connects.
> *b*) -**que** joins more closely than **et,** and is used especially where the two members have an internal connection with each other; as, —

> **parentēs līberīque,** *parents and children;*
> **cum hominēs aestū febrīque jactantur,** *when people are tossed about with heat and fever.*

    *c*) **atque (ac)** usually emphasizes the second of the two things connected, — *and also, and indeed, and in fact.* After words of *likeness* and *difference*, **atque (ac)** has the force of *as, than.* Thus : —

      **ego idem sentiō ac tū,** *I think the same as you ;*
      **haud aliter ac,** *not otherwise than.*

    *d*) **neque (nec)** means *and not, neither, nor.*

  **2.** *a*) **-que** is an enclitic, and is appended always to the second of two words connected. Where it connects phrases or clauses, it is appended to the first word of the second clause ; but when the first word of the second clause is a Preposition, **-que** is regularly appended to the next following word ; as, —

      **ob eamque rem,** *and on account of that thing.*

    *b*) **atque** is used before vowels and consonants ; **ac** never before vowels, and seldom before **c, g, qu.**

    *c*) **et nōn** is used for **neque** when the emphasis of the negative rests upon a special word ; as, —

      **vetus et nōn ignōbilis ōrātor,** *an old and not ignoble orator.*

    *d*) For *and nowhere, and never, and none,* the Latin regularly said **nec ūsquam, nec umquam, nec ūllus,** *etc.*

  **3. Correlatives.** Copulative Conjunctions are frequently used correlatively ; as, —

      **et . . . et,** *both . . . and ;*
      **neque (nec) . . . neque (nec),** *neither . . . nor ;*
      **cum . . . tum,** *while . . . at the same time ;*
      **tum . . . tum,** *not only . . . but also.*

  Less frequently : —

      **et . . . neque ;      neque . . . et.**

    *a.* Note that the Latin, with its tendency to emphasize antithetical relations, often uses correlatives, especially **et . . . et, et . . . neque, neque . . . et,** where the English employs but a single connective.

  **4. In enumerations —**

    *a*) The different members of a series may follow one another without connectives (Asyndeton; see § 346). Thus : —

      **ex cupiditātibus odia, discidia, discordiae, sēditiōnēs, bella nāscuntur,** *from covetous desires spring up hatred, dissension, discord, sedition, wars.*

*b*) The different members may severally be connected by **et** (Polysyndeton). Thus : —

> **hōrae cēdunt et diēs et mēnsēs et annī,** *hours and days and months and years pass away.*

*c*) The connective may be omitted between the former members, while the last two are connected by **-que** (rarely **et**) ; as, —

> **Caesar in Carnutēs, Andēs Turonēsque legiōnēs dēdūcit,** *Caesar leads his legions into the territory of the Carnutes, Andes, and Turones.*

**342. Disjunctive Conjunctions** indicate an *alternative.*

1. *a*) **aut** must be used when the alternatives are mutually exclusive ; as, —

> **cita mors venit aut victōria laeta,** (*either*) *swift death or glad victory comes.*

*b*) **vel, -ve** (enclitic) imply a choice between the alternatives ; as, —

> **quī aethēr vel caelum nōminātur,** *which is called aether or heaven.*

2. **Correlatives.** Disjunctive Conjunctions are often used correlatively ; as, —

> **aut** . . . **aut,** *either* . . . *or* ;
> **vel** . . . **vel,** *either* . . . *or* ;
> **sīve** . . . **sīve,** *if* . . . *or if.*

**343. Adversative Conjunctions.** These denote *opposition.*

1. *a*) **sed,** *but,* merely denotes opposition.

*b*) **vērum,** *but,* is stronger than **sed,** but is less frequently used.

*c*) **autem,** *but on the other hand, however,* marks a transition. It is always post-positive.

DEFINITION. A post-positive word is one that cannot begin a sentence, but is placed after one or more words.

*d*) **at,** *but,* is used especially in disputation, to introduce an opposing argument.

*e*) **atquī** means *but yet.*

*f*) **tamen,** *yet,* usually stands after the emphatic word, but not always.

*g*) **vērō,** *however, indeed, in truth,* is always post-positive.

2. Note the correlative expressions : —

**nōn sōlum (nōn modo)** . . . **sed etiam,** *not only* . . . *but also* ;
**nōn modo nōn** . . . **sed nē** . . . **quidem,** *not only not, but not*
*even* ; as, —

**nōn modo tibi nōn īrāscor, sed nē reprehendō quidem factum
tuum,** *I not only am not angry with you, but I do not even blame
your action.*

  *a.* But when the sentence has but one verb, and this stands with the second
  member, **nōn modo** may be used for **nōn modo nōn**; as,—
  **adsentātiō nōn modo amīcō, sed nē lībērō quidem digna
  est,** *flattery is not only not worthy of a friend, but not even of a
  free man.*

**344. Illative Conjunctions.** These represent the statement which they introduce as *following from* or as *in con-
formity with* what has preceded.

  1. *a)* **itaque** = *and so, accordingly.*
    *b)* **ergō** = *therefore, accordingly.*
    *c)* **igitur** (regularly post-positive [1]) = *therefore, accordingly.*

  2. **Igitur** is never combined with **et, atque, -que,** or **neque.**

**345. Causal Conjunctions.** These denote *cause,* or *give
an explanation.* They are **nam, namque, enim** (post-positive),
**etenim,** *for.*

**346. Asyndeton.** The conjunction is sometimes omitted between coördinate members, particularly in lively or impassioned
narration. Thus : —

  *a)* A copulative Conjunction is omitted ; as, —
    **avāritia īnfīnīta, īnsatiābilis est,** *avarice is boundless
    (and) insatiable;*
    **Cn. Pompejō, M. Crassō cōnsulibus,** *in the consulship of
    Gnaeus Pompey (and) Marcus Crassus.*
    The conjunction is regularly omitted between the names of
    consuls when the praenomen (*Mārcus, Gāius, etc.*) is expressed.

  *b)* An Adversative Conjunction may be omitted ; as, —
    **ratiōnēs dēfuērunt, ūbertās ōrātiōnis nōn dēfuit,** *argu-
    ments were lacking, (but) abundance of words was not.*

---

[1] Except in Sallust and Silver Latin.

## ADVERBS.

**347.** 1. The following particles, sometimes classed as Conjunctions, are more properly Adverbs : —

**etiam,** *also, even.*

**quoque** (always post-positive), *also.*

**quidem** (always post-positive) lays stress upon the preceding word. It is sometimes equivalent to the English *indeed, in fact*, but more frequently cannot be rendered, except by vocal emphasis.

**nē . . . quidem** means *not even;* the emphatic word or phrase always stands between ; as, **nē ille quidem,** *not even he.*

**tamen** and **vērō,** in addition to their use as Conjunctions, are often employed as Adverbs.

2. **Negatives.** Two negatives are regularly equivalent to an affirmative as in English, as **nōn nūllī,** *some;* but when **nōn, nēmō, nihil, numquam,** *etc.*, are accompanied by **neque . . . neque, nōn . . . nōn, nōn modo,** or **nē . . . quidem,** the latter particles simply take up the negation and emphasize it ; as, —

**habeō hīc nēminem neque amīcum neque cognātum,** *I have here no one, neither friend nor relative.*

**nōn enim praetereundum est nē id quidem,** *for not even that must be passed by.*

> *a.* **Haud** in Cicero and Caesar occurs almost exclusively as a modifier of Adjectives and Adverbs, and in the phrase **haud sciō an.** Later writers use it freely with verbs.

—•◦•—

CHAPTER VII. — *Word-order and Sentence-Structure.*

### A. WORD–ORDER.

**348.** In the normal arrangement of the Latin sentence the Subject stands at the beginning of the sentence, the Predicate at the end ; as, —

**Dārīus classem quīngentārum nāvium comparāvit,** *Darius got ready a fleet of five hundred ships.*

**349.** But for the sake of emphasis the normal arrangement is often abandoned, and the emphatic word is put
at the beginning, less frequently at the end of the sentence ; as, —

**magnus in hōc bellō Themistoclēs fuit,** GREAT *was Themistocles in this war* ;

**aliud iter habēmus nūllum,** *other course we have* NONE.

### SPECIAL PRINCIPLES.

**350.** 1. **Nouns.** A Genitive or other oblique case regularly follows the word upon which it depends. Thus : —

*a*) Depending upon a Noun : —

**tribūnus plēbis,** *tribune of the plebs* ;
**fīlius rēgis,** *son of the king* ;
**vir magnī animī,** *a man of noble spirit.*

Yet always **senātūs cōnsultum, plēbis scītum.**

*b*) Depending upon an Adjective : —

**ignārus rērum,** *ignorant·of affairs* ;
**dignī amīcitiā,** *worthy of friendship* ;
**plūs aequō,** *more than (what is) fair.*

2. **Appositives.** An Appositive regularly follows its Subject;
as, —

**Philippus, rēx Macedonum,** *Philip, king of the Macedonians* ;
**adsentātiō, vitiōrum adjūtrīx,** *flattery, promoter of evils.*

Yet **flūmen Rhēnus,** *the River Rhine* ; and always in good prose
**urbs Rōma,** *the city Rome.*

3. The **Vocative** usually follows one or more words ; as, —

**audī, Caesar,** *hear, Caesar !*

4. **Adjectives.** No general law can be laid down for the position of Adjectives. On the whole they precede the noun oftener
than they follow it.

*a.* Adjectives of *quantity* (including *numerals*) regularly precede their noun ; as, —

**omnēs hominēs,** *all men* ;
**septingentae nāvēs,** *seven hundred vessels.*

*b.* Note the force of position in the following: —

media urbs, *the middle of the city;*
urbs media, *the middle city;*
extrēmum bellum, *the end of the war;*
bellum extrēmum, *the last war.*

*c.* Rōmānus and Latīnus regularly follow; as, —

senātus populusque Rōmānus, *the Roman Senate and People;*
lūdī Rōmānī, *the Roman games;*
fēriae Latīnae, *the Latin holidays.*

*d.* When a Noun is modified both by an Adjective and by a Genitive, a favorite order is: Adjective, Genitive, Noun; as, —

summa omnium rērum abundantia, *the greatest abundance of all things.*

## 5. Pronouns.

*a.* The Demonstrative, Relative, and Interrogative Pronouns regularly precede the Noun; as, —

hīc homō, *this man;*
ille homō, *that man;*
erant duo itinera, quibus itineribus, *etc., there were two routes, by which, etc.*
quī homō? *what sort of man?*

*b.* But ille in the sense of '*that well known,*' '*that famous,*' usually stands after its Noun; as, —

testula illa, *that well-known custom of ostracism;*
Mēdēa illa, *that famous Medea.*

*c.* Possessive and Indefinite Pronouns usually follow their Noun; as, —

pater meus, *my father;*
homō quīdam, *a certain man;*
mulier aliqua, *some woman.*

But for purposes of contrast the Possessive often precedes its Noun; as, —

meus pater, MY *father* (*i.e.* as opposed to *yours, his, etc.*).

*d.* Where two or more Pronouns occur in the same sentence, the Latin is fond of putting them in close proximity; as, —

nisi forte ego vōbīs cessāre videor, *unless perchance I seem to you to be doing nothing.*

6. Adverbs and Adverbial phrases regularly precede the word they modify; as, —

> valdē dīligēns, *extremely diligent;*
> saepe dīxī, *I have often said;*
> tē jam diū hortāmur, *we have long been urging you;*
> paulō post, *a little after.*

7. **Prepositions** regularly precede the words they govern.

> *a.* But limiting words often intervene between the Preposition and its case; as, —
>
> > dē commūnī hominum memoriā, *concerning the common memory of men;*
> > ad beātē vīvendum, *for living happily.*

> *b.* When a noun is modified by an Adjective, the Adjective is often placed before the preposition; as, —
>
> > magnō in dolōre, *in great grief;*
> > summā cum laude, *with the highest credit;*
> > quā dē causā, *for which cause;*
> > hanc ob rem, *on account of this thing.*

> *c.* For Anastrophe, by which a Preposition is put after its case, see § 144, 3.

8. **Conjunctions.** Autem, enim, and igitur regularly stand in the second place in the sentence, but when combined with est or sunt they often stand third; as, —

> ita est enim, *for so it is.*

9. Words or Phrases referring to the preceding sentence or to some part of it, regularly stand first; as, —

id ut audīvit, Corcȳram dēmigrāvit, *when he heard that* (referring to the contents of the preceding sentence), *he moved to Corcyra;*

eō cum Caesar vēnisset, timentēs cōnfīrmat, *when Caesar had come thither* (*i.e.* to the place just mentioned), *he encouraged the timid.*

10. The Latin has a fondness for putting side by side words which are etymologically related; as, —

ut ad senem senex dē senectūte, sīc hōc librō ad amīcum amīcissimus dē amīcitiā scrīpsī, *as I, an old man, wrote to an old man. on old age, so in this book, as a fond friend, I have written to a friend, concerning friendship.*

11. Special rhetorical devices for indicating emphasis are the following : —

a) **Hypérbaton,** which consists in the separation of words that regularly stand together ; as, —

**septimus mihi Orīginum liber est in manibus,** *the seventh book of my ' Origines' is under way ;*

**receptō Caesar Ōricō proficīscitur,** *having recovered Oricus, Caesar set out.*

b) **Anáphora,** which consists in the repetition of the same word or the same word-order in successive phrases ; as, —

**sed plēnī omnēs sunt librī, plēnae sapientium vōcēs, plēna exemplōrum vetustās,** *but all books are full of it, the voices of sages are full of it, antiquity is full of examples of it.*

c) **Chiásmus,**[1] which consists in changing the relative order of words in two antithetical phrases ; as, —

**multōs dēfendī, laesī nēminem,** *many have I defended, I have injured no one ;*

**horrĭbilem illum diem aliīs, nōbīs faustum,** *that day dreadful to others, for us fortunate.*

d) **Sýnchysis,** or the interlocked arrangement. This is mostly confined to poetry, yet occurs in rhetorical prose, especially that of the Imperial Period ; as, —

**simulātam Pompejānārum grātiam partium,** *pretended interest in the Pompeian party.*

12. **Metrical Close.** At the end of a sentence certain cadences were avoided ; others were much employed. Thus : —

a) Cadences avoided.

$-\cup\cup-\cup$ ;    as, **esse vidētur** (close of hexameter).

$-\cup\cup\cup$ ;    as, **esse potest** (close of pentameter).

b) Cadences frequently employed.

$-\cup-$ ;    as, **auxerant.**

$-\cup-\cup$ ;    as, **comprobāvit.**

$-\cup\cup\cup-\cup$ ; as, **esse videātur.**

$\cup--\cup-$ ; as, **rogātū tuō.**

---

[1] So named from a fancied analogy to the strokes of the Greek letter X (*chi*) Thus : —

multōs    laesī

X

dēfendī   nēminem

## B. SENTENCE-STRUCTURE.

**351.** 1. **Unity of Subject.** — In complex sentences the Latin regularly holds to unity of Subject in the different members; as, —

**Caesar prīmum suō, deinde omnium ex cōnspectū remōtīs equīs, ut aequātō perīculō spem fugae tolleret, cohortātus suōs proelium commīsit,** *Caesar having first removed his own horse from sight, then the horses of all, in order, by making the danger equal, to take away hope of flight, encouraged his men and joined battle.*

2. A word serving as the common Subject or Object of the main clause and a subordinate one, stands before both; as, —

**Haeduī cum sē dēfendere nōn possent, lēgātōs ad Caesarem mittunt,** *since the Haedui could not defend themselves, they sent envoys to Caesar;*

**ille etsī flagrābat bellandī cupiditāte, tamen pācī serviendum putāvit,** *although he was burning with a desire to fight, yet he thought he ought to aim at peace.*

> *a.* The same is true also
>
> > 1) When the Subject of the main clause is Object (Direct or Indirect) of a subordinate clause; as, —
> >
> > **Caesar, cum hōc eī nūntiatum esset, mātūrat ab urbe proficīscī,** *when this had been reported to Caesar he hastened to set out from the city.*
> >
> > 2) When the Subject of a subordinate clause is at the same time the Object (Direct or Indirect) of the main clause; as, —
> >
> > **L. Mānliō, cum dictātor fuisset, M. Pompōnius tribūnus plēbis diem dīxit,** *M. Pomponius, tribune of the people, instituted proceedings against Lucius Manlius, though he had been dictator.*

3. Of subordinate clauses, temporal, conditional, and adversative clauses more commonly precede the main clause; indirect questions and clauses of purpose or result more commonly follow; as, —

**postquam haec dīxit, profectus est,** *after he said this, he set out;*

**sī quis ita agat, imprūdēns sit,** *if any one should act so, he would be devoid of foresight;*

**accidit ut ūnā nocte omnēs Hermae dēicerentur,** *it happened that in a single night all the Hermae were thrown down.*

4. Sometimes in Latin the main verb is placed within the subordinate clause; as, —

**sī quid est in mē ingenī, quod sentiō quam sit exiguum,** *if there is any talent in me, and I know how little it is.*

5. **The Latin Period.** The term Period, when strictly used, designates a compound sentence in which the subordinate clauses are inserted within the main clause; as, —

**Caesar etsī intellegēbat quā dē causā ea dīcerentur, tamen, nē aestātem in Trēverīs cōnsūmere cōgerētur, Indutiomārum ad sē venīre jussit,** *though Caesar perceived why this was said, yet, lest he should be forced to spend the summer among the Treveri, he ordered Indutiomarus to come to him.*

In the Periodic structure the thought is suspended until the end of the sentence is reached. Many Roman writers were extremely fond of this sentence-structure, and it was well adapted to the inflectional character of their language; in English we generally avoid it.

6. When there are several subordinate clauses in one Period, the Latin so arranges them as to avoid a succession of verbs. Thus : —

**At hostēs cum mīsissent, quī, quae in castrīs gererentur, cognōscerent, ubi sē dēceptōs intellēxērunt, omnibus cōpiīs subsecūtī ad flūmen contendunt,** *but the enemy when they had sent men to learn what was going on in camp, after discovering that they had been outwitted, followed with all their forces and hurried to the river.*

---

## CHAPTER VIII. — *Hints on Latin Style.*

**352.** In this chapter brief consideration is given to a few features of Latin diction which belong rather to style than to formal grammar.

### NOUNS.

**353.** 1. Where a distinct reference to several persons or things is involved, the Latin is frequently *much more exact in the use of the Plural* than is the English; as, —

domōs eunt, *they go home* (*i.e. to their homes*);
Germānī corpora cūrant, *the Germans care for the body*;
animōs mīlitum recreat, *he renews the courage of the soldiers*;
diēs noctēsque timēre, *to be in a state of fear day and night.*

2. In case of Neuter Pronouns and Adjectives used substantively, the Latin often employs the Plural where the English uses the Singular; as, —

omnia sunt perdita, *everything is lost*;
quae cum ita sint, *since this is so*;
haec omnibus pervulgāta sunt, *this is very well known to all.*

3. The Latin is usually *more concrete* than the English, and especially *less bold in the personification* of abstract qualities. Thus: —

ā puerō, ā puerīs, *from boyhood*;
Sullā dictātōre, *in Sulla's dictatorship*;
mē duce, *under my leadership*;
Rōmānī cum Carthāginiēnsibus pācem fēcērunt = *Rome made peace with Carthage*;
liber doctrīnae plēnus = *a learned book*;
prūdentiā Themistoclis Graecia servāta est = *Themistocles's foresight saved Greece.*

4. The Nouns of Agency in -tor and -sor (see § 147.1) denote a *permanent* or *characteristic activity*; as, —

accūsātōrēs (*professional*) *accusers*;
ōrātōrēs, *pleaders*;
cantōrēs, *singers*;
Arminius, Germāniae līberātor, *Arminius, liberator of Germany.*

> *a.* To denote **single instances** of an action, other expressions are commonly employed; as, —
>
> Numa, quī Rōmulō successit, *Numa, successor of Romulus*;
> quī mea legunt, *my readers*;
> quī mē audiunt, *my auditors.*

5. The Latin avoids the use of prepositional phrases as modifiers of a Noun. In English we say: '*The war against Carthage*'; '*a journey through Gaul*'; '*cities on the sea*'; '*the book in my hands*'; '*the fight at Salamis*'; etc. The Latin in such cases usually employs another mode of expression. Thus: —

> *a*) A Genitive; as, —
>
> dolor injūriārum, *resentment at injuries.*

*b*) An Adjective; as, —
> **urbēs maritimae,** *cities on the sea;*
> **pugna Salamīnia,** *the fight at Salamis.*

*c*) A Participle; as, —
> **pugna ad Cannās facta,** *the battle at Cannae.*

*d*) A Relative clause; as, —
> **liber quī in meīs manibus est,** *the book in my hands.*

NOTE. — Yet within certain limits the Latin does employ Prepositional phrases as Noun modifiers. This is particularly frequent when the governing noun is derived from a verb. The following are typical examples : —

> **trānsitus in Britanniam,** *the passage to Britain;*
> **excessus ē vītā,** *departure from life;*
> **odium ergā Rōmānōs,** *hatred of the Romans;*
> **liber dē senectūte,** *the book on old age;*
> **amor in patriam,** *love for one's country.*

## ADJECTIVES.

**354.** 1. **Special Latin Equivalents for English Adjectives** are —

*a*) A Genitive; as, —
> **virtūtēs animī** = *moral virtues;*
> **dolōrēs corporis** = *bodily ills.*

*b*) An Abstract Noun; as, —
> **novitās reī** = *the strange circumstance;*
> **asperitās viārum** = *rough roads.*

*c*) Hendiadys (see § 374, 4); as, —
> **ratiō et ōrdō** = *systematic order;*
> **ārdor et impetus** = *eager onset.*

*d*) Sometimes an Adverb; as, —
> **omnēs circā populī,** *all the surrounding tribes;*
> **suōs semper hostēs,** *their perpetual foes.*

2. Often a Latin Noun is equivalent to an English Noun modified by an Adjective; as, —

**doctrīna,** *theoretical knowledge;*
**oppidum,** *walled town;*

**prūdentia,** *practical knowledge;*
**libellus,** *little book.*

3. Adjectives are not used in immediate agreement with proper
names; but an Adjective may limit **vir, homō, ille**, or some other
word used as an Appositive of a proper name; as, —

> **Sōcratēs, homō sapiēns** = *the wise Socrates;*
> **Scīpiō, vir fortissimus** = *the doughty Scipio;*
> **Syrācūsae, urbs praeclārissima** = *famous Syracuse.*

4. An Adjective *may be* equivalent to a Possessive or Subjective
Genitive; as, —

> **pāstor rēgius,** *the shepherd of the king;*
> **tumultus servīlis,** *the uprising of the slaves.*

## PRONOUNS.

**355.** 1. In Compound Sentences the Relative Pronoun has a fondness for connecting itself with the subordinate clause rather than the
main one; as, —

**ā quō cum quaererētur, quid maximē expedīret, respondit,** *when
it was asked of him what was best, he replied.* (Less commonly,
**quī, cum ab eō quaererētur, respondit.**)

2. **Uterque, ambō.** **Uterque** means *each of two;* **ambō** means
*both;* as, —

**uterque frāter abiit,** *each of the two brothers departed* (*i.e.* separately);

**ambō frātrēs abiērunt,** *i.e.* the two brothers departed together.

> *a.* The Plural of **uterque** occurs —
>
> > 1) With Nouns used only in the Plural (see § 56); as, —
> > **in utrīsque castrīs,** *in each camp.*
> >
> > 2) Where there is a distinct reference to two groups of
> > persons or things; as, —
> > **utrīque ducēs clārī fuērunt,** *the generals on each side* (sev-
> > eral in number) *were famous.*

## VERBS.

**356.** 1. In case of Defective and Deponent Verbs, a Passive is
supplied : —

> *a*) By the corresponding verbal Nouns in combination with
> **esse,** *etc;* as, —
>
> > **in odiō sumus,** *we are hated;*
> > **in invidiā sum.** *I am envied;*

    admīrātiōnī est, *he is admired* ;

    oblīviōne obruitur, *he is forgotten* (lit. *is overwhelmed by oblivion*) ;

    in ūsū esse, *to be used.*

  *b*) By the Passive of Verbs of related meaning. Thus : —

    agitārī as Passive of **persequī** ;

    temptārī as Passive of **adorīrī.**

2. The lack of the Perfect Active Participle in Latin is supplied —

  *a*) Sometimes by the Perfect Passive Participle of the Deponent ; as, —

    adhortātus, *having exhorted* ;

    veritus, *having feared*.

  *b*) By the Ablative Absolute ; as, —

    **hostium agrīs vāstātīs Caesar exercitum redūxit,** *having ravaged the country of the enemy, Caesar led back his army.*

  *c*) By subordinate clauses ; as, —

    **eō cum advēnisset, castra posuit,** *having arrived there, he pitched a camp* ;

    **hostēs quī in urbem irrūperant,** *the enemy having burst into the city.*

3. The Latin agrees with English in the stylistic employment of the Second Person Singular in an indefinite sense ( = 'one'). *Cf.* the English ' *You can drive a horse to water, but you can't make him drink.*' But in Latin this use is mainly confined to certain varieties of the Subjunctive, especially the Potential (§ 280), Jussive (§ 275), Deliberative (§ 277), and the Subjunctive in conditional sentences of the sort included under § 302, 2, and 303. Examples : —

vidērēs, *you could see* ;

ūtāre vīribus, *use your strength* ,

quid hōc homine faciās, *what are you to do with this man ?*

mēns quoque et animus, nisi tamquam lūminī oleum īnstīllēs, exstinguuntur senectūte, *the intellect and mind too are extinguished by old age, unless, so to speak, you keep pouring oil into the lamp* ;

tantō amōre possessiōnēs suās amplexī tenēbant, ut ab eīs membra dīvellī citius posse dīcerēs, *they clung to their possessions with such an affectionate embrace, that you would have said their limbs could sooner be torn from their bodies.*

## PECULIARITIES IN THE USE OF THE ACCUSATIVE.

**357.** 1. To denote ' *so many years, etc.*, *afterwards* or *before*' the Latin employs not merely the Ablative of Degree of Difference with **post** and **ante** (see § 223), but has other forms of expression.  Thus : ⁓

post quīnque annōs, *five years afterward;*

paucōs ante diēs, *a few days before;*

ante quadriennium, *four years before;*

post diem quārtum quam ab urbe discesserāmus, *four days after we had left the city;*

ante tertium annum quam dēcesserat, *three years before he had died.*

2. The Latin seldom combines both Subject and Object with the same Infinitive ; as, —

### Rōmānōs Hannibalem vīcisse cōnstat.

Such a sentence would be ambiguous, and might mean either that the Romans had conquered Hannibal, or that Hannibal had conquered the Romans.   Perspicuity was gained by the use of the Passive Infinitive ; as, —

Rōmānōs ab Hannibale victōs esse cōnstat, *it is well established that the Romans were defeated by Hannibal.*

## PECULIARITIES IN CONNECTION WITH THE USE OF THE DATIVE.

**358.** 1. The English *for* does not always correspond to a Dative notion in Latin, but is often the equivalent of **prō** with the Ablative. *viz.* in the senses —

*a)* *In defense of*; as, —

prō patriā morī, *to die for one's country.*

*b)* *Instead of, in behalf of*; as, —

ūnus prō omnibus dīxit, *one spoke for all;*

haec prō lēge dicta sunt, *these things were said for the law.*

*c)* *In proportion to*; as, —

prō multitūdine hominum eōrum fīnēs erant angustī, *for the population, their territory was small.*

2. Similarly, English *to* when it indicates motion is rendered in Latin by **ad**.

> *a.* Note, however, that the Latin may say either **scrībere ad aliquem**, or **scrībere alicui**, according as the idea of motion is or is not predominant. So in several similar expressions.

3. In the poets, verbs of *mingling with, contending with, joining, clinging to, etc.,* sometimes take the Dative. This construction is a Grecism. Thus: —

> **sē miscet virīs**, *he mingles with the men* ;
> **contendis Homērō**, *you contend with Homer* ;
> **dextrae dextram jungere**, *to clasp hand with hand.*

## PECULIARITIES IN THE USE OF THE GENITIVE.

**359.** 1. The Possessive Genitive gives emphasis to the *possessor*, the Dative of Possessor emphasizes *the fact of possession* ; as, —

> **hortus patris est**, *the garden is my father's* ;
> **mihi hortus est**, *I possess a garden.*

2. The Latin can say either **stultī** or **stultum est dīcere**, *it is foolish to say* ; but Adjectives of one ending permit only the Genitive ; as, —

**sapientis est haec sēcum reputāre**, *it is the part of a wise man to consider this.*

# Part VI.

---◆---

## PROSODY.

---◆---

**360.** Prosody treats of metres and versification.

**361. Latin Verse.** Latin Poetry was essentially different in character from English. In our own language, poetry is based upon *accent*, and poetical form consists essentially in a certain succession of *accented* and *unaccented* syllables. Latin poetry, on the other hand, was based not upon accent, but upon *quantity*, so that with the Romans poetical form consisted in a certain succession of *long and short syllables*, *i.e.* of long and short intervals of time.

This fundamental difference in the character of English and Latin poetry is a natural result of the difference in character of the two languages. English is a strongly accented language, in which quantity is relatively subordinate. Latin, on the other hand, was a quantitative language, in which accent was relatively subordinate.

### QUANTITY OF VOWELS AND SYLLABLES.

#### GENERAL PRINCIPLES.

**362.** The general principles for the quantity of vowels and syllables have been given above in § 5. The following peculiarities are to be noted here : —

1. A vowel is usually short when followed by another vowel (§ 5. *A*. 2), but the following exceptions occur : —

*a*) In the Genitive termination -īus (except alterĭus) ; as, illīus, tōtīus.  Yet the i may be short in poetry ; as, illĭus, tōtĭus.

*b*) In the Genitive and Dative Singular of the Fifth Declension ; as, diēī, aciēī.  But fidĕī, rĕī, spĕī (§ 52, 1).

*c*) In fīō, excepting fit and forms where i is followed by er. Thus : fīēbam, fīat, fīunt ; but fĭerī, fĭerem.

*d*) In a few other words, especially words derived from the Greek ; as, dīus, Aenēās, Dārīus, hērōes, *etc.*

2. A diphthong is usually long (§ 5. *B*. 2), but the preposition **prae** in composition is often shortened before a vowel ; as, praĕacūtus

3. A syllable containing a short vowel followed by two consonants (§ 5. *B*. 2) is long, even when one of the consonants is in the following word ; as, **terret populum**.  Occasionally the syllable is long when both consonants are in the following word ; as, **prō segete spīcās**.

4. Compounds of jaciō, though written **inicit, adicit**, *etc.*, have the first syllable long, as though written **inj-, adj-**.

5. Before j, ă and ĕ made a long syllable, *e.g.* in **major, pejor, ejus, ejusdem, Pompejus, rejēcit**, *etc.*  These were pronounced, **mai-jor, pei-jor, ei-jus, Pompei-jus, rei-jēcit**, *etc.*  So also sometimes before i, *e.g.* **Pompe-ī**, pronounced **Pompei-ī** ; **re-iciō**, pronounced **rei-iciō**.

### Quantity of Final Syllables.

#### *A. Final Syllables ending in a Vowel.*

**363.** 1. Final **a** is mostly short, but is long : —

*a*) In the Ablative Singular of the First Declension ; as, **portā**.

*b*) In the Imperative ; as, **laudā**.

*c*) In indeclinable words (except ită, quiă) ; as, **trīgintā, con-trā, posteā, intereā**, *etc.*

2. Final **e** is usually short, but is long : —

*a*) In the Ablative Singular of the Fifth Declension ; as, **diē, rē** ; hence **hodiē, quārē**.  Here belongs also **famē** (§ 59. 2. *b*).

*b*) In the Imperative of the Second Conjugation ; as, **monē, habē**, *etc.* ; yet occasionally **cavĕ, valĕ**.

*c*) In Adverbs derived from Adjectives of the Second Declension, along with **ferē** and **fermē**.  **Benĕ, malĕ, temerĕ, saepĕ** have ĕ.

*d*) In ē, dē, mē, tē, sē, nē (*not, lest*), nē (*verily*).

3. Final **i** is usually long, but is short in **nisĭ** and **quasĭ**. **Mihi, tibi, sibi, ibi, ubi,** have regularly **ĭ**, but sometimes **ī**; yet always **ibīdem, ibīque, ubīque.**

4. Final **o** is regularly long, but is short: —

    *a*) In **egŏ, duŏ, modŏ** (*only*), **citŏ.**

    *b*) Rarely in the First Person Singular of the Verb, and in Nominatives of the Third Declension; as, **amŏ, leŏ.**

    *c*) In a few compounds beginning with the Preposition **pro,** especially before **f**; as **prŏfundere, prŏficīscī, prŏfugere.**

5. Final **u** is always long.

### B. Final Syllables ending in a Consonant.

**364.** 1. Final syllables ending in any other consonant than **s** are short. The following words, however, have a long vowel: **sāl, sōl, Lār, pār, vēr, fūr, dīc, dūc, ēn, nōn, quīn, sīn, sīc, cūr.** Also the adverbs **hīc, illīc, istic.**[1]

2. Final syllables in **-as** are long; as, **terrās, amās.**

3. Final syllables in **-es** are regularly long, but are short: —

    *a*) In the Nominative and Vocative Singular of dental stems (§ 33) of the Third Declension which have a short penult in the Genitive; as, **segĕs** (segetis), **obsĕs** (obsidis), **mīlĕs, dīvĕs.** But a few have **-ēs**; *viz.* **pēs, ariēs, abiēs, pariēs.**

    *b*) In **ĕs** (*thou art*), **penĕs.**

4. Final **-os** is usually long, but short in **ŏs** (ossis), **compŏs, impŏs.**

5. Final **-is** is usually short, but is long: —

    *a*) In Plurals; as, **portīs, hortīs, nōbīs, vōbīs, nūbīs** (Acc.).

    *b*) In the Second Person Singular Perfect Subjunctive Active; as, **amāverīs, monuerīs, audīverīs,** *etc.* Yet occasional exceptions occur.

    *c*) In the Second Person Singular Present Indicative Active of the Fourth Conjugation; as, **audīs.**

    *d*) In **vīs,** *force*; **īs,** *thou goest*; **fīs**; **sīs**; **velīs**; **nōlīs**; **vīs,** *thou wilt* (**māvīs, quamvīs, quīvīs,** *etc.*).

6. Final **-us** is usually short, but is long: —

    *a*) In the Genitive Singular and in the Nominative, Accusative, and Vocative Plural of the Fourth Declension; as, **frūctūs.**

---

[1] The pronouns **hic, hoc,** and the adverb **huc,** probably had a short *vowel.* The syllable was made long by pronouncing **hicc, hocc,** *etc.*

*b*) In the Nominative and Vocative Singular of those nouns of the Third Declension in which the **u** belongs to the stem; as, **palūs (-ūdis), servitūs (-ūtis), tellūs (-ūris).**

**365. Greek Nouns** retain in Latin their original quantity; as, **Aeneā, epitomē, Dēlos, Pallas, Simoīs, Salamīs, Dīdūs, Paridī, āēr, aethēr, crātēr, hērōǎs.** Yet Greek nouns in -ωρ (-ōr) regularly shorten the vowel of the final syllable; as, **rhētǒr, Hectǒr.**

## VERSE–STRUCTURE.

### GENERAL PRINCIPLES.

**366.** 1. The metrical unit in versification is a short syllable, technically called a mora (◡). A long syllable (—) is regarded as equivalent to two morae.

2. A **Foot** is a group of syllables. The following are the most important kinds of fundamental feet: —

| FEET OF THREE MORAE. | | FEET OF FOUR MORAE. | |
|---|---|---|---|
| — ◡ | Trochee. | — ◡ ◡ | Dactyl. |
| ◡ — | Iambus. | ◡ ◡ — | Anapaest. |

3. A **Verse** is a succession of feet.

4. The different kinds of verses are named Trochaic, Iambic, Dactylic, Anapaestic, according to the foot which forms the basis of their structure.

5. **Ictus.** In every fundamental foot the long syllable naturally receives the greater prominence. This prominence is called **ictus.**[1] It is denoted thus: ∠ ◡ ◡; ∠ ◡.

6. **Thesis and Arsis.** The syllable which receives the ictus is called the **thesis**; the rest of the foot is called the **arsis**.

7. **Elision.** Final syllables ending in a vowel, a diphthong, or -**m** are regularly elided before a word beginning with a vowel or **h**. In reading, we omit the elided syllable entirely. This may be indicated as follows: **corpore in ūnō; multum ille et; mōnstrum horrendum; causae īrārum.**

> *a.* Omission of elision is called **Hiátus.** It occurs especially before and after monosyllabic interjections; as, **Ō et praesidium.**

---

[1] Ictus was not accent, — neither stress accent nor musical accent, — but was simply the quantitative prominence inherent in the long syllables of *fundamental feet.*

8. The ending of a word within a foot is called a **Caesúra** (*cutting*)
Every verse usually has one prominent caesura. The ending of a word
and foot together within the verse is called a **diaeresis**.

9. Verses are distinguished as Catalectic or Acatalectic. A Catalectic verse is one in which the last foot is not complete, but lacks one
or more syllables; an Acatalectic verse has its last foot complete.

10. At the end of a verse a slight pause occurred. Hence the final
syllable may be either long or short (**syllaba anceps**), and may
terminate in a vowel or **m**, even though the next verse begins with a
vowel.

11. Iambic, Trochaic, and Anapaestic verses are further designated
as dimeter, trimeter, tetrameter, according to *the number of dipodies*
(pairs of feet) which they contain. Dactylic verses are measured *by
single feet*, and are designated as tetrameter, pentameter, hexameter,
accordingly.

### SPECIAL PECULIARITIES.

**367.** 1. **Synizésis (Synaéresis).** Two successive vowels in the
interior of a word are often united into a long syllable; as,—

aureīs, deinde, anteīre deesse.

2. **Diástole.** A syllable usually short is sometimes long; as,—
vidēt, audīt.

3. **Sýstole.** A syllable usually long is sometimes short; as,—
stetĕrunt.

 a. Diastole and Systole are not mere arbitrary processes. They
 usually represent an earlier pronunciation which had passed
 out of vogue in the ordinary speech.

4. After a consonant, **i** and **u** sometimes become **j** and **v**. The
preceding syllable then becomes long; as,—

abjete for abiete; genva for genua.

5. Sometimes **v** becomes **u**; as,—
silua for silva; dissoluō for dissolvō.

6. Sometimes a verse has an extra syllable. Such a verse is called
an **Hypérmeter**. The extra syllable ends in a vowel or -m, and is
united with the initial vowel or **h** of the next verse by **Synaphéia**.
Thus:—

. . . . . . . . . . ignāri hominumque locōrumque

errāmus.

7. **Tmesis** (*cutting*). Compound words are occasionally separated into their elements ; as, —

> **quō mē cumque rapit tempestās,** for **quōcumque,** *etc.*

8. **Sýncope.** A short vowel is sometimes dropped between two consonants ; as, —

> **repostus** for **repositus.**

### THE DACTYLIC HEXAMETER.

**368.** 1. The Dactylic Hexameter, or Heroic Verse, consists theoretically of six dactyls. But in all the feet except the fifth, a spondee (＿＿) may take the place of the dactyl. The sixth foot may be either a spondee or a trochee, since the final syllable of a verse may be either long or short (**syllaba anceps**). The following represents the scheme of the verse : —

$$\angle\,\overline{\smile\smile}, \angle\,\overline{\smile\smile}, \angle\,\overline{\smile\smile}, \angle\,\overline{\smile\smile}, \angle\,\smile\smile, \angle\,\underset{\smile}{\smile}.$$

2. Sometimes we find a spondee in the fifth foot. Such verses are called Spondaic. A dactyl usually stands in the fourth place, and the fifth and sixth feet are generally made up of a quadrisyllable ; as, —

> **armātum^que aurō circumspicit Ōrīōna.**
> **cāra deum subolēs, magnum Jovis incrēmentum.**

3. **Caesura.**

*a*) The favorite position of the caesura in the Dactylic Hexameter is after the thesis of the third foot ; as, —

> **arma virumque canō ‖ Trōjae quī prīmus ab ōrīs.**

*b*) Less frequently the caesura occurs after the thesis of the fourth foot, usually accompanied by another in the second foot ; as, —

> **inde torō ‖ pater Aenēās ‖ sīc ōrsus ab alt^ō est.**

*c*) Sometimes the caesura occurs between the two short syllables of the third foot ; as, —

> **Ō passī graviōra ‖ dabit deus hīs quoque fīnem.**

This caesura is called Feminine, as opposed to the caesura after a long syllable, which is called Masculine (as under *a* and *b*).

*d*) A pause sometimes occurs at the end of the fourth foot. This is called the Bucolic Diaeresis, as it was borrowed by the Romans from the Bucolic poetry of the Greeks. Thus: —

**sōlstitium pecorī dēfendite ; ‖ jam venit aestās.**

## DACTYLIC PENTAMETER.

**369.** 1. The Dactylic Pentameter consists of two parts, each of which contains two dactyls, followed by a long syllable. Spondees may take the place of the dactyls in the first part, but not in the second. The long syllable at the close of the first half of the verse always ends a word. The scheme is the following : —

$$\acute{-} \overline{\smile\smile} \acute{-} \overline{\smile\smile} \acute{-} \| \acute{-} \smile\smile \acute{-} \smile\smile \underline{\smile}$$

2. The Pentameter is never used alone, but only in connection with the Hexameter. The two arranged alternately form the so-called Elegiac Distich. Thus : —

**Vergilium vīdī tantum, nec amāra Tibullō**
**Tempus amīcitiae fāta dedēre meae.**

## IAMBIC MEASURES.

**370.** 1. The most important Iambic verse is the **Iambic Trimeter** (§ 366. 11), called also **Senarius**. This is an acatalectic verse. It consists of six Iambi. Its pure form is : —

$$\smile - \smile - \smile - \smile - \smile - \smile -$$

**Beātus ille quī procul negōtiīs.**

The Caesura usually occurs in the third foot; less frequently in the fourth.

2. In place of the Iambus, a Tribrach ($\smile\smile\smile$) may stand in any foot but the last. In the odd feet (first, third, and fifth) may stand a Spondee, Dactyl, or Anapaest, though the last two are less frequent. Sometimes a Proceleusmatic ($\smile\smile\smile\smile$) occurs.

3. In the Latin comic writers, Plautus and Terence, great freedom is permitted, and the various equivalents of the Iambus, *viz.* the Dactyl, Anapaest, Spondee, Tribrach, Proceleusmatic, are freely admitted in any foot except the last.

# SUPPLEMENTS TO THE GRAMMAR.

---◆---

## I. JULIAN CALENDAR.

**371.** 1. The names of the Roman months are: **Jānuārius, Februā-rius, Mārtius, Aprīlis, Majus, Jūnius, Jūlius (Quīntīlis**[1] prior to 46 B.C.), **Augustus (Sextīlis**[1] before the Empire), **September, Octō-ber, November, December.** These words are properly Adjectives in agreement with **mēnsis** understood.

2. Dates were reckoned from three points in the month:—

> *a*) The Calends, the first of the month.
> *b*) The Nones, usually the fifth of the month, but the seventh in March, May, July, and October.
> *c*) The Ides, usually the thirteenth of the month, but the fif-teenth in March, May, July, and October.

3. From these points dates were reckoned backward; consequently all days after the Ides of any month were reckoned as so many days before the Calends of the month next following.

4. The day before the Calends, Nones, or Ides of any month is designated as **prīdiē Kalendās, Nōnās, Īdūs.** The second day be-fore was designated as **diē tertiō ante Kalendās Nōnās,** *etc.* Simi larly the third day before was designated as **diē quārtō,** and so on. These designations are arithmetically inaccurate, but the Romans reckoned both ends of the series. The Roman numeral indicating the date is therefore always larger by one than the actual number of days before Nones, Ides, or Calends.

5. In indicating dates, the name of the month is added in the form of an Adjective agreeing with **Kalendās, Nōnās, Īdūs.** Various forms of expression occur, of which that given under *d*) is most common:—

> *a*) **diē quīntō ante Īdūs Mārtiās;**
> *b*) **quīntō ante Īdūs Mārtiās;**
> *c*) **quīntō (V) Īdūs Mārtiās;**
> *d*) **ante diem quīntum Īdūs Mārtiās.**

---

[1] Originally the Roman year began with March. This explains the names **Quīntīlis, Sextīlis, September,** *etc., fifth month, sixth month, etc.*

6. These designations may be treated as nouns and combined with the prepositions in, ad, ex; as, —

ad ante diem IV **Kalendās Octōbrēs**, *up to the* 28*th of September*.
ex ante diem quīntum **Īdūs Octōbrēs**, *from the* 11*th of October*.

7. In leap-year the 25th was reckoned as the extra day in February. The 24th was designated as **ante diem** VI **Kalendās Mārtiās**, and the 25th as **ante diem bis** VI **Kal Mārt**.

**372.** CALENDAR.

| Days of the month. | March, May, July, October. | January, August, December. | April, June, September, November. | February. |
|---|---|---|---|---|
| 1 | KALENDĪS. | KALENDĪS. | KALENDĪS. | KALENDĪS. |
| 2 | VI. Nōnās. | IV. Nōnās. | IV. Nōnās. | IV. Nōnās. |
| 3 | V. " | III. " | III. " | III. " |
| 4 | IV. " | Pridiē Nōnās. | Prīdie Nōnās. | Pridiē Nōnās. |
| 5 | III. " | NŌNĪS. | NŌNĪS. | NŌNĪS. |
| 6 | Prīdiē Nōnās. | VIII. Īdūs. | VIII. Īdūs. | VIII. Īdūs. |
| 7 | NŌNĪS. | VII. " | VII. " | VII. " |
| 8 | VIII. Īdūs. | VI. " | VI. " | VI. " |
| 9 | VII. " | V. " | V. " | V. " |
| 10 | VI. " | IV. " | IV. " | IV. " |
| 11 | V. " | III. " | III. " | III. " |
| 12 | IV. " | Prīdiē Īdūs. | Prīdiē Īdūs. | Prīdiē Īdūs. |
| 13 | III. " | ĪDIBUS. | ĪDIBUS. | ĪDIBUS. |
| 14 | Prīdiē Īdūs. | XIX. Kalend. | XVIII. Kalend. | XVI. Kalend. |
| 15 | ĪDIBUS. | XVIII. " | XVII. " | XV. " |
| 16 | XVII. Kalend. | XVII. " | XVI. " | XIV. " |
| 17 | XVI. " | XVI. " | XV. " | XIII. " |
| 18 | XV. " | XV. " | XIV. " | XII. " |
| 19 | XIV. " | XIV. " | XIII. " | XI. " |
| 20 | XIII. " | XIII. " | XII. " | X. " |
| 21 | XII. " | XII. " | XI. " | IX. " |
| 22 | XI. " | XI. " | X. " | VIII. " |
| 23 | X. " | X. " | IX. " | VII. " |
| 24 | IX. " | IX. " | VIII. " | VI. " |
| 25 | VIII. " | VIII. " | VII. " | V. (bis VI.) " |
| 26 | VII. " | VII. " | VI. " | IV. (V.) " |
| 27 | VI. " | VI. " | V. " | III. (IV.) " |
| 28 | V. " | V. " | IV. " | Prid. Kal. (III Kal ) |
| 29 | IV. " | IV. " | III. " | (Prīd. Kal.) |
| 30 | III. " | III. " | Prīdiē Kalend. | (Enclosed forms are for leap-year.) |
| 31 | Prīdiē Kalend. | Prīdiē Kalend. | | |

## II. PROPER NAMES.

**373.** 1. The name of a Roman citizen regularly consisted of three parts : the **praenōmen** (or given name), the **nōmen** (name of the *gens* or clan), and the **cognōmen** (family name). Such a typical name is exemplied by **Mārcus Tullius Cicerō**, in which **Mārcus** is the **praenōmen, Tullius** the **nōmen**, and **Cicerō** the **cognōmen**. Sometimes a second **cognōmen** (in later Latin called an **agnōmen**) is added — especially in honor of military achievements ; as, —

**Gāius Cornēlius Scīpiō Āfricānus.**

2. Abbreviations of Proper Names.

| | |
|---|---|
| A. = **Aulus.** | Mam. = **Māmercus.** |
| App. = **Appius.** | N. = **Numerius.** |
| C. = **Gāius.** | P. = **Pūblius.** |
| Cn. = **Gnaeus.** | Q. = **Quīntus.** |
| D. = **Decimus.** | Sex. = **Sextus.** |
| K. = **Kaesō.** | Ser. = **Servius.** |
| L. = **Lūcius.** | Sp. = **Spurius.** |
| M. = **Mārcus.** | T. = **Titus.** |
| M'. = **Mānius.** | Ti. = **Tiberius.** |

## III. FIGURES OF SYNTAX AND RHETORIC.

### A. Figures of Syntax.

**374.** 1. **Ellípsis** is the omission of one or more words ; as, — quid multa, *why (should I say) much ?*

2. **Brachýlogy** is a brief or condensed form of expression ; as, — **ut ager sine cultūrā frūctuōsus esse nōn potest, sīc sine doctrīnā animus,** *as a field cannot be productive without cultivation, so the mind (cannot be productive) without learning.*

Special varieties of Brachylogy are —

*a*) **Zeugma,** in which one verb is made to stand for two ; as, — **minīs aut blandīmentīs corrupta** = (*terrified*) *by threats or corrupted by flattery.*

*b*) **Compendiary Comparison,** by which a modifier of an object is mentioned instead of the object itself ; as, — **dissimilis erat Charēs eōrum et factīs et mōribus,** lit. *Chares was different from their conduct and character i.e.* Chares's conduct and character were different, *etc.*

3. **Pléonasm** is an unnecessary fullness of expression ; as, —

> **prius praedīcam**, lit. *I will first say in advance.*

4. **Hendíadys** (ἓν διὰ δυοῖν, *one through two*) is the use of two nouns joineᴅ by a conjunction, in the sense of a noun modified by a Genitive or an Adjective ; as, —

> **febris et aestus,** *the heat of fever ;*
> **celeritāte cursūque,** *by swift running.*

5. **Prolépsis,** or **Anticipation,** is the introduction of an epithet in advance of the action which makes it appropriate ; as, —

> **submersās obrue puppēs,** lit. *overwhelm their submerged ships,*
> *i.e.* overwhelm and sink their ships.

> a.  The name Prolepsis is also applied to the introduction of a noun or pronoun as object of the main clause where we should expect it to stand as subject of a subordinate clause.   Thus : —
>
> > **nōstī Mārcellum quam tardus sit,** *you know how slow Marcellus is* (lit. *you know Marcellus, how slow he is*).
>
> Both **v**arieties of Prolepsis are chiefly confined to poetry.

6. **Anacolúthon** is a lack of grammatical consistency in the construction of the sentence ; as, —

> **tum Ancī fīliī . . . impēnsius eīs indignitās crēscere,** *then the sons of Ancus . . . their indignation increased all the more.*

7. **Hýsteron Próteron** consists in the inversion of the natural order of two words or phrases ; as, —

> **moriāmur et in media arma ruāmus** = *let us rush into the midst of arms and die.*

### B. Figures of Rhetoric.

**375.**  1. **Lítotes** (literally *softening*) is the expression of an idea by the denial of its opposite ; as, —

> **haud parum labōris,** *no little toil* (*i.e.* much toil) ;
> **nōn ignōrō,** *I am not ignorant* (*i.e.* I am well aware).

2. **Oxymóron** is the combination of contradictory conceptions ; as, —  **sapiēns īnsānia,** *wise folly.*

3. **Alliteration** is the employment of a succession of words presenting frequent repetition of the same letter (mostly initial) ; as, —  **sēnsim sine sēnsū aetās senēscit.**

4. **Onomatopœia** is the suiting of sound to sense ; as, —

> **quadrupedante putrem sonitū quatit ungula campum,** '*And shake with horny hoofs the solid ground.*'

# INDEX OF THE SOURCES OF THE ILLUSTRATIVE EXAMPLES CITED IN THE SYNTAX.[1]

---

[1] For explanation of the abbreviations, see p. 257.

p. 163, numquam digne, *de Sen.* 2.
cognatio, *Arch.* 2.
mors est, *Tusc. Disp.* i, 27.
p. 164, justitia, *F.* i, 50.
si quisquam, *Lael.* 9.
potestne, *Tusc. Disp.* iv, 54.
si ullo, *Att.* xii, 23, 1.
taetrior, *Verr.* iv, 123.
quod cuique, *Off.* i, 21.
quinto quoque, *Verr.* ii, 139.
nemo Romanus, *Liv.* viii, 30, 3.
alter exercitum, *Planc.* 86.
alteri se, *B. G.* i, 26, 1.
p. 165, causidicus, *de Or.* i, 202.
p. 166, Tarquinii, *Liv.* i, 34, 7.
non omnis, *Div.* ii, 90.
Corioli, *Liv.* ii, 33, 8.
duo milia, *Curt.* iii, 2, 5.
temeritas, *F.* iii, 72.
p. 167, si tu, *Fam.* xiv, 5, 1.
velatus, *Ov. Met.* v, 110.
tunica, *Aen.* viii, 457.
p. 168, virtus, *Lael.* 100.
p. 169, dum vitant, *Hor. Sat.* i, 2, 24.
Caesar, *B. G.* vii, 90, 2.
jam pridem, *Att.* ii, 5, 1.
Duilium, *de Sen.* 44.
hostes, *B. G.* v, 9, 6.
domicilium, *Arch.* 7.
p. 170, Regulus, *Off.* iii, 100.
Caesar, *B. G.* iv, 17, 1.
p. 171, nihil habebam, *Att.* ix, 10, 1.
p. 172, videor, *N. D.* ii, 72.
Gallos, *B. G.* vii, 4, 4.
honestum, *F.* ii, 49.
si solos, *Tusc. Disp.* i, 9.
rex tantum, *Nep. Con.* 4.
p. 173, Verres, *Verr. Act. Pr.* 12.
ardebat, *Brut.* 302.
p. 174, Caesar, *B. G.* iii, 24, 1.
p. 175, hoc jam, *Cat.* i, 5.
dico me, *Sull.* 27.
p. 177, quare, *Cat.* 1, 32.
isto bono, *de Sen.* 33.
ne repugnetis, *Cluent.* 6.
tu vero, *Tusc. Disp.* i, 112.
impii ne, *Leg.* ii, 41.
cave ignoscas, *Lig.* 14.
p. 178, quid faciam, *Pl. Curc.* 589.
ego redeam, *Ter. Eun.* 49.
huic cedamus! *Phil.* xiii, 16.
quid facerem, *Ter. Eun.* 831.
hunc ego, *Arch.* 18.

ne sint, *de Sen.* 34.
fuerit, *Verr.* i, 37.
di istaec, *Ter. H. T.* 1038.
falsus utinam, *Liv.* xxi, 10, 10.
p. 179, dicat aliquis, *Ter. And.* 640.
fortunam, *Pub. Syr.* 193.
velim mihi, *Fam.* xiii, 75, 1.
nolim putes, *Fam.* ix, 15, 4.
dies deficiat, *N. D.* iii, 81.
p. 180, egredere, *Cat.* i, 20.
rem vobis, *Verr.* iv, 1.
si bene, *de Sen.* 3.
consules, *Leg.* iii, 8.
hominem, *Twelve Tables.*
amicitia, *Liv.* 38, 38, 1.
quin equos, *Liv.* i, 57, 7.
p. 181, adjuta, *Ter. Eun.* 150.
portas, *B. G.* ii, 33, 1.
haec, *And.* 472.
ut ne, *Off.* i, 103.
ut non, *Cat.* i, 23.
ut earum, *B. G.* iv, 17, 10.
p. 182, Helvetii, *B. G.* i, 7, 3.
haec habui, *de Sen.* 85.
non habebat, *B. G.* iv, 38, 2.
idoneus, *Verr.* iii, 41.
dignus, *Leg.* iii, 5.
multa, *Tusc. Disp.* i, 80.
p. 183, sunt qui, *Inv.* ii, 144.
nemo, *Fam.* i, 4, 2.
sapientia, *Fin.* i, 43.
quae, *Lael.* 23.
non is sum, *B. G.* v, 30, 2.
non longius, *B. G.* ii, 21, 3.
o fortunate, *Arch.* 24.
ut qui, *Phil.* xi, 30.
egomet, *de Or.* i, 82.
nemo est, *Verr.* iv, 115.
nemo fuit, *B. C.* iii, 53, 3.
quem audierim, *Nep. Ar.* 1, 2.
p. 184, quis tam, *Tusc. Disp.* iii, 71.
Siciliam, *Verr. Act. Pr.* 12.
mons, *B. G.* i, 6, 1.
non is, *Cat.* i, 22.
nemo est, *de Sen.* 24.
habetis, *Cat.* iv, 24.
nihil, *Ter. H. T.* 675.
nemo est, *B. G.* vi, 39, 3.
p. 185, Themistocles, *Nep. Them.* 8, 3.
neque, *de Sen.* 84.
quoniam, *Nep. Milt.* 7, 5.
noctu, *Tusc. Disp.* iv, 44.
Bellovaci, *B. G.* vii, 75.

## 254 INDEX TO THE EXAMPLES.

p. 186, id feci, *Caec.* 101.
    Crasso, *Fam.* xiii, 16, 3.
    hoc ita, *Leg.* iii, 31.
    Haeduos, *B. G.* i, 16, 6.
    id omitto, *Sall. Jug.* 110, 7.
p. 187, Epaminondas, *Nep. Ep.* 9, 4.
    id ut, *Nep. Them.* 8, 3.
    Caesar, *B. G.* iii, 9, 2.
    ubi de, *B. G.* i, 7, 3.
    ut quisque, *Verr.* v, 143.
    hostes, *B. G.* iv, 26, 2.
    id ubi, *Liv.* i, 32, 13.
p. 188, postquam occupatae, *Liv.* xxiv, 35, 4.
    postquam Romam, *Sall. Jug.* 28, 2.
    postquam structi, *Liv.* i, 23, 6.
    posteaquam, *Leg.* ii, 64.
    an tum, *Pis.* 26.
    credo tum, *Verr.* iv, 46.
    eo tempore, *Lig.* 20.
    illo die, *Mil.* 38.
p. 189, Lysander, *Div.* i, 96.
    Pythagoras, *N. D.* iii, 88.
    jam Galli, *B. G.* vii, 26, 3.
    Treveri, *B. G.* vi, 7, 1.
    cum ad, *Verr.* v, 27.
    cum equitatus, *B. G.* v, 19, 2.
    saepe cum, *Nep. Cim.* 4, 2.
    cum procucurrissent, *B. C.* ii, 41, 6.
p. 190, tum tua, *Hor. Epp.* i, 18, 84.
    cum videbis, *Pl. Bacch.* 145.
    stabilitas, *Lael.* 82.
    cum tacent, *Cat.* i, 21.
    cum te, *Att.* xiv, 17 A, 4.
    prius, *Pl. Merc.* 456.
    nihil contra, *Flacc.* 51.
    non prius, *Sall. C.* 51.
p. 191, priusquam, *Liv.* i, 24, 3.
    tempestas, *Sen. Ep.* 103, 2.
    priusquam telum, *B. C.* ii, 34, 6.
    animum, *Pl. Amph.* 240.
    sol antequam, *Phil.* xiv, 27.
    Alexander, *Quint. Curt.* iv, 6, 17.
    dum haec, *B. G.* iii, 17, 1.
    dum anima, *Att.* ix, 10, 3.
    Lacedaemoniorum, *Tusc. Disp.* i, 101.
    Cato, *Nep. Cat.* 2, 4.
p. 192, donec, *Liv.* xxiii, 31, 9.
    ferrum, *Nep. Ep.* 9, 3.

trepidationis, *Liv.* xxi, 28, 11.
exspectavit, *B. G.* iv, 23, 4.
dum litterae, *Fam.* xi, 23, 2.
postulo, *Ter. And.* 550.
orat, *Ter. Ad.* 882.
milites, *B. G.* ii, 21, 2.
Helvetiis, *B. G.* i, 2, 1.
p. 193, huic, *Rosc. Am.* 54.
    consuli, *Liv.* xxxv, 20, 4.
    ne lustrum, *Liv.* xxiv, 43, 4.
    prohibuit, *Liv.* xxv, 35, 6.
    nec quin, *Liv.* xxvi, 40, 4.
    constitueram, *Att.* xvi, 10, 1.
    decrevit, *Cat.* i, 4.
    convenit, *Liv.* x, 27, 2.
    fac ut, *Pl. Rud.* 1218.
    cura ut, *Cat.* iii, 12.
    laborabat, *B. G.* vii, 31, 1.
p. 194, sequitur, *N. D.* ii, 81.
    eos moneo, *Cat.* ii, 20.
    huic imperat, *B. G.* iv, 21, 8.
    opto, *Verr. Act. Pr.* 50.
p. 195, vereor ne, *Att.* vii, 12, 2.
    ex quo, *F.* ii, 24.
    ita fit, *Tusc. Disp.* ii, 16.
    est mos, *Brut.* 84.
p. 196, quis, *Par.* 48.
    illud, *Off.* iii, 111.
    hoc uno, *de Or.* i, 32.
    bene mihi, *Tusc. Disp.* i, 97.
    quod, *B. G.* i, 44, 6.
    quod me, *Nep. Ep.* 5, 6.
p. 197, oculis, *B. G.* i, 12, 1.
    bis bina, *N. D.* ii, 49.
    effugere, *N. D.* iii, 14.
    saepe autem, *N. D.* iii, 14.
    Epaminondas, *F.* ii, 97.
    ex Socrate, *Tusc. Disp.* v, 34.
    nescio, *Pl. Amph.* 1056.
p. 198, conantur, *B. G.* i, 8, 4.
    pergit, *Liv.* i, 7, 6.
    quaeritur, *N. D.* i, 61.
    haud scio, *Tusc. Disp.* ii, 41.
p. 199, naturam, *Off.* i, 100.
    memoria, *de Sen.* 21.
    si quis, *B. G.* i, 48, 6.
    si dicendo, *Tac. Dial.* 19.
p. 200, mentiar, *Lael.* 10.
    haec si, *Cat.* i, 19.
    sapientia, *F.* i, 42.
    consilium, *de Sen.* 19.
    Laelius, *Arch.* 16.
    num igitur, *de Sen.* 19.

# ABBREVIATIONS USED IN INDEX TO THE ILLUSTRATIVE EXAMPLES.

Ac., Cicero, *Academica.*
Acc., Accius.
ad Her., ad Herennium.
Aen., Virgil, *Aeneid.*
Arch., Cicero, *pro Archia.*
Att., Cicero, *Epistulae ad Atticum.*
B. C., Caesar, *de Bello Civili.*
B. G., Caesar, *de Bello Gallico.*
Brut., Cicero, *Brutus.*
Caec., Cicero, *pro Caecina.*
Cat., Cicero, *in Catilinam.*
Cluent., Cicero, *pro Cluentio.*
Curt., Quintus Curtius.
de Dom., Cicero, *de Domo Sua.*
de Or., Cicero, *de Oratore.*
de Sen., Cicero, *de Senectute.*
D., Cicero, *de Divinatione.*
Div. Caec., Cicero, *Divinatio in Caecilium.*
Ecl., Virgil, *Eclogues.*
Eut., Eutropius.
F., Cicero, *de Finibus.*
Fam., Cicero, *Epistulae ad Familiares.*
Flac., Cicero, *pro Flacco.*
Gell., Aulus Gellius.
Hor., Horace.
    Epp., *Epistles.*
    Od., *Odes.*
    Sat., *Satires.*
Inv., Cicero, *de Inventione.*
Juv., Juvenal.
Lael., Cicero, *Laelius, de Amicitia.*
Leg., Cicero, *de Legibus.*
Lig., Cicero, *pro Ligario.*
Liv., Livy.
Lucr., Lucretius.
Marc., Cicero, *pro Marcello.*
Mil., Cicero, *pro Milone.*
N. D., Cicero, *de Natura Deorum.*
Nep., Nepos.
    Alc., *Alcibiades.*
    Ar., *Aristides.*
    Att., *Atticus.*
    Cat., *Cato.*

Chab. *Chabrias.*
Cim., *Cimon.*
Con., *Conon.*
Dat., *Datames.*
Ep., *Epaminondas.*
Milt., *Miltiades.*
Paus., *Pausanias.*
Them., *Themistocles.*
Thras., *Thrasybulus.*
Tim., *Timoleon.*
Off., Cicero, *de Officiis.*
Or., Cicero, *Orator.*
Ov., Ovid.
    Am., *Amores.*
    Met., *Metamorphoses.*
Par., Cicero, *Paradoxa.*
Phil., Cicero, *Philippics.*
Pis., Cicero, *in Pisonem.*
Planc., Cicero, *pro Plancio.*
Pl., Plautus.
    Amph., *Amphitruo.*
    Aul., *Aulularia.*
    Bacch., *Bacchides.*
    Capt., *Captivi.*
    Curc., *Curculio.*
    Men., *Menaechmi.*
    Merc., *Mercator.*
    M. G., *Miles Gloriosus.*
    Pers., *Persa.*
    Poen., *Poenulus.*
    Rud., *Rudens.*
    Tr., *Trinummus.*
    Vid., *Vidularia.*
Plin. Epp., Pliny the Younger, **Letters.**
Pub. Syr., Publilius Syrus.
Q. F., Cicero, *ad Quintum Fratrem.*
Rosc. Am., Cicero, *pro Roscio Amerino.*
Sall., Sallust.
    C., *Catiline.*
    Fr., *Fragments.*
    Jug., *Jugurtha.*
Sen., Seneca.
    Ep., *Epistles.*
    N. Q., *Naturales Quaestiones.*

Sest., Cicero, *pro Sestio.*
Sex. Rosc., Cicero, *pro Sexto Roscio.*
Sil., Silius Italicus.
Stat., Caecilius Statius.
Sull., Cicero, *pro Sulla.*
Tac., Tacitus.
    A., *Annals.*
    Agr., *Agricola.*
    Dial., *Dialogus de Oratoribus.*
    Ger., *Germania.*
    H., *Histories.*
Ter., Terence.
    Ad., *Adelphoi.*

And., *Andria.*
Eun., *Eunuchus.*
Hec., *Hecyra.*
H. T., *Hautontimoroumenos.*
Phor., *Phormio.*
Tusc. Disp., Cicero, *Tusculan Disputations.*
Twelve Tables, Laws of the Twelve Tables.
Vatin., Cicero, *in Vatinium.*
Verr., Cicero, *in Verrem.*
Verr., Act. Pr., Cicero, *Actio Prima in C. Verrem.*

# INDEX TO THE PRINCIPAL PARTS OF THE MOST IMPORTANT VERBS.

NOTE. — Compounds are not given unless they present some special irregularity. The references are to sections.

The references are to sections.

The references are to sections.

misceō, 121, II, *b.*
miseret, 138, II.
misereor, 121, VII.
mittō, 122, I, 1, *b.*
molō, 122, I, 5.
moneō, 121, II, *a.*
mordeō, 121, IV.
morior, 122, V.
moveō, 121, V.

## N.

nancīscor, 122, V.
nāscor, 122, V.
nectō, 122, I, 1, *b.*
neglegō, 122, I, 3.
ningit, 138, I.
niteō, 121, II, *a,* N. 1.
nītor, 122, V.
noceō, 121, II, *a.*
nōlō, 130.
nōscō, 122, IV, 1.
nūbō, 122, I, 1, *a.*

## O.

obdūrēscō, 122, IV, 3.
oblinō, 122, I, 6.
oblīvīscor, 122, V.
obmūtēscō, 122, IV, 3.
obruō, 122, II.
obsolēscō, 122, IV, 1.
obsum, 125.
obtineō, 121, II, *b.*
ōdī, 133.
offerō, 129.
oleō, 121, II, *a,* N. 1.
operiō, 123, II.
oportet, 138, II.
opperior, 123, VII.
ōrdior, 123, VII.
orior, 123, VII.

## P.

paenitet, 138, II.
palleō, 121, II, *a,* N. 1.
pandō, 122, I, 4.
parcō, 122, I, 2.
pāreō, 121, II, *a.*
pariō, 122, III.
pāscō, 122, IV, 1.
pāscor, 122, IV, 1.

patefaciō, 122, III.
patefīō, 122, III.
pateō, 121, II, *a,* N. 1.
patior, 122, V.
paveō, 121, V.
pelliciō, 122, III.
pellō, 122, I, 2.
pendeō, 121, IV.
pendō, 122, I, 2.
peragō, 122, I, 3.
percellō, 122, I, 2, N.
percrēbrēscō, 122, IV, 3.
perdō, 122, I, 2.
perficiō, 122, III.
perfringō, 122, I, 3.
perfruor, 122, V.
perlegō, 122, I, 3.
permulceō, 121, III.
perpetior, 122, V.
pervādō. p. 87, footnote.
petō, 122, I, 6.
piget, 138, II.
pingō, 122, I, 1, *a.*
placeō, 121, II, *a.*
plaudō, 122, I, 1, *b.*
pluit, 138, I.
polleō, 121, II, *a,* N. 2.
polliceor, 121, VII.
polluō, 122, II.
pōnō, 122, I, 6.
poscō, 122, IV, 1.
possīdō, 122, I, 4.
possum, 126.
pōtō, 120, I.
praebeō, 121, II, *a.*
praestat, 138, III.
praesum, 125.
prandeō, 121, VI.
prehendō, 122, I, 4.
premō, 122, I, 1, *b.*
prōdō, 122, I, 2.
prōmō, 122, I, 3.
prōsum, 125.
prōsternō, 122, I, 6.
pudet, 138, II.
pungō, 122, I, 2.

## Q.

quaerō, 122, I, 6.
quatiō, 122, III.
queror, 122, V.
quiēscō, 122, IV, 1.

## R.

rādō, 122, I, 1, *b.*
rapiō, 122, III.
reddō, 122, I, 2.
redimō, 122, I, 3.
referciō, 123, III.
referō, 129.
rēfert, 138, II.
regō, 122, I, 1, *a.*
relinquō, 122, I, 3.
reminīscor, 122, V.
reor, 121, VII.
reperiō, 123, V.
rēpō, 122, I, 1, *a.*
resistō, 122, I, 2.
respuō, 122, II.
restinguō, p. 87, footnote.
retineō, 121, II, *b.*
rīdeō, 121, III.
rōdō, 122, I, 1, *b.*
rubeō, 121, II, *a,* N. 1.
rumpō, 122, I, 3.
ruō, 122, II.

## S.

saepiō, 123, III.
saliō, 123, II.
sanciō, 123, III.
sapiō, 122, III.
sarciō, 123, III.
scindō, 122, I, 2, N.
scīscō, 122, IV, 2.
scrībō, 122, I, 1, *a.*
sculpō, 122, I, 1, *a.*
secō, 120, II.
sedeō, 121, V.
sentiō, 123, III.
sepeliō, 123, I.
sequor, 122, V.
serō, 122, I, 6.
serpō, 122, I, 1, *a.*
sileō, 121, II, *a,* N.
sinō, 122, I, 6.
solvō, 122, I, 4.
sonō, 120, II.
spargō, 122, I, 1, *b.*
spernō, 122, I, 6.
splendeō, 121, II, *a,* N. t
spondeō, 121, IV.
statuō, 122, II.
sternō, 122, I, 6.
-stinguō, 122, I, 1, *a.*

The references are to sections.

# GENERAL INDEX.

The references are to sections and paragraphs.

ABBREVIATIONS. — Abl., ablative; acc., accusative; adj., adjective; adv., adverb, adverbial, or adverbially; cf., compare; comp., comparison or comparative; conj., conjunction or conjugation; const., constr., construction; dat., dative; decl., declension; gen., genitive; ind., indicative; indir. disc., indirect discourse; loc., locative; N., note; nom., nominative; plu., plural; prep., preposition; pron., pronoun or pronunciation; sing., singular; subj., subject; subjv., subjunctive; voc., vocative; w., with.

## A.

ă, vowel, 2, 1; pronunciation, 3, 1; development of ă, before a single consonant, 7, 1, a; before two consonants, 7, 1, b; ă as ending of nom. sing. of 1st decl., 20; in voc. sing. of Greek nouns in -ēs of 1st decl., 22; in nom. sing. of Greek nouns in -ē of 1st decl., 22, 3; termination of nom. and acc. plu. of neuters, 23; 35; 48; termination of nom. sing. of nouns of 3d decl., 28; gender of nouns in -ă of 3d decl., 43, 3; ending of acc. sing, of Greek nouns of 3d decl., 47, 1; regular quantity of final a, 363, 1; exceptions to quantity of final a, 363, 1, a-c.

ā, pronunciation, 3, 1; arising by contraction, 7, 2; as ending of stem in 1st decl., 18; ā-stems inflected, 20; in voc. sing. of Greek nouns of 1st decl., 22; in voc. sing. of Greek nouns in -ās of 3d decl., 47, 4; distinguishing vowel of 1st conjugation, 98; ending of imperative act. of 1st conj., 101; final a long by exception, 363, 1, a-c.

ā, ab, abs, use, 142, 1; with town names, 229, 2.

ā to denote agency, 216.
—— to denote separation, 214.
—— place from which, 229.
—— with town names, 229, 2.
—— with abl. of gerund, 338, 4, b.

ā-stems, 20; 98; 101.

Abbreviations of proper names, 373.
Ablative case, 17; 213 f.
—— in -ābus, 21. 2, e.
—— in -d in prons., 84, 3; 85, 3.
—— formation of sing. of adjs. of 3d decl., 67, a; 70, 1-5.
—— of ĭ-stems, 37; 38.
—— genuine abl. uses, 214 f.
—— absolute, 227.
—— of agent, 216.
—— of accompaniment, 222.
—— of accordance, 220, 3.
—— of association, 222, A.
—— of attendant circumstance, 221; 227, 2, e).
—— of cause, 219.
—— of comparison, 217.
—— of degree of difference, 223.
—— of fine or penalty, 208, 2, b.
—— of manner, 220.
—— of material, 224, 3.
—— of means, 218.
—— of penalty, 208, 2, b.
—— of place where, 228.
—— of place whence, 229.
—— of price, 225.
—— of quality, 224.
—— of separation, 214; with compounds of dis- and sē-, 214, 3.
—— of source, 215.
—— of specification, 226.
—— of time at which, 230.
—— of time during which, 231, ᴌ

263

The references are to sections and paragraphs.

The references are to sections and paragraphs.

Anaphora, 350, 11, *b*).
Anastrophe of prep., 141, 2; 142, 3; 144, 3.
*anceps* (*syllaba anceps*), defined, 366, 10.
*Androgeōs*, decl., 27.
*animal*, decl., 39.
Animals, as agents, 216, 2.
*animī*, locative, 232, 3.
*annōn*, in double questions, 162, 4.
Answers, 162, 5.
*ante*, prep. w. acc., 141; as adv., 144, 1; dat. w. verbs compounded w. *ante*, 187, III; in expressions of time, 357, 1; 371, 5; *ante diem*, 371, 5; 6.
Antecedent of rel., 251.
—— attraction of, 251, 4.
—— incorporated with rel., 251, 4.
Antecedent omitted, 251, 1.
—— repeated with rel., 251, 3.
Antepenult, 6, 2.
*antepōnō*, with dat., 187, III, 2.
*antequam*, with ind., 291; with subjv., 292.
Anticipation, denoted by subjv., w. *antequam* and *priusquam*, 292; by subjv. with *dum*, *dōnec*, *quoad*, 293, III, 2; 374, 5.
*-ānus*, suffix, 151, 2; 152, 1; 3.
Aorist tense, see Historical perfect.
Apodosis, 301 ff.
—— in conditional sent. of 1st type, 302, 4; result clauses as apodoses, 322; *quīn*-clauses as apodoses, 322; ind. questions as apodoses, 322, *b*; *potuerim* in apodosis, 322, *c*; apodosis in indir. disc., 319–321; in expressions of obligation, ability, *etc.*, 304, 3, *a*; with periphrastic conjugations, 304, 3, *b*.
Apposition, 169; agreement, 169, 2; partitive, 169, 5; with voc. in nom., 171, 2; genitive w. force of appositive, 202; *id* as appositive of clause, 247, 1, *b*; inf. as appositive, 326; 329; subst. clauses as appositives, 282, 1, *f*; 294; 297, 3.
Appositive of locative, 169, 4; with acc. of limit of motion, 182, 2, *a*; with town names, in abl. of place whence, 229, 2.
—— position of, 350, 2.
*aptus*, w. dat., 192, 2.
*apud*, prep. w. acc., 141.

*Archiās*, declension of, 22.
*-ar*, declension of nouns in, 39.
*arguō*, constr., 178, 1, *d*).
*-āris*, suffix, 151, 2.
*-ārium*, suffix, 148, 3.
*-ārius*, suffix, 151, 2.
*armiger*, decl., 23, 2.
Arrangement of words, 348–350; of clauses, 351.
Arsis, defined, 366, 6.
*artūs*, dat. and abl. plu. of, 49, 3.
*arx*, decl., 40.
*-ăs*, acc. plu. in Greek nouns, 47, 3.
*-ās*, old gen. sing., 1st decl., case-ending, 21, 2, *a*).
—— ending of Greek nouns, nom. sing. in, 22.
—— gender of nouns in *-ās*, 43, 2; 45, 1.
—— voc. of Greek nouns in *-ās*, *antis*, 47, 4.
—— *-ătis*, abl. of patrials in, 70, 5, *c*).
Asking, case const. with verbs of, 178,1, *c*; subst. clauses w., 295, 1; ind. questions, 300, 1.
Aspirates, 2, 3, *c*.
Assimilation of consonants, 8, 4 f.; 9, 2.
Association, abl. of, 222, *A*.
Asyndeton, 341, 4, *a*); 346.
*at*, 343, 1, *d*).
*-ătim*, suffix, 157, 2.
*Atlās*, decl., 47, 4.
*atomus*, gender of, 26, 1, *c*).
*atque*, 341, 2, *b*); = *as*, 341, 1, *c*).
*atquī*, 343, 1, *e*).
Attendant circumstance, abl. of, 221; 227, 2, *e*).
Attraction of demonstratives, 246, 5; of relatives, 250, 5; subjunctive by attraction, 324; of adjectives, 327, 2, *a*; 328, 2.
Attributive adjs., 233, 2.
*-ātus*, its force as suffix, 151, 4.
*audăcter*, formation and comparison, 76, 2.
*audeō*, conj., 114, 1.
*audiō*, conj., 107; with pres. partic., 337, 3.
*aulāī*, archaic gen., 21, 2, *b*.
*ausus*, force as participle, 336, 5.
*aut*, 342, 1, *a*).
*autem*, 343, 1, *c*); 350, 8.
Auxiliary omitted in infin., 116, 5; in finite forms, 166, 3.

The references are to sections and paragraphs.

*auxilium, auxilia*, 61.
*-āx*, suffix, 150, 2.

## B.

*balneum, balneae*, 60, 2.
*barbitos*, decl., 27.
Believing, verbs of, with dat., 187, II.
*bellī*, locative, 232, 2.
*bellum*, decl., 23.
*bene*, comparison, 77, 1.
Benefiting, verbs of, w. dat., 187, II.
*benevolus*, comparison, 71, 5, *a*).
*-ber*, declension of month names in, 68, 1.
*-bilis*, suffix, 150, 4.
*bonus*, decl., 63; comparison, 72.
*bōs*, decl., 41.
Brachylogy, 374, 2.
Bucolic diaeresis, 368, 3, *d*.
*-bulum*, suffix, 147, 4.
*-bundus*, suffix, 150, 1.
*būris*, decl., 38, 1.

## C.

C., for G. as abbreviation of *Gāius*, 373.
*caedēs*, decl., 40.
Caesura, 366, 8: in dactylic hexameter, 368, 3.
*calcar*, decl., 39.
Calendar, 371; 372.
Calends, 371, 2, *a*).
*campester*, decl., 68, 1.
*canis*, decl., 38, 2.
*capiō*, conj., 110.
*carbasus*, gender of, 26, 1, *b*).
*carcer, carcerēs*, 61.
Cardinals, defined, 78, 1; list of, 79; decl., 80; with and without *et*, 81, 1; 3; expressed by subtraction, 81, 2; replaced by distributives in poetry, 81, 4, *d*.
*cārē*, comparison, 76, 2.
*carō*, decl., 42.
*carrus, carrum*, 60, 1.
Cases, 17; alike in form, 19; 170 ff.
Case-endings, 17, 3.
*castrum, castra*, 61.
Catalectic verses, 366, 9.
*causā*, with gen., 198, 1; *nūlla causa est cūr*, with subjv., 295, 7.
Causal clauses, 285; 286; clause of characteristic with accessory notion of cause, 283, 3.

—— conjunctions, 345.
Cause, abl. of, 219; 227, 2, *d*).
*cavĕ*, 363, 2, *b*).
*cavĕ, cavē nē* in prohibitions, 376, *b*.
*-ce*, 6, 3 f.; 87, footnote 2.
*cedo, cette*, 137, 3.
*cēdō*, with dat., 187, II.
*celeber*, decl., 68, 1.
*celer*, decl., 68, 2.
*cēlō*, constr., 178, 1, *e*).
*cēnātus*, force, 114, 2.
*cētera*, adverbial acc., 185, 2.
*cēterī*, use, 253, 4.
Characteristic, clauses of, 283; denoting cause or opposition ('although'), 283, 3; gen. of, 203, 1; abl., 224.
Charge, gen. of, 208, 1; 2.
Chiasmus, 350, 11, *c*).
Choosing, const. w. verbs of, 177, 1-3.
*circā, circiter, circum*, preps. w. acc., 141.
*circum*, compounds of, w. dat., 187, III.
*circumdō*, const., 187, 1, *a*.
Circumstance, abl. of attendant, 221.
*cis*, prep. w. acc., 141.
*citerior*, comparison, 73, 1.
*cito*, 77, 2, *a*.
*citrā*, prep. w. acc., 141.
*cīvitās*, decl., 40, 1, *e*.
*clam*, with acc., 144, 2.
Clauses, coörd. and subord., 164, 165.
Clauses of characteristic, 283; purpose, 282; result, 284; causal, 285; temporal with *postquam, ut, ubi, simul ac*, etc., 287; with *cum*, 288; substantive clauses, 294 f.; condition, 301 f.; conditional comparison, 307; concessive, 308; adversative, 309; wish or proviso, 310; relative, 311 f.; 283 f.
*clāvis*, decl., 38, 1.
Clinging, construction of verbs of, 258, 3.
*clipeus, clipeum*, 60, 1.
Close of sentences, cadences used, 350, 12.
*coepī*, conj., 133; *coeptus est*, 133, 1.
Cognate acc., 176, 4.
*cognōmen*, 373.
*cōgō*, w. acc., 178, 1, *d*); w. infin., 331, VI.
Collective nouns, 12, 2, *a*); w. plu. verb, 254, 4.
*colus*, gender of, 26, 1, *b*).
*com-*, compounds of, w. dat., 187, III.

The references are to sections and paragraphs.

The references are to sections and paragraphs.

The references are to sections and paragraphs.

# GENERAL INDEX. 273

The references are to sections and paragraphs.

for -*ārum*, 21, 2, *d*); -*um* for- *ōrum*,
25, 6; 63, 2; -*um* for -*ium*, 70, 7; gen.
plu. lacking, 57, 7; syntax of, 194 f.
—— of characteristic, 203, 1.
—— of charge with judicial verbs, 208.
—— of indefinite price, 203, 4.
—— of indefinite value, 203, 3.
—— of material, 197.
—— of measure, 203, 2.
—— of origin, 196.
—— of possession, 198.
—— of quality, 203.
—— of the whole, 201.
—— appositional, 202.
—— objective, 200.
—— of separation, 212, 3.
—— subjective, 199.
—— with adjs., 204; with participles,
204, 1, *a*.
—— with *causā*, *grātiā*, 198, 1.
—— with verbs, 205 f.; of plenty and
want, 212; with impers. verbs, 209.
—— position of gen., 350, 1.
*genus*, decl., 36; *id genus*, 185, 1.
-*ger*, decl. of nouns in, 23, 2; adjs., 65, 1.
Gerund, 95, 1; 1st conj., 101; 2d conj.,
103; 3d conj., 105; 4th conj., 107;
syntax, 338; with object, 338, 5.
Gerundive, 95, 1; 1st conj., 102; 2d
conj., 104; 3d conj., 106; 4th conj.,
108; in periphrastic conj., 115; 337, 8.
Gerundive, const., 339, 1–6; in passive
periphrastic conj., 337, 8 f.; gen. denoting purpose, 339, 6; with dat. of
purpose, 191, 3; 339, 7.
*gnārus*, not compared, 75, 2.
Gnomic present, 259, 1; perfect, 262, 1.
*gradior*, conj., 109, 2, *c*.
Grammatical gender, 15.
*grātiā*, with gen., 198, 1; *grātia*, *grātiae*,
61.
Greek nouns, 1st decl., 22; 2d decl., 27;
exceptions in gender, 26, 1, *c*); 3d
decl., 47; Greek acc., 180; Greek nouns
in verse, 365.
*grūs*, decl., 41, 2.
*gu* = *gv*, 3, 3.
Guttural mutes, 2, 4.
—— stems, 32.

## H.

*h*, pron., 3, 3; *ph, ch, th*, 2, 4; 3, 3.
*habeō*, with perf. pass. partic., 337, 6.

*Hadria*, gender, 21, 1.
Happening, verbs of, w. ind., 299, 1, 2;
w. subjv., 297, 2.
Hard consonants, 2, 3, *a*), footnote 1.
Hardening, 367, 4.
*haud*, use, 347, 2, *a*; *haud sciō an*,
300, 5.
*havē*, 137, 5.
Help, verbs signifying, w. dat., 187,
II.
Hendiadys, 374, 4.
*herī*, locative, 232, 2.
Heteroclites, 59.
Heterogeneous nouns, 60.
Hexameter, dactylic, 368.
Hiatus, 366, 7, *a*.
*hīc*, 87; 246, 1; 246, 2; *hĭc*, 364, footnote.
*hiems*, 35, footnote.
Hindering, verbs of, with subjv., 295,
3.
Historical tenses, 258; historical present
259, 3; 268, 3; historical perfect, 262
*B*; historical infinitive, 335.
*honor*, decl., 36.
Hoping, verbs of, w. inf., 331, I.
Hortatory subjv., 274.
*hortus*, decl., 23.
*hōscine*, 87, footnote 1.
*hostis*, decl., 38.
*hūjusce*, 87, footnote 1.
*humī*, locative, 232, 2.
*humilis*, comp., 71, 4.
*humus*, gender of, 26, 1, *b*).
*huncine*, 87, footnote 1.
Hyperbaton, 350, 11, *a*).
Hypermeter, 367, 6.
Hysteron proteron, 374, 7.

## I.

*ĭ*, 1, 1; in diphthongs, 2, 1; pron., 3, 1
from *ĕ*, 7, 1, *a*; from *ŭ*, 7, 1, *b*; dropped
by syncope, 7, 4; for *ŭ* in some words,
9, 1; changes to *ĕ*, 39; dropped, 39;
final *i* short, 363, 3; becomes *j*, 367,
4.
*ĭ*-stems, 37; 39; not always ending in -*is*,
38, 3.
-*ī*, gen. and voc. of 2d decl. nouns in -*ius*
and -*ium* in, 25, 1 and 2.
—— gen. of 4th decl. nouns in -*us*, 49, 1.
—— gen. of 5th decl. nouns, 52, 2.

inf. for subjv. in indir. disc., 314, 4; subj. acc. omitted, 314, 5; implied indir. disc., 323.

—— questions, 300; particles introducing, 300, 1, *a*; deliberative subjv. in indir. quest., 300, 2; indir. quest. w. *sī*, 300, 3; double indir. questions, 300, 4; in indir. quest., 300, 6; in conditional sents. of 3d type, 322, *b*.

—— reflexives, 244, 2.

—— object, 187.

*īnferum, īnferior*, 73, 2.

*īnfimus*, 241, 1.

Infinitive, gender of, 15, *A*, 3; in -*ier*, 116, 4, *a*; force of tenses in, 270; 326 ff.

—— fut. perf. inf., 270, 4; periphrastic future, 270, 3.

—— without subj. acc., 326–328; 314, 5.

—— with subj. acc., 329–331.

—— as obj., 328; 331.

—— as subj., 327; 330.

—— with adjs., 333.

—— denoting purpose, 326, N.

—— in abl. abs., 227, 3.

—— in exclamations, 334.

—— historical inf., 335.

*īnfitiās*, constr., 182, 5.

Inflection, 11.

Inflections, 11 ff.

*īnfrā*, prep. w. acc., 141.

*ingēns*, comp., 73, 4.

*injūriā*, abl. of manner, 220, 2.

*injussū*, defective, 57, 1; the abl., 219, 2.

*inl-* = *ill-*, 9, 2.

*innīxus*, w. abl., 218, 3.

*inops*, decl., 70, 2.

*inquam*, conj., 134.

Inseparable prepositions, 159, 3, N.

*īnsidiae*, plu. only, 56, 3.

*īnstar*, 58.

Instrumental uses of abl., 213; 218 ff.

Intensive pron., 88.

Intensives (verbs), 155, 2.

*inter*, prep. w. acc., 141; compounded w. verbs, governing dat. 187, III; to express reciprocal relation, 245.

*interdīcō*, const., 188, 1, *a*.

*interest*, constr., 210; 211.

*interior*, comp., 73, 1.

Interjections, 145.

Interlocked order, 350, 11, *d*.

Interrogative pronouns, 90.

—— sentences, 162; particles, 162, 2; omitted, 162, 2, *d*); in indir. disc., 315.

*intrā*, prep. w. acc., 141.

Intransitive verbs, with cognate acc., 176, 4; in passive, 256, 3; 187, II, *b*; impersonal intransitives, 138, IV.

-*īnus*, suffix, 151, 2; 152, 1; 152, 3.

-*iō*, verbs of 3d conj., 109.

-*ior, ius*, comparative ending, 71.

*ipse*, 88; 249; as indir. reflexive, 249, 3.

*ipsīus* and *ipsōrum*, with possessive pronouns, 243, 3.

-*ir*, decl. of nouns in, 23.

Irregular comparison, 72 ff.; nouns, 42; verbs, 124 f.

*is*, 87; 247; as personal pron., 247, 2.

-*is*, as patronymic ending, 148, 6, *b*); nouns in -*is* of 3d decl., 37 f.; adjs. in -*is*, 69.

-*īs*, acc. plu., 3d decl., 37; 40.

——, -*ītis*, abl. of partials in, 70, 5, *c*).

*istaec*, 87, footnote 2.

*iste*, 87; 246, 4.

*istīc*, 6, 4.

*īstūc*, 6, 4; 87, footnote 2.

*ita*, in answers, 162, 5.

*itaque*, 344, 1, *a*).

*iter*, 42, 1.

-*itia*, 149.

-*itō*, frequentatives in, 155, 2, *a*.

-*ium*, gen. of nouns in, 25, 2; ending of gen. plu., 3d decl., 37 f.; 39; 40; 147, 3, *b*); 148, 2.

-*ius*, gen. and voc. sing. of nouns in, 25, 1 and 2; of adjs., 63, *a*; 151, 2; 152, 2; 152, 3; -*ĭus* for *īus*, 362, 1, *a*).

-*īvus*, suffix, 151, 2.

## J.

*j*, 1, 2.

*jaciō*, conj., 109, 2, *a*); compounds of, 9, 3; 362, 5.

*jam*, etc., with present tense, 259, 4; with imperfect, 260, 4.

*jecur*, decl., 42, 3.

*jocō*, abl. of manner, 220, 2.

*jocus*, plu. of, 60, 2.

Joining, verbs of, construction, 358, 3.

*jubeō*, constr., 295, 1, *a*; 331, II.

## 276 GENERAL INDEX.

The references are to sections and paragraphs.

*jūdicor*, w. inf., 332, *c*.
*jūgerum*, 59, 1.
Julian calendar, 371.
*jungō*, w. abl., 222, *A*.
*Juppiter*, decl., 41.
*jūrātus*, 114, 2.
*jūre*, abl. of manner, 220, 2.
*jūs est*, with substantive clause, 297, 3.
*jussū*, 57, 1; the abl., 219, 2.
Jussive subjv., 275; equiv. to a protasis, 305, 2.
*juvat*, w. acc., 175, 2, *c*); with inf., 327, 1.
*Juvenāle*, abl., 70, 5, *b*.
*juvenis*, a cons. stem, 38, 2; comparison, 73, 4.
*juvō*, with acc., 187, II, N.
*jūxtā*, prep. w. acc., 141.

## K.
*k*, 1, 1.
Knowing, verbs of, w. inf., 331, I.
Knowledge, adjs. of, w. gen., 204.

## L.
*l*, pron., 3, 3.
Labial mutes, 2, 4.
—— stems, 31; gender of, 43, 3; 46, 1.
*lacer*, decl., 65, 1.
*lacus*, decl., 49, 3.
*laedō*, w. acc., 187, II, N.
*laetus*, w. adverbial force, 239.
*lapis*, decl., 33.
*largior*, 113.
Latin period, 351, 5.
Length of syllables, 5, *B*.
Length of vowels, 5, *A*.
*-lentus*, suffix, 151, 3.
*leō*, decl., 35.
*Līber*, decl., 23, 2.
*līber*, adj., decl., 65, 1.
*līberō*, constr., 214, 1, N. 1.
*līberta*, *lībertābus*, 21, 2, *e*).
*līberum*, gen. plu., 25, 6, *c*).
*licet*, with subjv., 295, 6 and 8; 308, *a*; with inf., 327, 1; 330.
*licet*, adversative, 309, 4.
Likeness, adjs. of, w. dat., 192, 1.
Limit of motion, acc. of., 182.
Lingual mutes, 2, 4.
*linter*, decl., 40.
Liquids, 2, 5.
—— stems, 34.

*līs*, decl., 40, 1, *d*).
Litotes, 375, 1.
*littera*, *litterae*, 61.
Locative, 17, 1; in *-ae*, 21, 2, *c*); in *-ī*, 25, 5; syntax, 232; apposition with, 169, 4; loc. uses of abl., 213; 228 f.
*locō*, *locīs*, the abl., 228, 1, *b*.
*locus*, plurals of, 60, 2.
Long syllables, 5, *B*, 1.
—— vowels, 5, *A*, 1.
*longius = longius quam*, 271, 3.
*longum est* = Eng. potential, 217, 1, *b*.
*lubet*, *lubīdō*, spelling, 9, 1.
*lūdīs*, the abl., 230, 1.
*-lus, -la, -lum*, diminutives in, 148, 1.
*lūx*, 57, 7.

## M.
*m*, pron., 3, 3; changed to *n* before *d, c*, 8, 5, *c*; *m*-stem, 35, footnote; *m*-final in poetry, 366, 10.
*maereō*, w. acc., 175, 2, *b*.
*magis*, comparison, 77, 1; comparison with, 74.
*magnī*, gen. of value, 203, 3.
*magnopere*, compared, 77, 1.
*magnus*, compared, 72.
Making, verbs of, w. two accusatives, 177.
*male*, comparison, 77, 1.
*maledīcēns*, comparison, 71, 5, *a*).
*mālim*, potential subjv., 280, 2, *a*.
*māllem*, potential subjv., 280, 4.
*magnus*, compared, 72.
*mālō*, 130; with inf., 331, IV, and *a*; with subjv., 296, 1, *a*.
*malus*, comparison, 72.
*māne*, indeclinable, 58.
Manner, abl. of, 220.
*mare*, decl., 39, 2; *marī*, 228, 1, *c*).
*mās*, decl., 40, 1, *d*).
Masculine, see Gender.
Masculine caesura, 368, 3, *c*.
Material, abl. of, 224, 3.
*māteriēs*, *māteria*, 59, 2, *a*).
*mātūrē*, compared, 77, 1.
*mātūrus*, compared, 71, 3.
*maximē*, adjs. compared with, 74.
*maximī*, as gen. of value, 203, 3.
*maxumus*, 9, 1.
Means, abl. of, 218, abl. abs. denoting, 227, 2; denoted by partic., 337, 2, *d*.
*mēd*, for *mē*, 84, 3.

The references are to sections and paragraphs.

The references are to sections and paragraphs.

# GENERAL INDEX. 279

The references are to sections and paragraphs.

Operations of nature, impersonal verbs expressing, 138, I.
*opīniōne* with comparatives, 217, 4.
*opis*, 57, 6; *opēs*, 61.
*oportet*, 138, II; w. subjv., 295, 6; 8; w. inf., 327, 330.
*oportuit*, with pres. inf. 'ought to have,' 270, 2; with perf. inf., 270, 2, *a*.
*oppidum* (*Genavam ad oppidum*), 182, 2, *a*.
Optative subjv., 272; 279; substantive clauses developed from, 296.
*optimātēs*, decl., 40, 1, *d*).
*optimus*, comp., 72.
*optō*, w. subst. cl. developed from optative, 296, 1.
*optumus*, spelling, 9, 1.
*opus est*, w. abl., 218, 2; w. partic., 218, 2, *c*.
-*or*, nouns in, 34; 36; -*or* for -*os*, 36; gender of nouns in, 43, 1; exceptions in gender, 44, 2; as suffix, 147, 2.
Oratio Obliqua, 313 f.
Order of words, 348 f.
Ordinals, 78, 1; 79.
*orior*, conjugation, 123, VII.
*oriundus*, constr., 215, 2.
*ōrō*, with acc., 178, 1, *a*).
*Orpheus*, decl. 47, 6.
Orthography, peculiarities, 9.
*ortus*, constr., 215.
*ōs*, decl., 57, 7.
*os*, decl., 42.
-*os*, later -*us* in 2d decl., 23.
-*ōs*, later -*or* in 3d decl., 36, 1.
——— -*ōs*, Greek nouns, 2d decl. in, 27.
-*ōsus*, form of suffix, 151, 3.
*ovis*, decl., 38, 1.
Oxyꞷoron, 375, 2.

## P.

*p*, pron., 3, 3; by assimilation, 8, 4; by partial assimilation, 8, 5.
*paenitet*, 138, II; with gen., 209.
*palam*, as prep. w. abl., 144, 2.
Palatal mutes, 2, 4.
*palūster*, decl., 68, 1.
Parasitic vowels, 7, 3.
*parātus*, with infin., 333.
Pardon, verbs signifying, w. dat., 187, II.
*pariō*, 109, 2, *a*).

*pars*, *partēs*, 61.
*parte*, abl. of place, 228, 1, *b*.
*partem*, adverbially used, 185, 1.
Participation, adjs. of, w. gen., 204, 1.
Participial stem, 97, III; formation, 119.
Participles, in -*āns* and -*ēns*, 70, 3; gen. plu. of in -*um*, 70, 7; pres. act. partic., 97, I, 5; 101; 103; 105; 107; 110; 113; fut. act. partic., 97, III; as one of the principal parts of the verb, p. 55, footnote; 100; 101; 103; 105; 107; 110; 113; perf. pass. partic., 97, III; 102; 104; 106; 108, 111; 113; gerundive, see Gerundive; fut. act., peculiar formation of, 119, 4; perf. pass., w. act. or neuter meaning, 114, 2; of deponents, 112, *b*; syntax, 336 ff.
Participles, fut. act., 119, 4; denoting purpose, 337, 4.
——— perf. act., how supplied, 356, 2.
——— perf. pass., 336, 3; as pres., 336, 5.
——— pres. partic., 336, 2; with conative force, 336, 2, *a*.
——— perf. pass., with active meaning, 114, 2; pred. use of partic., 337, 2; participles equivalent to subordinate clauses, 337, 2; to coördinate clauses, 337, 5; w. *opus est*, 218, 2, *c*; with noun, equivalent to abstract noun, 337, 6; with *habeō*, 337, 7.
——— with *videō*, *audiō*, *faciō*, etc., 337, 3.
Particles, 139 f.; 341 f.
Partitive apposition, 169, 5.
Partitive gen., so called, 201.
Parts of speech, 10.
*parum*, comparison, 77, 1.
*parvī*, gen. of value, 203, 3.
*parvus*, comparison, 72.
Passive, verbs in, with middle meaning, 175, 2, *d*); 256; verbs governing dat. used in pass. only impersonally, 187, II, *b*; constr. of passive verbs of saying, etc., 332, and note; how supplied when missing, 356, 1.
*patior*, conj., 109, 2, *c*); 113; with inf., 331, III.
Patrial adjs., 70, 5, *c*).
Patronymics, 148, 6.
*paulum*, formation, 77, 3.
*paulus*, spelling, 9, 1.
*pauper*, decl., 70, 1.
*pedester*, decl., 68, 1.
*pejor*, quantity of first syllable, 362, 5.

*pelagus*, gender of, 26, 2.

Penalty, abl. of, 208, 2, *b*.

*penātēs*, decl., 40, 1, *d*).

*penes*, prep. w. acc., 141.

Pentameter, dactylic, 369.

Penult, 6, 2.

*per*, prep. w. acc., 141; with acc. of time and space, 181, 2.

Perceiving, verbs of, w. inf., 331, I.

Perfect active ptc., how supplied in Latin, 356, 2.

Perfect pass. partic., force of w. deponent verbs, 112, *b*; dat. of agency sometimes used w., 189, 2; *opus*, 218, 2, *c*.

Perfect stem, 97, II; formation, 118.

—— in *-āvī, -ēvī, -īvī* contracted, 116, 1.

—— historical perf., 262.

—— with force of pres., 262; 133, 2; pres. perf. and hist. perf. distinguished, 237, 1 and 2; gnomic perf., 262, 1; perf. subjv. as historical tense, 268, 6 and 7, *b*; perf. inf. w. *oportuit*, 270, 2; perf. prohibitive, 279, *a*; perf. potential, 280, 1 and 2; perf. concessive, 278; sequence of tenses after perf. inf., 268, 2.

Periodic structure, 351, 5.

Periphrastic conj., 115; 269, 3; in conditional sentences of the 3d type, 304, 3, *b*); in indir. disc., 322; in passive, 337, 8, *b*, 1.

—— fut. inf., 270, 3.

Persons, 95, 4; 2d sing. of indefinite subject, 356, 3.

Personal pronouns, 84; 242; as subject, omission of, 166, 2; as objective genitives, 242, 2.

—— endings, 96.

*persuādeō*, with dat., 187, II, *a*; with subjv., 295, 1.

Persuading, verbs of, w. dat., 187, II.

*ph*, 2, 3, *c*; 2, 4; 3, 3.

*piget*, with gen., 209.

Pity, verbs of, w. gen., 209, 1 and 2.

Place to which, 182; whence, 229; place where, 228.

*placitus*, force, 114, 2.

Pleasing, verbs of, w. dat., 187, II, *a*; w. acc., 187, II, *a*, N.

*plēbēs*, heteroclite, 59, 2, *d*).

*plēbī*, gen., 52, 2.

Plenty and Want, verbs of, constr., 212; cf. 218, 8.

*plēnus*, w. gen., 218, 8, *a*.

Pleonasm, 374, 3.

*plēráque*, 6, 5.

*pluit*, 138, I.

Pluperfect tense, formation, 100; syntax, 263; 265; 287, 2; 288, 3; with imperfect meaning, 133, 2.

Plural, 16; in 5th decl., 52, 4; of proper names, 55, 4, *a*); of abstract nouns, 5, 4, *c*); nouns used in, only, 56; with change of meaning, 61; stylistic use, 353, 1; 2.

*Pluralia tantum*, 56; 81, 4, *b*).

*plūris*, gen. of value, 203, 3; of price, 203, 4.

*plūs*, decl., 70; 70, 4; = *plūs quam*, 217, 3.

*poēma*, decl., 47, 5.

Polysyndeton, 341, 4, *b*).

*por-*, inseparable prep., 159, 3, *e*.

*porticus*, gender, 50.

*portus*, decl., 49, 3.

*poscō*, constr., 178, 1, *a*).

Position of clauses, 351, 3.

—— of words, 348; 350; 351.

Possessive dat., 190; gen., 198; contrasted with dat. of poss., 359, 1.

Possessive pronouns, 86; 243; = objective gen., 243, 2; position of, 243, 1, *a*.

Possibility, verbs of, put in indic. in cond. sentences, 304, 3, *a*.

*possum*, 126; with present infin., 'I might,' 271, 1, *a*); in cond. sentences, 304, 3, *a*.

*post*, prep. w. acc., 144, 1; in expressions of time, 357, 1.

Post-positive words, 343, 1, *c*).

*posteāquam*, 287; separated, 287, 3; with imperf. ind., 287, 4; w. pluperf. ind., 287, 3; with subjv., 287, 5.

*posterus, posterior*, comp., 73. 2.

*postrēmus*, use, 241, 2.

*postrīdiē*, with gen., 201, 3, *a*.

*postulō*, constr., 178, 1, *a*.

Potential subjv., 272; 280.

*potior*, with gen., 212, 2; with abl., 218 1; in gerundive constr., 339, 4.

——, adj., 73, 1.

*potius*, compared, 77, 1.

*potuī, poteram*, in apodosis of conditiona'

The references are to sections and paragraphs.

*neus*, 282, 3; independent of principal verb, 282, 4; inf., denoting purpose, 326, N.; fut. partic., denoting purpose, 337, 4; gerund, w. *ad*, 338, 3; gerundive, 339, 2; supine, 340.

### Q.

*-qu-*, pron., 3, 3; both letters consonants, 74, *a*.

*quaerō*, w. indir. questions, 300, 1, *b*), N.

*quaesō*, 137, 2.

Quality, gen., 203; abl., 224.

*quam*, in comparisons, 217, 2; with superl., 240, 3; *ante . . . quam, post . . . quam, prius . . . quam*, see *antequam, postquam, priusquam*; *quam quī*, 283, 2, *a*.

*quam sī*, 307, 1.

*quam ut*, with subjv., 284, 4.

*quamquam*, with ind., 309, 2; with subjv., 309, 6; = 'and yet,' 309, 5.

*quamvīs*, with subjv., 309, 1; 6; denoting a fact, 309, 6.

*quandō*, 286, 3, *b*.

*quantī*, as gen. of price, 203, 4; of value, 203, 3.

Quantity, 5.

—— of syllables, 5, *B*; 363 f.

—— of vowels, 5, *A*; 362; in Greek words, 365.

*quasi*, 307, 1.

*quatiō*, conj., 109, 2, *a*).

*-que*, accent of word preceding, 6, 3; 6, 5; 341, 1, *b*); 2, *a*); 4, *c*).

*queō*, 137, 1.

Questions, word, sentence, 162 f.; rhetorical, 162, 3; double (alternative), 162, 4; indirect, 300; questions in indir. disc., 315.

*quī*, rel., 89; interr., 90; indef., 91; for *quis* in indir. questions, 90, 2, *b*; with *nē, sī, nisi, num*, 91, 5; in purpose clauses, 282, 2; abl., 90, 2, *a*.

*quia*, in causal clauses, 286, 1.

*quīcum*, 89.

*quīcumque*, decl., 91, 8.

*quīdam*, decl., 91; syntax, 252, 3.

*quidem*, post-positive, 347, 1.

*quīlibet*, decl., 91.

*quīn*, in result clauses, 284, 3; in substantive clauses, 295, 3; 298; = *quī nōn* in clauses of characteristic, 283, 4;

with ind., 281, 3; in indir. disc., 321 and *a*; *nūlla causa est quīn*, 295, 7.

*quīnam*, 90, 2, *d*.

*Quīntīlis* (= *Jūlius*), 371.

*quippe quī*, in clauses of characteristic, 283, 3.

*Quirītēs*, decl., 40, 1, *d*.

*quis*, indef., 91; interr., 90; 90, 2, *c*; 252, 1; *nesciō quis*, 253, 6; with *nē, sī, nisi, num*, 91, 5.

*quis est quī*, 283, 2.

*quīs* = *quibus*, 89.

*quisnam*, inflection, 90, 2, *d*.

*quispiam*, inflection, 91.

*quisquam*, inflection, 91; usage, 252, 4.

*quisque*, inflection, 91; usage, 252, 5.

*quisquis*, inflection, 91, 8.

*quīvīs*, inflection, 91.

*quō*, in purpose clauses, 282, 1, *a*.

*quoad*, with ind., 293; with subjv., 293, III, 2.

*quod*, in causal clauses, 286, 1; in substantive clauses, 299; 331, V, *a*; 'as regards the fact,' 299, 2.

*quod audierim*, 283, 5; *quod sciam*, 283, 5.

*quod (sī)*, adverbial acc., 185, 2.

*quom*, early form of *cum*, 9, 1.

*quō minus*, after verbs of hindering, 295, 3.

*quoniam*, in causal clauses, 286, 1.

*quoque*, post-positive, 347.

*-quus*, decl. of nouns in, 24.

### R.

*r*, pron., 3, 3; for *s* between vowels ('Rhotacism'), 8, 1.

*rapiō*, conj., 109, 2, *a*).

*rāstrum*, plurals of, 60, 2.

*ratus*, 'thinking,' 336, 5.

Reciprocal pronouns, 85, 2; 245; cf. 253, 3.

Reduplication in perf., 118, 4, *a*); in pres., 117, 7.

Reference, dat. of, 188.

*rēfert*, constr., 210; 211, 4.

Reflexive pronouns, 85; 244; 249, 3.

*regō*, conj., 105.

Regular verbs, 101–113.

*rĕī*, 362, 1, *b*).

*reiciō*, quantity, 362, 5.

Relative adverbs, in rel. clauses of purp., 282, 2.

—— clauses, of purp., 282, 2; w. *dignus, indignus, idōneus,* 282, 3; of characteristic, 283; denoting cause or opposition, 283, 3; restrictive, 283, 5; introduced by *quīn,* 283, 4; 284, 3; conditional rel. clauses, 311; 312, 1 and 2; relative as subj. of inf., 314, 4; rel. clause standing first, 251, 4, *a.*

—— pronouns, inflection, 89; use, 250 ff.; = Eng. demonstrative, 251, 6; agreement, 250; not omitted as in Eng., 251, 5; fondness for subordinate clauses, 355.

*relinquitur ut,* 297, 2.

*reliquī,* use, 253, 5.

*reliquum est,* with subjv., 295, 6.

*rēmex,* decl., 32.

Remembering, verbs of, cases used w., 206.

Reminding, verbs of, const., 207.

*reminīscor,* constr., 206, 2.

Removing, verbs of, w. abl., 214, 2.

*reposcō,* constr., 178, 1, *a*).

*Repraesentātiō,* 318.

*requiēs, requiem, requiētem,* 59, 2, *c*).

*rēs,* decl., 51.

Resisting, verbs of, w. dat., 187, II.

Restrictive clauses, 283, 5.

Result, acc. of, 173, *B*; 176; clauses of, 284; 297; in dependent apodosis, 322, and *a*; sequence of tense in, 268, 6.

*revertor,* semi-deponent, 114, 3.

Rhetorical questions, 162, 3; 277, *a*; in indir. disc., 315, 2.

Rhotacism, 8, 1; 36, 1.

Rivers, gender of names of, 15, *A*, 1.

*rogātū,* abl. of cause, 219, 2.

*rogō,* constr., 178, 1, *c*); 178, 1, *a*).

Roman pronunciation, 3.

Root, 17, 3, footnote 1.

*-rs,* decl. of nouns in, 40, 1, *c*).

*rūre,* abl., place from which, 229, 1, *b.*

*rūrī,* abl., place in which, 228, 1, *c.*

*-ūs.* 57, 7; acc., limit of motion, 182, 1, *b.*

## S.

*s,* pron., 3, 3; changed to *r* between vowels, 8, 1; *s, ss* from *dt, tt, ts,* 8, 2.

*-s,* decl. of monosyllables in, preceded by one or more consonants, 40, 1 *b*).

*s-*stems, 36.

*sacer,* decl., 65; comparison, 73, 3.

*saepe,* compared, 77, 1.

*sāl,* 57, 7; *sălēs,* 61.

*salūbris,* decl., 68, 3.

*salūtāris,* comp., 73, 4.

*salvē, salvēte,* 137, 4.

*Samnītēs,* decl., 40, 1, *d*).

*sānē,* in answers, 162, 5.

*sapiō,* conj., 109, 2, *a*).

*satur,* decl., 65, 2.

Saying, verbs of, w. inf. of ind. disc., 331, I.

*sciō, quod sciam,* 283, 5.

*-scō-*class of verbs, 117, 6; 155.

*scrībere ad aliquem,* 358, 2.

*sē,* use, 244.

*sē-,* compounds of, 159, 3, *e.*

Second conj., 103; decl., 23; peculiarities 25; second person indefinite, 280, 3; 356, 3; 302, 2.

Secondary tenses, see Historical tenses.

*secundum,* prep. w. acc., 141.

*secūris,* decl., 38, 1.

*secus,* compared, 77, 1.

*secus (virīle secus),* 185, 1; 58.

*secūtus,* 'following,' 336, 5.

*sed, sē,* 85, 3.

*sēd-,* compounds of, 159, 3, *e.*

*sēd,* 343, 1, *a*).

*sedīle,* decl., 39.

*sēmentis,* decl., 38, 1.

Semi-deponent verbs, 114.

Semivowels, 2, 8.

*senex,* decl., 42; compared, 73, 4.

Sentences, classification, 160 f.; simple and compound, 164; sentence-structure, 351; sentence questions, 162, 2.

*sententiā,* abl. of accordance, 220, 3.

Separation, dat. of, 188, 2, *d*); gen., 212, 3; abl., 214.

Sequence of tenses, 267; 268.

*sequester,* decl., 68, 1.

*sequitur ut,* 297, 2.

*sequor,* conj., 113.

Serving, verbs of, w. dat., 187, II.

*servos,* decl., 24.

*sēsē,* decl., 85.

*Sextīlis* ( = *Augustus*), 371.

Sharing, adjs. of, w. gen., 204, 1.

Short syllables, 5, *B*, 2; vowels, 5, *A*, 2.

The references are to sections and paragraphs.

Supine, 340.

*suprā*, prep. w. acc., 141.

*-sūra*, suffix, 147, 3, *a*.

Surd consonants, 2, 3, *a*), footnote 1.

*sūs*, decl., 41.

*sustulī*, p. 99, footnote.

*suus*, decl., 86, 1; 244;. *suus quisque*, 244, 4, *a*.

*Syllaba anceps*, 366, 10.

Syllables, division, 4; quantity of, 5, *B*.

Synapheia, 367, 6.

Synaeresis, 367, 1.

Synchysis, 350, 11, *d*).

Syncope, 7, 4; 367, 8.

Synecdochical acc., 180.

Synizesis, 367, 1.

Syntax, 160 f.

Systole, 367, 3.

# T.

*t*, pron., 3, 3; *th*, 2, 3, *c*; 3, 3; changes, 8, 2; dropped, 8, 3.

*taedet*, 138, II; w. gen., 209.

Taking away, verbs of, w. dat., 188, 2, *d*.

*talentum*, gen. plu., 25, 6, *a*).

*tamen*, 343, 1, *f*.

*tametsī*, 309, 2.

*tamquam, tamquam sī*, w. subjv.. 307.

*tantōn*, 6, 4.

*-tas*, 149; gen. *-tātis*, decl. of nouns in. 40, 1, *e*).

Tasting, verbs of, constr., 176, 5.

Teaching, verbs of, constr., 178, 1, *b*.

*tēd* = *tē*, 84, 3.

Temporal clauses, w. *postquam, ut, ubi, simul ac*, 287; w. *cum*, 288; 289; w. *antequam* and *priusquam*, 291; 292; with *dum, dōnec, quoad*, 293.

*temporis* (*id temporis*), 185, 2.

Tendency, dat. of, 191.

*tener*, decl., 64.

Tenses, 94, 3; 257 ff.; of inf., 270; of inf. in indir. disc., 317; of participles, 336; of subjv., 266; sequence of, 266–268; in indir. disc., 317; 318.

Tenues (consonants), 2, 3, *a*), **footnote 1**.

*tenus*, position, 142, 3.

Terminations, 17, 3.

*ternī*, how used, 81, 4, *b*.

*-ternus*, 154.

*terrā marīque*, 228, 1, *c*.

*terrester*, 68, 3.

Tetrameter verses, 366, 11.

Thematic verbs, 101–113.

—— vowels, 117, footnote.

Thesis, 366, 6.

Third conj., 105'; 109 f.; decl., 28 f.; gender in, 43 f.

Threatening, verbs of, 187, **II**.

*-tim*, adverbs in, 157, 2.

Time, at which, 230; during which, 181, 231, 1; within which, 231.

*timeō nē* and *ut*, 296, 2.

*-tinus*, suffix, 154.

*-tiō*, suffix, 147, 3.

Tmesis, 367, 7.

*-to* as suffix of verbs, 155, 2.

*-tor*, use of nouns in, 353, 4.

*tōtus*, 66; preposition absent w., in expression of place relations, 228, 1, *b*).

Towns, gender of names of, 15, 2; names of, denoting limit of motion, 182, 1, *a*; denoting place where, 228, 1, *a*; place from which, 229, 1, *a*; appositives of town names, 169, 4; 229, 2.

*trāditur, trāditum est*, w. inf., 332, N.

*trāns*, prep. w. acc., 141; constr. of verbs compounded with, 179.

Transitive verbs, 174.

Trees, gender of names of, 15, 2.

*trēs*, decl., 80, 3.

Tribrach, 370, 2.

*tribus*, decl., 49, 3; gender, 50.

Trimeter verses, 366, 11.

*trīnī*, use, 81, 4, *b*).

*triumvir*, gen. plu. of, 25, 6, *b*).

*-trīx*, suffix, 147, 1.

Trochee, 366, 2.

*-trum*, suffix, 147, 4.

Trusting, verbs of, w. dat., 187, **II**.

*tū*, decl., 84.

*-tūdō*, suffix, 149.

*tuī*, as objective gen., 242, 2.

*-tūra*, suffix, 147, 3, *a*).

*tūs*, decl., 57, 7.

*-tus*, suffix, 147, 3; 151, 4.

*tussis*, decl., 38.

*tūte, tūtemet, tūtimet*, 84, 2.

Two accusatives, 177; 178.

Two datives, 191, 2.

# U.

*u*, instead of *i* in some words, 9, 1; in stead of *a*, 9, 1; 9, 4.

*vērō*, 343, 1, *g*); in answers, 162, 5.
Verse, 366, 3.
Verse-structure, 366 f.
Versification, 361.
*versus*, prep. w. acc., 141; follows its case, 141, 2.
*vērum*, 343, 1, *b*).
*vescor*, with abl., 218, 1.
*vesper*, decl., 23, 2.
*vesperī*, locative, 232, 2.
*vestrī*, as obj. gen., 242, 2.
*vestrum*, as gen. of whole, 242, 2; as possessive gen., 242, 2, *a*.
*vetō*, with inf., 331, II.
*vetus*, decl., 70; compared, 73, 3.
*vī*, 220, 2.
*vicem*, used adverbially, 185, 1; *vicis, vice*, 57, 5, *b*.
*victor*, decl., 34.
*videō*, with pres. partic., 337, 3.
*vigil*, decl., 34.
*violenter*, formation, 77, 4, *a*.
*vir*, decl., 23.
——, gen. plu. of nouns compounded with, 25, 6, *b*).
*virīle secus*, constr., 185, 1.
*vīrus*, gender of, 26, 2.
*vīs*, decl., 41.
*vīscera*, used in plu. only, 56, 3.
Vocative case, 17; 19, 1; of Greek proper names in -*ās*, 47, 4; of adjs. in -*ius*, 63, 1; 171; in -*ī* for -*ie*, 25, 1; position of, 350, 3.
Voiced sounds, 2, 3, *a*.
Voiced consonants, 2, 3, *b*).
Voiceless consonants, 2, 3, *a*.
Voices, 94; 256; middle voice, 256, 1.
Volitive subjunctive, 272 f.
*volnus*, spelling, 9, 1.
*volō*, 130; with inf., 331, IV and *a*; 270, 2, *a*; with subjv., 296, 1, *a*.
*volt*, spelling, 9, 1.
*voltis*, spelling, 8, 1.
*volucer*, decl., 68, 1.
*voluntāie*, 220, 2.

-*volus*, comparison of adjs. in, 71, 5.
Vowels, 2, 1; sounds of the, 3, 1; quantity of, 5, *A*; contraction of, 7, 2; parasitic, 7, 3.
Vowel changes, 7.
*vulgus*, gender of, 26, 2.
-*vum, -vus*, decl. of nouns in, 24.

### W.

Want, verbs and adjs. of, w. abl., 214, 1, *c*; *d*.
Way by which, abl. of, 218, 9.
We, editorial, 242, 3.
Whole, gen. of, 201.
Wills, use of fut. imperative in, 281, 1, *b*.
Winds, gender of names of, 15, 1.
Wish, clauses with *dum*, etc., expressing a, 310.
Wishes, subjunctive in, 279; see Optative subjunctive.
Wishing, verbs of, with subst. clause, 296, 1; with obj. inf., 331, IV.
Word-formation, 146 f.
Word-order, 348 f.
Word questions, 162, 1.

### X.

*x*, 2, 9; = *cs* and *gs*, 32.
-*x*, decl. of monosyllables in, preceded by one or more cons., 40, 1, *b*); gender of nouns in -*x* of 3d decl., 43, 2; exceptions, 45, 4.

### Y.

*y*, 1, 1.
Yes, how expressed, 162, 5.
'You,' indefinite, 356, 3; 280, 3; 302, 2

### Z.

*z*, 1, 1; 2, 9.
Zeugma, 374, 2, *a*).